MW01265612

1 MONTH OF
FREE
READING

at

www.ForgottenBooks.com

By purchasing this book you are
eligible for one month membership to
ForgottenBooks.com, giving you
unlimited access to our entire
collection of over 1,000,000 titles via
our web site and mobile apps.

To claim your free month visit:

www.forgottenbooks.com/free810759

ISBN 978-0-265-52206-6
PIBN 10810759

THE

RISE AND PROGRESS

OF

RELIGION IN THE SOUL

ILLUSTRATED IN A COURSE OF

SERIOUS AND PRACTICAL ADDRESSES,

SUITED TO PERSONS OF EVERY CHARACTER AND CIRCUMSTANCE.

WITH A

DEVOUT MEDITATION AND PRAYER,

ADDED TO EACH CHAPTER.

By PHILIP DODDRIDGE, D. D.

PHILADELPHIA:
PRESBYTERIAN BOARD OF PUBLICATION.

CONTENTS.

CHAPTER I.

CHAPTER II.

CHAPTER III.

CHAPTER IV.

CHAPTER V.

3

CHAPTER XII.

CHAPTER XIII.

CHAPTER XIV.

CHAPTER XV.

CHAPTER XVI.

PREFACE.

THE several hints given in the first chapter of this Treatise, which contains a particular plan of the design, render it unnecessary to introduce it with a long preface. My much-honoured friend, Dr. Watts, had laid the scheme, especially of the former part. But as those indispositions, with which (to the unspeakable grief of the churches) God has been pleased to exercise him, had forbid his hopes of being able to add this to his many labours of love to immortal souls, he was pleased, in a very affectionate and importunate manner, to urge me to undertake it. And I bless God, with my whole heart, not only that he hath carried me through this delightful task, (for such indeed I have found it,) but also that he hath spared that worthy and amiable person to see it accomplished, and given him strength and spirit to review so considerable a part of it. His approbation, expressed in stronger terms than modesty will permit me to repeat, encourages me to hope that it is executed in such a manner as may by the divine blessing, render it of some general service. And I the rather hope it will be so, as it now comes abroad into the world, not only with my own prayers and his, but also with those of many other pious friends, which I have been particularly careful to engage for its success.

Into whatever hands this work may come, I must desire that, before any pass their judgment, they

would please o read it through, that they **may**
discern the connexion between one part of it and
another.   This I the rather request, because I have
ιong observed, that Christians of different parties
have been eagerly laying hold on particular parts of
the system of divine truth, and have been contending about them, as if each had been all; or, as if
the separation of the members from each other, and
from the head, were the preservation of the body
instead of its destruction.   They have been zealous
to espouse the defence, and to maintain the honour
and usefulness of each apart; whereas their honour
as well as usefulness, seems to me to lie much in
their connexion : and suspicions have often arisen
betwixt the respective defenders of each, which have
appeared as unreasonable and absurd, as if all the
preparations for securing one part of a ship in a
storm were to be censured as a contrivance to sink
the rest.   I pray God to give to all his ministers and
people more and more of the spirit of wisdom, and
of love, and of a sound mind; and to remove far
from us those mutual jealousies and animosities,
which hinder our acting with that unanimity which
is necessary in order to the successful carrying on
our common warfare against the enemies of Christianity.   We may be sure these enemies will never
fail to make their own advantage of our multiplied
divisions and severe contests with each other.   But
they must necessarily lose both their ground and
their influence, in proportion to the degree in which
the energy of Christian principles is felt, to unite and
transform the hearts of those by whom they are
professed.

I have studied the greatest plainness of speech,
that the lowest of my readers may, if possible, be
able to understand every word; and I hope persons

of a more elegant taste and refined education, will pardon what appeared to me so necessary a piece of charity. Such a care in practical writers, seems one important instance of that honouring all men, which our amiable and condescending religion teaches; and I have been particularly obliged to my worthy patron, for what he has done to shorten some of the sentences, and to put my meaning into plainer and more familiar words. Yet, I dare say, the world will not suspect it of having contracted any impropriety or inelegance of language by passing through the hands of Dr. Watts.

I must add one remark here, viz. That though I do in this book consider my reader as successively in a great variety of supposed circumstances, beginning with those of a thoughtless sinner, and leading him through several stages of conviction, terror, &c., as what may be previous to his sincerely accepting the gospel, and devoting himself to the service of God; yet I would by no means be thought to insinuate that every one who is brought to that happy resolution, arrives at it through those particular steps, or feels agitations of mind equal, in any degree, to those I have described. Some sense of sin, and some serious and humbling apprehension of our danger and misery in consequence of it, must indeed be necessary, to dispose us to receive the grace of the gospel, and the Saviour who is there exhibited to our faith: but God is pleased sometimes to begin the work of his grace on the heart almost from the first dawning of reason, and to carry it on by such gentle and insensible degrees, that very excellent persons, who have made the most eminent attainments in the divine life, have been unable to recount any remarkable history of their conversion. And, so far as I can learn, this is most frequently the case with those of them who have enjoyed the benefit of a pious education, when it has not been succeeded by a vicious and licentious youth. God forbid, therefore, that any should be so insensible of their own happiness as to fall into perplexity with relation to their spiritual state, for want of being able to trace such a rise of religion in their minds as it was necessary, on my plan, for me to describe and exemplify here. I have spoken my sentiments on this head so fully in the eighth of my sermons on Regeneration, that I think none who has read, and remembers the general contents of it, can be in danger of mistaking my meaning here. But as it is very possible this book may fall into the hands of many who have not read the other, and have no opportunity of consulting it, I thought proper to insert this caution in the preface to this; and I am much obliged to that worthy and excellent person who kindly reminded me of the expediency of doing it.

PHILIP DODDRIDGE.

THE RISE AND PROGRESS

OF

RELIGION IN THE SOUL.

———◆———

CHAPTER I.

THE INTRODUCTION TO THE WORK, WITH SOME GENFRAL
ACCOUNT OF ITS DLSIGN.

That true religion is very rare, appears from comparing the nature
of it with the lives and characters of men around us, 1, 2. The
want of it is matter of just lamentation, 3. To remedy this evil
is the design of the ensuing treatise, 4. To which, therefore, the
author earnestly bespeaks the attention of the reader, as his own
heart is deeply interested in it, 5, 6. A general plan of the work,
of which the first fifteen chapters relate chiefly to the RISE of religion, and the remaining chapters to its PROGRESS, 7—12. The
chapter concludes with a prayer for the success of the work.

1. WHEN we look around us with an attentive eye,
and consider the characters and pursuits of men, we
plainly see, that though, in the original constitution
of their natures, they only, of all the creatures that
dwell on the face of the earth, are capable of religion,
yet many of them shamefully neglect it. And whatever different notions people may entertain of what
they call religion, all must agree in owning, that it is
very far from being a universal thing.

2. Religion, in its most general view, is such a
sense of God on the soul, and such a conviction of
our obligations to him, and of our dependence upon
him, as shall engage us to make it our great care to
conduct ourselves in a manner which we have rea-

son to believe will be pleasing to him.   Now, when
we have given this plain account of religion, it is by
no means necessary that we should search among the
savages of the African or American nations, to find
instances of those who are strangers to it.   When we
view the conduct of the generality of people at home,
in a Christian and Protestant nation, in a nation
whose obligations to God have been singular, almost
beyond those of any other people under heaven, will
any one presume to say, that religion has a universal
reign among us?   Will any one suppose that it prevails in every life; that it reigns in every heart?
Alas! the avowed infidelity, the profanation of the
name and day of God, the drunkenness, the lewd-
ness, the injustice, the falsehood, the pride, the pro-
digality, the base selfishness, the stupid insensibility
about the spiritual and eternal interests of themselves
and others, which so generally appear among us,
loudly proclaim the contrary.   So that one would
imagine, upon this view, that thousands and tens of
thousands thought the neglect, and even the contempt of religion, a glory rather than a reproach.
And where is the neighbourhood, where is the society, where is the happy family, consisting of any
considerable number, in which, on a more exact examination, we find reason to say, " Religion fills even
this little circle?"   There is, perhaps, a freedom from
any gross and scandalous immoralities, an external
decency of behaviour, an attendance on the outward
forms of worship in public, and, here and there, in
the family; yet amidst all this, there is nothing which
looks like the genuine actings of the spiritual and
divine life.   There is no appearance of love to God,
no reverence for his presence, no desire of his favour
as the highest good: there is no cordial belief of the
gospel of salvation; no eager solicitude to escape that
condemnation which we have incurred by sin; no
hearty concern to secure that eternal life which Christ
has purchased and secured for his people, and which
he freely promises to all who will receive him.   Alas!
whatever the love of a friend, or even of a parent,

can do; whatever inclination there may be to hope all things, and believe all things, the most favourable; evidence to the contrary will force itself upon the mind, and extort the unwilling conclusion, that, whatever else may be amiable in this dear friend, in that favourite child, " religion dwells not in his breast."

3. To a heart that firmly believes the gospel, and views persons and things in the light of eternity, this is one of the most mournful considerations in the world. And indeed, to such a one, all the other calamities and evils of human nature appear trifles when compared with this, the absence of real religion, and that contrariety to it, which reigns in so many thousands of mankind. Let this be cured, and all the other evils will easily be borne; nay, good will be extracted out of them: but if this continue, it " bringeth forth fruit unto death," Rom. vii. 5, and in consequence of it, multitudes, who share the entertainments of an indulgent Providence with us, and are at least allied to us by the bond of the same common nature, must, in a few years, be swept away into utter destruction, and be plunged beyond redemption " into everlasting burnings."

4. I doubt not but that there are many, under the various forms of religious profession, who are not only lamenting this in public, if their office in life calls them to an opportunity of doing it, but are likewise mourning before God in secret, under a sense of this sad state of things; and who can appeal to him that searches all hearts, as to the sincerity of their desires to revive the languishing cause of vital Christianity and substantial piety, and, among the rest, the author of this treatise, may with confidence say, it is this which animates him to the present attempt, in the midst of so many other cares and labours; for this, he is willing to lay aside many of those curious amusements in science which might suit his own private taste, and perhaps open a way to some reputation in the learned world: for this, he is willing to wave the laboured ornaments of speech,

that he may, if possible, descend to the capacity of the lowest part of mankind: for this, he would endeavour to convince the judgment, and to reach the heart, of every reader: and in a word, for this, with out any dread of the name of an enthusiast, whoever may at random throw it out upon the occasion, he would, as it were, enter with you into your closet from day to day, and with all plainness and freedom, as well as seriousness, would discourse to you of the great things which he has learned from the Christian revelation, and on which he assuredly knows your everlasting happiness to depend: that if you hitherto have lived without religion, you may now be awa kened to the consideration of it, and may be instruct ed in its nature and importance; or that, if you are already, through divine grace, experimentally acquainted with it, you may be assisted to make a greater progress.

5. But he earnestly entreats this favour of you, that, as it is plainly a serious business we are entering upon, you would be pleased to give him a serious and an attentive hearing. He entreats that these addresses, and these meditations, may be perused at leisure, and be thought over in retirement; and that you would do him and yourself the justice to believe the representations which are here made, and the warnings which are here given, to proceed from sincerity and love; from a heart which would not designedly give one moment's unnecessary pain to the meanest creature on the face of the earth, and much less to any human mind. If he be importunate, it is, because he at least imagines that there is just reason for it; and fears, lest amidst the multitudes who are undone by the utter neglect of religion, and among those who are greatly damaged for want of a more resolute and constant attention to it, this may be the case of some into whose hands this treatise may fall.

6. He is a barbarian, and deserves not to be called a man, who can look on the sorrows of his fellow-creatures without drawing out his soul unto them,

and wishing, at least, that it were in the power of his hand to help them. Surely earth would be a heaven to that man who could go about from place to place, scattering happiness wheresoever he came, though it were only the body that he was capable of relieving, and though he could impart nothing better than the happiness of a mortal life. But the happiness rises in proportion to the nature and degree of the good which he imparts. Happy, are we ready to say, were those honoured servants of Christ, who in the early days of his church, were the benevolent and sympathizing instruments of conveying miracuious healing to those whose cases seemed desperate; who poured in upon the blind and the deaf the pleasures of light and sound, and called up the dead to the powers of action and enjoyment. But this is an honour and happiness which it is not fit for God commonly to bestow on mortal men. Yet there have been in every age, and, blessed be his name, there still are those, whom he has condescended to make his instruments in conveying nobler and more lasting blessings than these to their fellow-creatures. Death has long since veiled the eyes, and stopped the ears of those who were the subjects of miraculous healing, and recovered his empire over those who vere once recalled from the grave. But the souls who were prevailed on to receive the gospel, live for ever. God has owned the labours of his faithful ministers in every age to produce these blessed effeets; and some of them being dead, yet speak, Heb. xi. 4, with power and success in this important cause. Wonder not then if, living and dying, I be ambitious of this honour; and if my mouth be freely opened, where I can truly say, " My heart is enlarged," 2 Cor. vi. 11.

7. In forming my general plan, I have been solicitous that this little treatise might, if possible, be useful to all its readers, and contain something suitable to each. I will therefore take the man, and the Christian, in a great variety of circumstances. I will first suppose myself addressing one of the vast

number of thoughtless creatures, who have hitlierto been utterly unconcerned about religion; and will try what can be done, by all plainness and earnestness of address, to awaken him from this fatal lethargy, to a care, (chap. 2.) an affectionate and an immediate care about it, (chap. 3.) I will labour to fix a deep and awful conviction of guilt upon his conscience, (chap. 4.) and to strip him of his vain excuses and his flattering hopes, (chap. 5.) I will read to him, oh! that I could fix on his heart, that sentence, that dreadful sentence, which a righteous and an almighty God has denounced against him as a sinner; (chap. 6.) and endeavour to show him in how helpless a state he lies under this condemnation, as to any capacity he has of delivering himself, (chap. 7.) But I do not mean to leave any in so terrible a situation; I will joyfully proclaim the glad tidings of pardon and salvation by Christ Jesus our Lord, which is all the support and confidence of my own soul; (chap. 8.) and then I will give some general view of the way by which this salvation is to be obtained, (chap. 9.) urging the sinner to accept of it, as affectionately as I can, (chap. 10.) though nothing can be sufficiently pathetic, where, as in this matter, the life of an immortal soul is in question.

8. Too probable it is, that some will, after all this, remain insensible; and therefore, that their sad case may not encumber the following articles, I shall here take a solemn leave of them, (chap. 11.) and then shall turn and address myself as compassionately as I can, to a most contrary character; I mean to a soul overwhelmed with a sense of the greatness of its sins, and trembling under the burden, as if there were no more hope for him in God; (chap. 12.) and that nothing may be omitted which may give solid peace to the troubled spirit, I shall endeavour to guide its inquiries as to the evidences of sincere repentance and faith, (chap. 13.) which will be further illustrated by a more particular view of the several branches of the Christian temper, such as may serve at once to assist the reader in judging what he is, and to show him

what he should labour to be, (chap. 14.) This wil.
naturally lead to a view of the need we have of the
influences of the blessed Spirit to assist us in the important and difficult work of the true Christian; and
of the encouragement we have to hope for these
divine assistances, (chap. 15.) In an humble dependence on which I shall then enter on the consideration of several cases, which often occur in the Christian life, in which, particular addresses to the conscience may be requisite and useful.

9. As some peculiar difficulties and discouragements attend the first entrance on a religious course,
it will here be our first care to animate the young
convert against them, (chap. 16.) And that it may
be done more effectually, I shall urge a solemn dedication of himself to God, (chap. 17.) to be confirmed
by entering into the full communion of the church
by an approach to the sacred table, (chap. 18.) That
these engagements may be more happily fulfilled, we
shall endeavour to draw a more particular plan of
that devout, regular, and accurate course, which ought
daily to be attended to, (chap. 19.) and because the
idea will probably rise so much higher than what
is the general practice, even of good men, we shall
endeavour to persuade the reader to make the attempt, hard as it may seem, (chap. 20.) and shall
caution him against various temptations, which
might otherwise draw him aside to negligence and
sin, (chap. 21.)

10. Happy will it be for the reader, if these exhortations and cautions be attended to with becoming
regard; but as it is, alas! too probable, that notwithstanding all, the infirmities of nature will sometimes
prevail, we shall consider the case of deadness and
languor in religion, which often steals upon us by insensible degrees, (chap. 22.) from whence there is too
easy a passage to that terrible one of a return unto
known and deliberate sin, (chap. 23.) And as the one
or the other of these tends, in a proportionable degree,
to provoke the blessed God to hide his face, and his
njured Spiri to withdraw. that melancholy condition

will be taken into a particular survey, (chap. 24.)   I
shall then take notice also of the case of great and
heavy afflictions in life, (chap. 25.) a discipline which
the best of men have reason to expect, especially
when they backslide from God, and yield to their
spiritual enemies.

11. Instances of this kind will, I fear, be too frequent; yet, I trust, there will be many others, whose
path, like the dawning light, will "shine more and
more unto the perfect day," Prov. iv. 13. And there
fore we shall endeavour, in the best manner we can,
to assist the Christian in passing a true judgment on
the growth of grace in his heart, (chap. 26.) as we
had done before in judging of its sincerity.   And as
nothing conduces more to the advancement of grace
than the lively exercise of love to God, a holy joy in
him, we shall here remind the real Christian of those
mercies which tend to excite that love and joy, (chap.
27.) and, in the views of them, to animate him to
those vigorous efforts of usefulness in life which so
well become his character, and will have so happy
an efficacy on brightening his crown, (chap. 28.) Supposing him to act accordingly, we shall then labour
to illustrate and assist the delight with which he may
look forward to the awful solemnities of death and
judgment: (chap. 29.) and shall close the scene by
accompanying him, as it were, to the nearest confines
of that dark valley, through which he is to pass to
glory; giving him such directions as may seem most
subservient to his honouring God, and adorning religion, by his dying behaviour, (chap. 30.)   Nor am
I without a pleasing hope, that through the divine
blessing and grace, I may be, in some instances, so
successful as to leave those triumphing in the views
of judgment and eternity, and glorifying God by a
truly Christian life and death, whom I found trembling in the apprehensions of future misery; or,
perhaps, in a much more dangerous and miserable
condition than that; I mean, entirely forgetting the
prospect, and sunk into the most stupid insensibility
of those things, for an attention to which the hu·

man mind was formed, and in comparison of which all the pursuits of this transitory life are emptier than wind, and lighter than a feather.

12. Such a variety of heads must, to be sure, be handled but briefly, as we intend to bring them within the bulk of a moderate volume. I shall not, therefore, discuss them, as a preacher might properly do in sermons, in which the truths of religion are professedly to be explained and taught, defended and improved in a wide variety, and long detail of propositions, arguments, objections, replies, and inferences, marshalled and numbered under their distinct generals. I shall here speak in a looser and freer manner, as a friend to a friend; just as I would do, if I were to be in person admitted to a private audience, by one whom I tenderly loved, and whose circumstances and character I knew to be like that which the title of one chapter or another of this treatise describes. And when I have discoursed with him a little while, which will seldom be so long as half an hour, I shall, as it were, step aside, and leave him to meditate on what he has heard, or endeavour to assist him in such fervent addresses to God, as it may be proper to mingle with those meditations. In the mean time, I will here take the liberty to pray over my reader and my work, and to commend it solemnly to the divine blessing, in token of my deep conviction of an entire dependence upon it. And I am well persuaded, that sentiments like these are common, in the general, to every faithful minister, to every real Christian

A PRAYER FOR THE SUCCESS OF THIS WORK IN PROMOTING THE RISE AND PROGRESS OF RELIGION.

Oh thou great eternal Original, and Author of all created being and happiness! I adore thee, who hast made man a creature capable of religion; and hast bestowed this dignity and felicity upon our nature, that it may be taught to say, "Where is God our Maker?" Job xxxv. 10. I lament that degeneracy spread over the whole human race, which has "turned our glory into shame," Hos. iv. 7, and has rendered the forgetfulness of God (unnatural as it is) so common, and so universal a disease. Holy Father, we know it is thy presence, and thy teaching alone that can reclaim thy wandering children; can impress a sense of divine things on the heart, and render that sense lasting and effectual. From thee proceed all good purposes and desires; and this desire above all, of diffusing wisdom, piety, and happiness in this world, which, (though sunk in such deep apostasy,) thine infinite mercy has not utterly forsaken.

"Thou knowest, O Lord, the hearts of the children of men," 2 Chron. vi. 30, and an upright soul, in the midst of all the censures and suspicions it may meet with, rejoices in thine intimate knowledge of its most secret sentiments and principles of action. Thou knowest the sincerity and fervency with which thine unworthy servant desires to spread the knowledge of thy name, and the favour of thy gospel, among all to whom this work may reach. Thou knowest, that hadst thou given him an abundance of this world, it would have been, in his esteem, the noblest pleasure that abundance could have afforded to have been thine almoner, in distributing thy bounties to the indigent and necessitous, and so causing the sorrowful heart to rejoice in thy goodness dispensed through his hands. Thou knowest, that hadst thou given him either by ordinary or extraordinary methods, the gift of healing, it would have been his daily delight to relieve the pains, the maladies, and the infirmities of men's bodies; to have seen the languishing countenance brightened by returning health and cheerfulness; and much more, to have beheld the roving distracted mind reduced to calmness and serenity in the exercise of its rational faculties. Yet happier, far happier, will he think himself, in those humble circumstances in which thy Providence has placed him, if thou vouchsafe to honour these his feeble endeavours as the means of relieving and enriching men's minds; of recovering them from the madness of a sinful state, and bringing back thy reasonable crea-

tures to the knowledge, the service, and the enjoyment of their God; or of improving those who are
already reduced.

O may it have that blessed influence on the person, whosoever he be, that is now reading these lines,
and on all who may read or hear them! Let not
my Lord be angry, if I presume to ask, that however
weak and contemptible this work may seem in the
eyes of the children of this world, and however imperfect it really be, as well as the author of it unworthy, it may, nevertheless, live before thee; and,
through a divine power, be mighty to produce the
rise and progress of religion in the minds of multitudes in distant places, and in generations yet to
come! Impute it not, O God, as a culpable ambition, if I desire, that whatever becomes of my name,
about which I would not lose one thought before
thee, this work, to which I am now applying myself
in thy strength, may be completed, and propagated
far abroad; that it may reach to those that are yet
unborn, and teach them thy name and thy praise
when the author has long dwelt in the dust: that so,
when he shall appear before thee in the great day
of final account, his joy may be increased, and his
crown brightened, by numbers before unknown to
each other, and to him! But if this petition be too
great to be granted to one who pretends no claim,
but thy sovereign grace, to hope for being favoured
with the least, give him to be, in thine almighty
hand, the blessed instrument of converting and saving
one soul: and, if it be but one, and that the weakest
and meanest of those who are capable of receiving
this address, it shall be most thankfully accepted as
a rich recompense for all the thought and labour it
may cost; and though it should be amidst a thousand disappointments with respect to others, yet it
shall be the subject of immortal songs of praise to
thee, O blessed God, for and by every soul, whom,
through the blood of Jesus, and the grace of thy
Spirit, thou hast saved: and everlasting honours shall
be ascribed to the Father, and to the Son, and to the

Holy Spirit, by the innumerable company of angels
and by the general assembly and church of the first-
born in heaven. Amen.

———◆———

CHAPTER II.

THE CARELESS SINNER AWAKENED.

It is too supposable a case that this treatise may come into such
hands, 1, 2. Since many, not grossly vicious, fall under that
character, 3, 4. A more particular illustration of this case, with
an appeal to the reader whether it be not his own, 5, 6. Expos-
tulation with such, 7—9; more particularly, (1.) from acknowledged principles, relating to the nature of God, his universal presence, agency, and perfections, 10—12. (2.) From a view of personal obligations to him, 13. (3.) From the danger of this neglect,
when considered in its aspect on a future state, 14. An appeal
to the conscience, as already convinced, 15. Transition to the
subject of the next chapter, 16. The meditation of a sinner, who,
having been long thoughtless, begins to be awakened.

1. SHAMEFULLY and fatally as religion is neglected
in the world, yet blessed be God, it has some sincere
disciples; children of wisdom, by whom, even in this
foolish and degenerate age, it " is justified," Matt.
xi. 19; who having, by divine grace, been brought
to the knowledge of God in Christ, have faithfully
devoted their hearts to him, and, by a natural couse-
quence, are devoting their lives to his service. Could
I be sure this treatise would fall into no hands but
theirs, my work would be shorter, easier, and plea-
santer.

2. But, among the thousands that neglect religion,
it is more than possible that some of my readers may
be included; and I am so deeply affected with their
unhappy case, that the temper of my heart, as well
as the proper method of my subject, leads me, in the
first place, to address myself to such; to apply to
every one of them: and therefore, to you, O reader,
whoever you are, who may come under the denomi
nation of " a careless sinner."   .

3. Be not, I beseech you, angry at the name. The physicians of souls must speak plainly, or they may murder those whom they should cure. I would make no harsh and unreasonable supposition. I would charge you with nothing more than is abso· lutely necessary to convince you that you are the person to whom I speak. I will not, therefore, imagine you to be a profane and abandoned profligate. I will not suppose that you allow yourself to blaspheme God, to dishonour his name by customary swearing, or grossly to violate the Sabbath, or commouly to neglect the solemnities of his public worship: I will not imagine that you have injured your neighbours in their lives, their chastity, or their possessions, either by violence, or by fraud; or that you have scandalously debased the rational nature of man by that vile intemperance which transforms us into the worst kind of brutes, or something beneath them.

4. In opposition to all this, I will suppose that you believe the existence and providence of God, and the truth of Christianity as a revelation from him; of which, if you have any doubt, I must desire that you would immediately seek your satisfaction elsewhere.* I say, immediately: becau e not to believe it, is in effect, to disbelieve it; and will make your ruin equally certain, though, perhaps, it may leave it less aggravated, than if contempt and opposition had been added to suspicion and neglect. But, supposing you to be a nominal Christian, and not a deist or a sceptic; I will also suppose your conduct among men to be not only blameless, but amiable, and that they who know you most intimately, must acknowledge that you are just and sober, humane and courteous, compassionate and liberal; yet, with all this, you may " lack that one thing," Mark x. 21, on which your eternal happiness depends.

* In such a case, I beg leave to refer the reader to my three sermons on the Evidence of Christianity; the last of the ten on the Power and Grace of Christ: in which he may see the hitherto un. shaken foundations of my own faith, in a short, and, I hope, a clear view.

5. I beseech you, reader, whoever you are, that you would look seriously into your own heart, and ask it this one plain question, " Am I truly religious?" Is the love of God the governing principle of my life? Do I walk under a sense of his presence? Do I converse with him from day to day, in the exercise of prayer and praise? And am I, on the whole, making his service my business and my delight, regarding him as my Master and my Father?

6. It is my present business only to address myself to the person whose conscience answers in the negative. And I would address with equal plainness, and equal freedom, to high and low, to rich and poor: to you who (as the Scripture, with a dreadful propriety, expresses it,) " live without God in the world," Eph. ii. 12, and while, in words and forms, you " own God, deny him in your actions," Tit. i. 16, and behave yourselves in the main, (a few external ceremonies only excepted,) just as you would do if you believed, and were sure, there was no God. Unhappy creature, whoever you are, your own heart condemns you immediately; and how much more that " God who is greater than your heart, and knoweth all things!" 1 John iii. 20. He is " in secret," Matt. vi. 6, as well as in public; and words cannot express the delight with which his children converse with him alone: but in secret you acknowledge him not; you neither pray to him, nor praise him in your retirements. Accounts, correspondences, studies, may often bring you into your closet : but if nothing but devotion were to be transacted there, it would be to you quite an unfrequented place. And thus you go on from day to day, in a continual forgetfulness of God; and are as thoughtless about religion, as if you had long since demonstrated it to yourself that it was a mere dream. If, indeed, you are sick, you will perhaps cry to God for health; in any extreme danger you will lift up your eyes and voice for deliverance; but as for the pardon of sin, and the other blessings of the gospel, you are not at all inwardly solicitous about them, though you profess to believe

that the gospel is divine, and the blessings of it eternal. All your thoughts, and all your hours are divided between the business and amusements of life: and if, now and then, an awful providence, or a serious ser·mon or book, awakens you, it is but a few days, or it may be, a few hours, and you are the same careless creature you ever were before. On the whole, you act as if you were resolved to put it to the venture, and, at your own expense, to make the experiment, whether the consequences of neglecting religion be indeed as terrible as its ministers and friends have represented. Their remonstrances do, indeed, sometimes force themselves upon you, as (considering the age and country in which you live) it is hardly possible entirely to avoid them; but you have, it may be, found out the art of Isaiah's people, " Hearing to hear, and not understand; and seeing to see, and not perceive; your heart is waxed gross, your eyes are closed, and your ears heavy," Isaiah vi. 9, 10. Under the very ordinances of worship, your thoughts " are at the ends of the earth," Prov. xvii. 24. Every amusement of the imagination is welcome, if it may but lead away your mind from so insipid and disagreeable a subject as religion. And, probably, the very last time you were in a worshiping assembly, you managed just as you would have done, if you thought God knew nothing of your behaviour; or as if you did not think it worth one single care, whether he were pleased or displeased with it.

7. Alas! is it then come to this, with all your belief of God, and providence, and Scripture, that religion is not worth a thought; that it is not worth one hour's serious consideration and reflection, " what God and Christ are, and what you yourself are, and what you must hereafter be?" Where then are all your rational faculties? How are they employed; or rather, how are they stupefied and benumbed?

8. The certainty and importance of the things of which I speak are so evident, from the principles which you yourself grant, that one might almost set a child or an idiot to reason upon them; and yet

they are neglected by those who are grown up to understanding, and perhaps, some of them to such refinement of understanding, that they would think themselves greatly injured, if they were not to be reckoned among the politer and the more learned part of mankind.

9. But it is not your neglect, that can destroy the being or importance of such things as these. It may indeed destroy you, but it cannot in the least affect them. Permit me, therefore, having been myself awakened, to come to you, and say, as the mariners did to Jonah, while asleep in the midst of a much less dangerous storm, "what meanest thou, O sleeper? Arise and call upon thy God," Jonah i. 6. Do you doubt as to the reasonableness, or necessity, of doing it? "I will demand, and answer me," Job xxxviii. 3. Answer me to your own conscience. as one that must, ere long, render another kind of account.

10. You own that there is a God, and well you may: for you cannot open your eyes but you must see the evident proofs of his being, his presence, and his agency. You behold him around you in every object: you feel him within you, if I may so speak, in every vein, and in every nerve: you see, and you feel, not only that he has formed you with an exquisite wisdom which no mortal man could ever fully explain or comprehend; but that he is continually near you, wherever you are, and however you are employed, by day or by night; "in him you live, and move, and have your being," Acts xvii. 28. Common sense will tell you that it is not your own wisdom, and power, and attention, that causes your heart to beat, and your blood to circulate; that draws in, and sends out, that breath of life, that precarious breath of a most uncertain life, "that is in your nostrils," Isaiah ii. 22. These things are done when you sleep, as well as in those waking moments, when you think not of the circulation of the blood, nor of the necessity of breathing, nor so much as recollect that you have a heart and lungs. Now, what is this but the

hand of God perpetually supporting and actuating those curious machines that he has made?

11. Nor is this his care limited to you; but, if you look all around you, far as your views can reach, you see it extending itself on every side; and, oh, how much further than you can trace it! Reflect on the light and heat which the sun every where dispenses; on the air which surrounds our globe, on the right temperature of which the life of the whole human race depends, and that of all the inferior creatures which dwell on the earth. Think of the suitable and plentiful provision made for man and beast; the grass, the grain, the variety of fruits, and herbs, and flowers; every thing that nourishes us, every thing that delights us; and say, whether it does not speak plainly and loudly that our Almighty Maker is near, and that he is careful of us, and kind to us. And while all these things proclaim his goodness, do they not also proclaim his power? For what power has any thing comparable to that which furnishes out these gifts of royal bounty; and which, unwearied and unchanged, produces continually, from day to day, and from age to age, such astonishing and magnificent effects over the face of the whole earth, and through all the regions of heaven?

12. It is then evident, that God is present, present with you at this moment; even God, your Creator and Preserver; God, the Creator and Preserver of the whole visible and invisible world. And is he not present as a most observant and attentive Being? " He that formed the eye, shall not he see? He that planted the ear, shall not he hear? He that teaches man knowledge," that gives him his rational faculties, and pours in on his opening mind all the light it receives by them, " shall not he know?" Psalm xciv. 9, 10. He who sees all the necessities of his creatures, so seasonably to provide for them, shall he not see their actions too; and seeing, shall he not judge of them? Has he given us a sense and discernment of what is good and evil, of what is true and false, of what is fair and deformed in temper and conduct;

and has he himself no discernment of these things?
Trifle not with your conscience, which tells you at
once, that he judges of it, and approves or condemns,
as it is decent or indecent, reasonable or unreasonable; and that the judgment which he passes is of infinite importance to all his creatures.

13. And now, to apply all this to your own case,
let me seriously ask you, is it a decent and reasonable
thing that this great and glorious Benefactor should
be neglected by his rational creatures; by those
that are capable of attaining to some knowledge of
him, and presenting to him some homage? Is it decent and reasonable that he should be forgotten and
neglected by you? Are you alone, of all the works
of his hands, forgotten and neglected by him? Oh
sinner, thoughtless as you are, you cannot dare to say
that, or even to think it. You need not go back to
the helpless days of your infancy and childhood to
convince you to the contrary; you need not, in order
to this, to recollect the remarkable deliverances which,
perhaps, were wrought out for you many years ago.
The repose of the last night, the refreshment and comfort you have received this day; yea, the mercies you
are receiving this very moment, bear witness to him;
and yet you regard him not. Ungrateful creature
that you are! could you have treated any human
benefactor thus? Could you have borne to neglect
a kind parent, or any generous friend that had but
for a few months acted the part of a parent to you;
to have taken no notice of him, while in his presence;
to have returned him no thanks; to have had no contrivances to make some little acknowledgment for all
his goodness? Human nature, bad as it is, is not
fallen so low; nay, the brutal nature is not so low,
as this. Surely every domestic animal around you,
must shame such ingratitude. If you do but for
a few days take a little kind notice of a dog, and
feed him with the refuse of your table, he will
wait upon you, and love to be near you; he will be
eager to follow you from place to place: and when
after a little absence, you return home, will try, by a

thousand fond transported motions, to tell you how much he rejoices to see you again. Nay brutes, far less sagacious and apprehensive, have some sense of our kindness, and express it after their way; as the blessed God condescends to observe, in this very view in which I mention it, the dull " ox knows his owner, and the" stupid " ass his master's crib," Isaiah i. 3. What lamentable degeneracy therefore is it that you do not know, that you, who have been numbered among God's professed people, do not, and, will not, consider your numberless obligations to him?

14. Surely, if you have any ingenuousness of tem per, you must be ashamed and grieved in the review; but if you have not, give me leave further to expostulate with you on this head, by setting it in something of a different light. Can you think yourself safe while you are acting a part like this? Do you not in your conscience believe there will be a future judgment? Do you not believe there is an invisible and eternal world? As professed Christians we all believe it; for it is no controverted point, but displayed in Scripture with so clear an evidence, that, subtle and ingenious as men are in error, they have not yet found out a way to evade it. And believing this, do you not see, that while you are thus wandering from God, " destruction and misery are in your ways?" Rom. iii. 16. Will this indolence and negligence of temper, be any security to you? will it guard you from death? will it excuse you from judgment? You might much more reasonably expect, that shutting your eyes would be a defence against the rage of a devouring lion; or that looking another way should secure your body from being pierced by a bullet or a sword. When God speaks of the extravagant folly of some thoughtless creatures, who would hearken to no admonition now, he adds, in a very awful manner, " in the latter day they shall consider it perfectly." Jer. xxiii. 20. And is not this applicable to you? Must you not, sooner or later, be brought to think of these things whether you will or no? And, in the mean time, do you not certainly know, that

timely and serious reflection upon them is, through
divine grace, the only way to prevent your ruin?

15. Yes, sinner, I need not multiply words on a
subject like this.   Your conscience is already in.
wardly convinced, though your pride may be unwilling to own it.   And, to prove it, let me ask you one
question more: would you, upon any terms and considerations whatever, come to a resolution, absolutely
to dismiss all further thought of religion, and all care
about it, from this day and hour, and to abide by the
consequences of that neglect?   I believe hardly any
man living would be bold enough to determine upon
this; I believe most of my readers would be ready to
tremble at the thought of it.

16. But if it be necessary to take these things into
consideration at all, it is necessary to do it quickly;
for life itself is not so very long, nor so certain, that
a wise man should risk much upon its continuance.
And I hope to convince you, when I have another
hearing, that it is necessary to do it immediately;
and that next to the madness of resolving you will
not think of religion at all, is that of saying you will
think of it hereafter.   In the mean time, pause on
the hints which have been already given, and they
will prepare you to receive what is to be added on
that head.

**THE MEDITATION OF A SINNER, WHO WAS ONCE THOUGHT-
LESS, BUT BEGINS TO BE AWAKENED.**

Awake, oh my forgetful soul, awake from these
wandering dreams; turn thee from this chase of vanity, and for a little while be persuaded, by all these
considerations, to look forward, and to look upward,
at least, for a few moments.   Sufficient are the hours
and days given to the labours and amusements of
life; grudge not a short allotment of minutes to view
thyself and thine own more immediate concerns: to
reflect who, and what thou art; how it comes to pass
that thou art here, and what thou must quickly be.

It is indeed as thou hast now seen it represented.

Oh my soul. thou art the creature of God, formed and furnished by him, and lodged in a body which he provided, and which he supports; a body in which he in'ends thee only a transitory abode. Oh, tnink how soon " this tabernacle must be dissolved," 2 Cor v. 1, and "thou must return to God," Eccles. xii. 7. And shall He, the one infinite, eternal, ever blessed, and ever glorious Being, shall He be least of all regarded by thee? Wilt thou live and die with this character, saying by every action of every day unto God, " Depart from me, for I desire not the knowledge of thy ways?" Job xxi. 14. The morning, the day, the evening, the night, every period of time, has its excuses for this neglect. But, oh my soul, what will these excuses appear when examined by his penetrating eye! They may delude me, but they cannot impose upon him.

Oh, thou injured, neglected, provoked Benefactor! when I think but for a moment or two, of all thy greatness, and of all thy goodness, I am astonished at this insensibility which has prevailed in my heart, and even still prevails. " I blush, and am confounded to lift up my face before thee," Ezra ix. 6. On the most transient review, I see that " I have played the fool, that I have erred exceedingly," 1 Sam. xxvi. 21, and yet this stupid heart of mine would make its having neglected thee so long, a reason for going on to neglect thee. I own it might justly be expected that, with regard to thee, every one of thy rational creatures should be all duty and love; that each heart should be full of a sense of thy presence; and that a care to please thee should swallow up every other care; yet thou " hast not been in all my thoughts," Psal. x. 4; and religion, the end and glory of my nature, has been so strangely overlooked, that I have hardly ever seriously asked my own heart what it is I know, if matters rest here, I perish; and yet I feel in my perverse nature a secret indisposition to pursue these thoughts; a proneness, if not entirely to dismiss them, yet to lay them aside for the present My mind is perplexed and divided; but I am sur

thou who madest me knowest what is best for me.
I therefore beseech thee, that thou wilt, " for thy
name's sake, lead me and guide me," Psal. xxxi. 3.
Let me not delay till it is for ever too late; " pluck
me as a brand out of the burning," Amos iv. 11.
Oh, break this fatal enchantment that holds down my
affections to objects which my judgment comparatively despises; and let me, at length, come into so
happy a state of mind, that I may not be afraid to
think of thee and of myself, and may not be tempted
to wish, that thou hadst not made me, or that thou
couldst forever forget me; that it may not be my best
hope to perish like the brutes.

If what I shall further read here be agreeable to
truth and reason; if it be calculated to promote my
happiness, and is to be regarded as an intimation of
thy will and pleasure to me, oh God, let me hear
and obey; let the words of thy servant, when pleading thy cause, be like goads to pierce into my mind;
and let me rather feel and smart, than die.   Let them
be as " nails fastened in a sure place," Eccles. xii. 11,
that whatever mysteries as yet unknown, or whatever difficulties there be in religion, if it be necessary,
I may not finally neglect it; and that if it be expedient to attend immediately to it, I may no longer
delay that attention.   And, oh, let thy grace teach
me the lesson I am so slow to learn, and conquer that
strong opposition which I feel in my heart against
the very thought of it!   Hear these broken cries for
the sake of thy Son, who has taught and saved many
a creature as untractable as I, and can " of stones
raise up children to Abraham," Matt. iii. 9. Amen.

CHAPTER III.

THE AWAKENED SINNER URGED TO IMMEDIATE CONSIDERA TION, AND CAUTIONED AGAINST DELAY.

Sinners when awakened, inclined to dismiss convictions for the present, 1. An immediate regard to religion urged, 2. (1.) From the excellency and pleasure of the thing itself, 3. (2.) From the uncertainty of that future time on which sinners presume, compared with the sad consequences of being cut off in sin, 4. (3.) From the immutability of God's present demands, 5. (4.) From the tendency which delay has to make a compliance with these demands more difficult than it is at present, 6. (5.) From the danger of God's withdrawing his Spirit, compared with the dreadful case of a sinner, given up by it, 7. which probably is now the case of many, 8. Since, therefore, on the whole, whatever the event be, delays must prove matter of lamentation, 9. The chapter concludes with an exhortation against yielding to them, 10. and a prayer against temptations of that kind.

1. I HOPE my last address so far awakened the convictions of my reader, as to bring him to this purpose, "That some time or other he would attend to religious considerations." But give me leave to ask earnestly and pointedly, "When shall that be?"— "Go thy way for this time, and at a more convenient season I will send for thee," was the language and the ruin of unhappy Felix, Acts xxiv. 25, when he trembled under the reasonings and expostulations of the apostle. The tempter presumed not to urge that he should give up all thoughts of repentance and reformation; but only that, considering the present hurry of his affairs, (as no doubt they were many) he should defer it to a longer day. The artifice succeeded, and Felix was undone.

2. Will you, reader, dismiss me thus? For your own sake, and out of tender compassion to your perishing immortal soul, I would not willingly take up with such a dismission and excuse. No, not though you should fix a time; though you should determine on the next year, or month, or week, or day. I would turn upon you with all the eagerness and tenderness of friendly importunity, and entreat you to bring the

matter to an issue even now; for if you say, "I will think on these things to-morrow," I shall have little hope, and shall conclude, that all that I have hitherto urged, and all that you have read, has been offered and viewed in vain.

3. When I invite you to the care and practice of religion, it may seem strange that it should be necessary for me affectionately to plead the cause with you, in order to your immediate regard and compliance What I am inviting you to is so noble and excellent in itself, so well worthy the dignity of our rational nature, so suitable to it, so manly, and so wise, that one would imagine you should take fire, as it were, at the first hearing of it; yea, that so delightful a view should presently possess your whole soul with a kind of indignation against yourself that you pursued it no sooner. "May I lift up mine eyes and my soul to God? may I devote myself to him? may I even now commence a friendship with him, a friendship which shall last for ever, the security, the delight, the glory of this immortal nature of mine? And shall I draw back, and say, Nevertheless, let me not commence this friendship too soon: let me live at least a few weeks, or a few days longer, without God in the world?" Surely it would be much more reasonable to turn inward, and say, "Oh my soul, on what vile husks hast thou been feeding, while thine heavenly Father has been forsaken and injured? Shall I desire to multiply the days of my poverty, my scandal, and my misery?" On this principle, surely, an immediate return to God should, in all reason, be chosen, rather than to play the fool any longer, and go on a little more to displease God, and thereby to starve and to wound your own soul, even though your continuance in life were ever so certain, and your capacity to return to God and your duty ever so entirely in your own power now, and in every future moment, through scores of years yet to come.

4. But who, or what are you, that you should lay your account for years, or for months to come? "What is your life?" Is it not "even a vapour

that appeareth for a little time, and then vanisheth away?" James iv. 14. And what is your security, or what is your peculiar warrant, that you should thus depend upon the certainty of its continuance; and that so absolutely, as to venture, as it were, to pawn your soul upon it? " Why," you will perhaps say, "I am young, and in all my bloom and vigour: I see hundreds about me, who are more than double my age, and not a few of them who seem to think it too soon to attend to religion yet." You view the living, and you talk thus: but I beseech you think of the dead. Return in your thoughts to those graves, in which you have left some of your young companions and your friends. You saw them awhile ago, gay and active; warm with life, and hopes, and schemes; and some of them would have thought a friend strangely importunate that should have interrupted them in their business, and their pleasures, with a solemn lecture of death and eternity: yet they were then on the very borders of both. You have since seen their corpses, or at least their coffins; and probably carried about with you the badges of mourning which you received at their funerals. Those once vigorous and perhaps beautiful bodies of theirs, now lie mouldering in the dust, as senseless and helpless as the most decrepid pieces of human nature which fourscore years ever brought down to it. And, what is infinitely more to be regarded, their souls, whether prepared for this great change, or thoughtless of it, have made their appearance before God, and are, at this moment, fixed either in heaven or in hell. Now, let me seriously ask you, would it be miraculous, or would it be strange, if such an event should befall you? How are you sure that some fatal disease shall not this day begin to work in your veins? How are you sure that you shall ever be capable of reading or thinking any more, if you do not attend to what you now read, and pursue the thought which is now offering itself to your mind? This sudden alteration may, at least, possibly happen; and if it does, it will be to you a terrible one indeed. To be thus surprised into

the presence of a forgotten God; to be torn away, at
once, from a world, to which your whole heart and
soul has been riveted; a world, which has engrossed
all your thoughts and cares, all your desires and pursuits; and be fixed in a state which you could never
be so far persuaded to think of, as to spend so much
as one hour in serious preparation for it; how must
you even shudder at the apprehension of it, and with
what horror must it fill you?   It seems matter of
wonder, that, in such circumstances, you are not al
most distracted with the thoughts of the uncertainty
of life, and are not even ready to die for fear of death.
To trifle with God any longer, after so solemn an
admonition as this, would be a circumstance of additional provocation, which, after all the rest, might be
fatal: nor is there any thing that you can expect in
such a case, but that he should cut you off immediately, and teach other thoughtless creatures, by
your ruin, what a hazardous experiment they make,
when they act as you are acting.

5. And will you, after all, run this desperate risk?
For what imaginable purpose can you do it?   Do
you think the business of religion will become less
necessary, or more easy, by your delay? You know
that it will not. You know, that whatever the blessed God demands now, he will also demand twenty
or thirty years hence, if you should live to see the
time.   God has fixed the method, in which he will
pardon and accept sinners, in his gospel.   And will
he ever alter that method? or, if he will not, can men
alter it? You like not to think of repenting, and
humbling yourself before God, to receive righteousness and life from his free grace in Christ; and you
above all dislike to think of returning to God in the
ways of holy obedience. But will he ever dispense
with any of these, and publish a new gospel, with
promises of life and salvation to impenitent unbelieving sinners, if they will but call themselves Christians, and submit to a few external rites? How long
do you think you might wait for such a change in
the constitution of things? You know death will

come upon you; and you cannot but know in your own conscience, that a general dissolution will come upon the world long before God can thus deny himself, and contradict all his perfections, and all his declarations.

6. Or, if his demands continue the same, as they assuredly will, do you think any thing, which is now disagreeable to you in them, will be less disagreeable hereafter than it is at present? Shall you love sin less, when it is become more habitual to you, and when conscience is yet more enfeebled and debauched? If you are "running with the footmen and fainting, shall you be able to contend with the horsemen?" Jer. xii. 5. Surely you cannot imagine it. You would not say in any distemper which threatened your life, "I will stay till I grow a little worse, and then I will apply to a physician: I will let my disease get a little more rooting in my vitals, and then I will try what can be done to remove it." No: it is only where the life of the soul is concerned, that men think thus wildly: the life and health of the body appear too precious to be thus trifled away.

7. If, after such desperate experiments, you are ever recovered, it must be by an operation of divine grace on your soul, yet more powerful and more wonderful, in proportion to the increasing inveteracy of your spiritual maladies. And can you expect that the Holy Spirit should be more ready to assist you, in consequence of your having so shamefully trifled with him and affronted him? He is now, in some measure, moving on your heart: if you feel any secret relentings in it upon what you read, it is a sign you are not yet utterly forsaken: but who can tell whether these are not the last touches he will ever give to a heart so long hardened against him? Who can tell but God may this day "swear in his wrath, that you shall not enter into his rest?" Heb. iii. 1s. I have been telling you that you may immediately die. You own it is possible you may. And can you think of any thing more terrible? Yes, sinner, I will tell you of one thing more dreadful than immediate

death and immediate damnation. The blessed **God** may say, " as for that wretched creature, who has so long trifled with me, and provoked me, let him still live: let him live in the midst of prosperity and plenty: let him live under the purest and most powerful ordinances of the gospel too; that he may abuse them, to aggravate his condemnation, and die under seven-fold guilt, and a seven-fold curse. I will not give him the grace to think of his ways for one serious moment more; but he shall go on from bad to worse, filling up the measure of his iniquities, till death and destruction seize him in an unexpected hour, and wrath come upon him to the uttermost," 1 Thess. ii. 16.

8. You think this is an uncommon case; but I fear it is much otherwise. I fear there are few congregations where the word of God has been faithfully preached, and where it has been long despised, especially by those whom it had once awakened, in which the eye of God does not see a number of such wretched souls; though it is impossible for us to pronounce who they are.

9. I pretend not to say how he will deal with you, oh reader; whether he will immediately cut you off, or seal you up under final hardness and impenitency of heart; or whether his grace may, at length, awaken you, to consider your ways, and to return to him, even when your heart is grown yet more obdurate than it is at present: for to his almighty grace nothing is hard, not even to transform a rock of marble into a man and a saint. But this I will confidently say that if you delay any longer, the time will come when you will bitterly repent of that delay; and either lament it before God in the anguish of your heart here, or curse your own folly and madness in hell; yea, when you will wish that, dreadful as hell is, you had rather fallen into it sooner than have lived in the midst of so many abused mercies, to render the degree of your punishment more insupportable, and your sense of it more exquisitely tormenting.

10. I do, therefore, earnestly exhort you, in the name of our Lord Jesus Christ, and by the worth, and, if I may so speak, by the blood of your immortal and perishing soul, that you delay not a day or an hour longer. Far from " giving sleep to your eyes, or slumber to your eye-lids," Prov. vi. 4, in the continued neglect of this important concern, "take with you," even now, " words, and turn unto the Lord," Hos. xiv. 2, and before you quit the place where you now are, fall upon your knees in his sacred presence, and pour out your heart in such language, or at least to some such purpose as this.

A PRAYER FOR ONE WHO IS TEMPTED TO DELAY APPLYING TO RELIGION, THOUGH UNDER SOME CONVICTIONS OF ITS IMPORTANCE.

Oh thou righteous and holy Sovereign of heaven. and earth! thou "God in whose hand my breath is, and whose are all my ways," Dan. v. 23, I confess I have been far from glorifying thee, or conducting myself according to the intimations, or the declarations of thy will. I have therefore reason to adore thy forbearance and goodness, that thou hast not long since stopped my breath, and "cut me off from the land of the living." I adore thy patience, that I have not months and years ago been an inhabitant of hell; where ten thousand delaying sinners are now lamenting their folly, and will be lamenting it for ever. But, O God, how possible is it, that this trifling heart of mine may, at length, betray me into the same ruin! and then, alas, into a ruin aggravated by all this patience and forbearance of thine! I am convinced that, sooner or later, religion must be my serious care, or I am undone; and yet my foolish heart draws back from the yoke: yet I stretch myself upon the bed of sloth, and cry out for " a little more sleep, a little more slumber, a little more folding of the hands to sleep," Prov. vi. 10. Thus does my corrupt heart plead for its own indulgence against the convictions of my better judgment. What shall

4*

I say? O Lord, save me from myself! save me from.
the artifices and deceitfulness of sin; save me from.
the treachery of this perverse and degenerate nature
of mine, and fix upon my mind what I have now
been reading.

O Lord, am I not now instructed in truths which
were before quite unknown?   Often have I been
warned of the uncertainty of life, and of the greater
uncertainty of the day of salvation: and I have formed some light purposes, and have begun to take a few
irresolute steps in my way towards a return unto
thee.   But, alas! I have been only, as it were, flut-
tering about religion, and have never fixed upon it.
All my resolutions have been scattered like smoke,
or dispersed like a cloudy vapour before the wind.
Oh, that thou wouldst now bring these things home
to my heart with a more powerful conviction than it
has ever yet felt!   Oh, that thou wouldst pursue me
with them, even when I flee from them, if I should
even grow mad enough to endeavour to escape them
any more!   May thy Spirit address me in the language of effectual terror; and add all the most powerful methods which thou knowest to be necessary,
to awaken me from this lethargy, which must otherwise be mortal.   May the sound of these things be
in mine ears, "when I go out, and when I come in,
when I lie down, and when I rise up," Deut. vi. 7.
And if the repose of the night, and the business of
the day, be for a while interrupted by the impression,
be it so, O God! if I may but thereby carry on my
business with thee to better purpose, and at length
secure a repose in thee, instead of all that terror which
I now find, when " I think upon God, and am troubled," Psal. lxxvii. 3.

O Lord, " my flesh trembleth for fear of thee, and
I am afraid of thy judgments," Psal. cxix. 120.   I
am afraid, lest, even now, that I have begun to think
of religion, thou shouldst cut me off in this critical
and important moment, before my thoughts grow to
any ripeness; and blast in eternal d ith, the first bud-
dings and openings of it in my mind.   But oh, spare

me, I earnestly entreat thee; .or thy me. cy's s. ke, spare me a little longer! It may be, through thy grace, I shall return. It may be, if thou continuest thy patience towards me a while longer, there may be some better fruit produced by this "cumberer of the ground," Luke xiii. 7, 8. And may the remembrance of that long forbearance, which thou hast already exercised towards me, prevent my continuing to trifle with thee, and with my own soul; from this day, O Lord, from this hour, from this moment, may I be able to date more lasting impressions of religion than have ever yet been made upon my heart by all that I have ever read, or all that I have heard. Amen.

———————

CHAPTER IV.

THE SINNER ARRAIGNED AND CONVICTED.

Conviction of guilt necessary, 1. A charge of rebellion against God advanced, 2. Where it is shown, (1.) That all men are born under God's law, 3. (2.) That no man has perfectly kept it, 4. An appeal to the reader's conscience on this head, that he has not, 5. (3.) That to have broken it is an evil inexpressibly great, 6: Illustrated by a more particular view of the aggravations of this guilt, arising, (1.) From knowledge, 7. (2.) From divine favours received, 8. (3.) From convictions of conscience overborne, 9. (4.) From the strivings of God's Spirit resisted, 10. (5.) From vows and resolutions broken, 11. The charges summed up, and left upon the sinner's conscience, 12. The sinner's confession under a general conviction of guilt.

1. As I am attempting to lead you to true religion, and not merely to some superficial form of it, I am sensible I can do it no otherwise than in the way of deep humiliation. And therefore, supposing you are persuaded, through the divine blessing on what you have before read, to take it into consideration, I would now endeavour, in the first place, with all the seriousness I can, to make you heartily sensible of your guilt before God. For I well know, that unless you

are convinced of this, and affected with the convic
tion, all the provisions of gospel grace will be slight
ed, and your soul infallibly destroyed in the midst of
the noblest means appointed for its recovery.   I am
fully persuaded that thousands live and die in a course
of sin, without feeling upon their hearts any sense
that they are sinners; though they cannot for shame,
but own it in words.   And therefore let me deal
faithfully with you, though I may seem to deal rough-
ly; for complaisance is not to give law to addresses
in which the life of your soul is concerned.

2. Permit me, therefore, O sinner, to consider myself at this time as an advocate for God; as one employed in his name to plead against thee, and to
charge thee with nothing less than being a rebel and
a traitor against the sovereign Majesty of heaven and
earth.   However thou mayest be dignified or distinguished among men; if the noblest blood run in thy
veins; if thy seat were among princes, and thine arm
were "the terror of the mighty in the land of the living," Ezek. xxxii. 27, it would be necessary thou
shouldst be told, and told plainly, thou hast broken
the "laws of the King of kings," and by the breach
of them art become obnoxious to his righteous con--
demnation.

3. Your conscience tells you, that you were born
the natural subject of God: born under the indispen-
sable obligations of his law.   For it is most apparent,
that the constitution of your rational nature, which
makes you capable of receiving law from God, binds
you to obey it.   And it is equally evident and certain, that you have not exactly obeyed this law;
nay, that you have violated it in many aggravated
instances.

4. Will you dare to deny this?   Will you dare to
assert your innocence?   Remember, it must be a
complete innocence; yes, and a perfect righteousness
too; or it can stand you in no stead, further than to
prove that, though a condemned sinner, you are not
quite so criminal as some others, and will not have
quite so hot a place in hell as they.   And when this is

considered, will you plead not guilty to the charge? Search the records of your own conscience, for God searches them: ask it seriously, "Have you never in your lives sinned against God?" Solomon declared, that, in his day there was "not a just man upon earth, who did good, and sinned not," Eccles. vii. 20, and the apostle Paul, that "all had sinned and had come short of the glory of God," Rom. iii. 25: that "both Jews and Gentiles," (which, you know comprehended the whole human race,) "were all under sin," Rom. ii. 9. And can you pretend any imaginable reason to believe the world is grown so much better since their days, that any should now plead their own case as an exception? Or will you, however, presume to rise in the face of the omniscient Majesty of heaven, and say, "I am the man?"

5. Supposing, as before, you have been free from those gross acts of immorality, which are so pernicions to society, that they have generally been punishable by human laws; can you pretend that you have not, in smaller instances, violated the rules of piety, of temperance, and of charity? Is there any one person, who has intimately known you, that would not be able to testify you had said or done something amiss? Or, if others could not convict you, would not your own heart do it? Does it not prove you guilty of pride, of passion, of sensuality, of an excessive fondness for the world and its enjoyments; of murmuring, or at least of secretly repining against God under the strokes of an afflictive providence; of misspending a great deal of your time; of abusing the gifts of God's bounty to vain, if not, in some instances, to pernicious purposes; of mocking him when you have pretended to engage in his worship, "drawing near to him with your mouth and your lips, while your heart has been far from him?" Isa. xxix. 13. Does not conscience condemn you of some one breach of the law at least? And, by one breach of it you are, in a sense, a scriptural sense, "become guilty of all," Jam. ii. 10, and are as incapable of being justified before God by any obedience of your

own, as if you had committed ten thousand offei.ces
But, in reality, there are ten thousand and more
chargeable to your account.   When you come to reflect on all your sins of negligence, as well as on those
of commission; on all the instances in which you
have " failed to do good, when it was in the power
of your hand to do it," Prov. iii. 27; on all the instances in which acts of devotion have been omitted.
especially in secret; and on all those cases in which
you have shown a stupid disregard to the honour of
God, and to the temporal and eternal happiness of
your fellow-creatures; when all these, I say, are reviewed, the number will swell beyond all possibility
of account, and force you to cry out, " Mine iniquities
are more than the hairs of my head," Psal. xl. 12.
They will appear in such a light before you, that
your own heart will charge you with countless multitudes; and how much more then " that God who is
greater than your heart, and knoweth all things?" 1
John iii. 20.

6. And say, sinner, is it a little thing that you have
presumed to set light by the authority of the God of
heaven, and to violate his law, if it had been by mere
carelessness and inattention? how much more heinous,
therefore, is the guilt, when in so many instances you
have done it knowingly and wilfully? Give me leave
seriously to ask you, and let me intreat you to ask
your own soul, "against whom hast thou magnified
thyself? against whom hast thou exalted thy voice,"
2 Kings xix. 22, or lifted up thy rebellious hand? On
whose law, oh sinner, hast thou presumed to trample?
And whose friendship and whose enmity hast thou
therefore dared to affront? Is it a man like thyself
that thou hast insulted? is it only a temporal monarch? only one, " who can kill thy body, and then
hath no more that he can do?" Luke xii. 4. Nay,
sinner, thou wouldst not have dared to treat a temporal prince as thou hast treated the " King eternal,
immortal, and invisible," 1 Tim. i. 17. No price
could have hired thee to deal by the majesty of an
earthly sovereign, as thou hast dealt by that God be-

fore wnom the cherubim and seraphim are continually bowing. Not one opposing or complaining, dis-
puting or murmuring word is heard among all the
celestial legions when the intimations of his will are
published to them; and who art thou, oh wretched
man, who art thou, that thou shouldst oppose him?
that thou shouldst oppose and provoke a God of infinite power and terror, who needs but exert one single
act of his sovereign will, and thou art in a moment
stripped of every possession; cut off from every hope;
destroyed and rooted up from existence, if that were
his pleasure; or, what is inconceivably worse, con-
signed over to the severest and most lasting agonies?
Yet this is the God whom thou hast offended; whom
thou hast affronted to his face, presuming to violate
his express laws in his very presence; this is the God
before whom thou standest as a convicted criminal;
convicted, not of one or two particular offences, but
of thousands and of ten thousands; of a course and
series of rebellions and provocations, in which thou
hast persisted, more or less, ever since thou wast
born; and the particulars of which have been attended with almost every conceivable circumstance of
aggravation. Reflect on particulars, and deny the
charge if you can.

7. If knowledge be an aggravation of guilt, thy guilt,
O sinner, is greatly aggravated! For thou wast born in
Emmanuel's land, and God has " written to thee the
great things of his law, yet thou hast accounted them
as a strange thing," Hosea vii. 12. " Thou hast
known to do good, and hast not done it," James iv.
17, and therefore to thee the omission of it has been
sin indeed. " Hast thou not known? hast thou not
heard," Isa. xl. 28, wast thou not early taught the
will of God in thine infant years? Hast thou not
since received repeated lessons, by which it has been
inculcated again and again, in public and in private,
by preaching and reading the word of God? nay, has
thy duty not been, in some instances, so plain, that
even without any instruction at all, thine own reason
might easily have inferred it? and hast thou not also

been warned of the consequences of disobedience Hast thou not "known the righteous judgment of God, that they who commit such things are worthy of death? yet thou hast, perhaps, not only done the same, but hast taken pleasure in those that do them," Rom. i. 32, hast chosen them for thy most intimate friends and companions; so as thereby to strengthen by the force of example and converse, the hands of each other in your iniquities.

8. Nay, more, if divine love and mercy be an aggravation of the sins committed against it, thy crimes, O sinner, are heinously aggravated. Must thou not acknowledge it, O foolish creature, and unwise? hast thou not been " nourished and brought up by him as his child, and yet hast rebelled against him?" Isa. i. 2. Did not God " take you out of the womb?" Psal. xxii. 9; did he not watch over you in your infant days, and guard you from a multitude of dangers, which the most careful parent or nurse could not have observed or warded off? Has he not given you your rational powers? and is it not by him you have been favoured with every opportunity of improving them? Has he not every day supplied your wants with an unwearied liberality; and added, with respect to many who will read this, the delicacies of life to its necessary supports? Has he not " heard you cry when trouble came upon you," Job xxvii. 9; and frequently appeared for your deliverance, when in the distresses of nature you had called upon him for help? Has he not rescued you from ruin, when it seemed just ready to swallow you up; and healed your diseases, when it seemed to all about you that the " residue of your days was cut off in the midst?" Psal. cii. 24. Or, if it has not been so, is not this long continued and uninterrupted health, which you have enjoyed for so many years, to be acknowledged as an equivalent obligation? Look around upon all your possessions, and say what one thing have you in the world which his goodness did not give you, and which he has not thus far preserved to you. Add to all this, the kind notices of his will

which he has sent you; the tender expostulations which he has used with you to bring you to a wiser and a better temper; and the discoveries and gracious invitations of his gospel, which you have heard, and which you have despised: and then say whether your rebellion has not been aggravated by the vilest ingratitude, and whether that aggravation can be accounted small.

9. Again, if it be any aggravation of sin to be committed against conscience, thy crimes, O sinner, have been so aggravated. Consult the records of it, and then dispute the fact if you can. "There is a spirit in man, and the inspiration of the Almighty giveth him understanding," Job xxxii. 8, and that understanding will act, and a secret conviction of being accountable to its Maker and Preserver is inseparable from the actings of it. It is easy to object to human remonstrances, and to give things false colourings before men; but the heart often condemns, while the tongue excuses. Have you not often found it so? has not conscience remonstrated against your past conduct, and have not these remonstrances been very painful too? I have been assured by a gentleman of undoubted credit, that when he was in the pursuit of all the gayest sensualities of life, and was reckoned one of the happiest of mankind, when he has seen a dog come into the room where he was among his merry companions, he has groaned inwardly, and said, "Oh, that I had been that dog!" And hast thou, O sinner, felt nothing like this? has thy conscience been so stupefied, so "seared with a hot iron," 1 Tim. iv. 2, that it has never cried out of any of the violences which have been done it? has it never warned thee of the fatal consequences of what thou hast done in opposition to it? These warnings are, in effect, the voice of God; they are the admonitions which he gave thee by his vicegerent in thy breast. And when his sentence for thy evil works is executed upon thee in everlasting death, thou shalt hear that voice speaking to thee again in a louder tone and a severer accent than before: and

thou shalt be tormented with its upbraidings through
eternity, because thou wouldst not in time hearken
to its admonitions.

10. Let me add further: If it be any aggravation
that sin has been committed after God has been moving by his Spirit on the mind, surely your sin has
been attended with that aggravation too. Under the
Mosaic dispensation, dark and imperfect as it was,
the Spirit strove with the Jews; else Stephen could
not have charged it upon them that, through all their
generations " they had always resisted him," Acts
vii. 51. Now, surely we may much more reasonably apprehend that he strives with sinners under
the gospel. And have you never experienced any
thing of this kind, even when there has been no external circumstance to awaken you, nor any pious
teacher near you; have you never perceived some
secret impulse upon your mind, leading you to think
of religion, urging you to an immediate consideration
of it, sweetly inviting you to make trial of it, and
warning you that you would lament this stupid neglect? O sinner, why were not these happy motions
attended to? why did you not, as it were, spread out
all the sails of your soul to catch that heavenly, that
favourable breeze? But you have carelessly neglected it: you have overborne these kind influences:
how reasonably then might the sentence have gone
forth in righteous displeasure, " My Spirit shall no
more strive," Gen. vi. 3. And, indeed, who can say
that it is not already gone forth? If you feel no
secret agitation of mind, no remorse, no awakening,
while you read such a remonstrance as this, there
will be room, great room, to suspect it.

11. There is indeed one aggravation more, which
may not attend your guilt; I mean that of being
committed against solemn covenant engagements: a
circumstance which has lain heavy on the consciences
of many, who perhaps, in the main series of their
lives, have served God with great integrity. But let
me call you to think to what this is owing. Is it not,
that you have never personally made any solemn

profession of devoting yourself to God at all? have never done any thing which has appeared to your own apprehension an action by which you made a covenant with him; though you have heard so much of his covenant, though you have been so solemnly and so tenderly invited to it? And in this view, how monstrous must this circumstance appear, which at first was mentioned as some alleviation of guilt! yet I must add, that you are not, perhaps, altogether so free from guilt on this head as you may at first imagine. I will not insist on the covenant which your parents made in your name when they devoted you to God in baptism; though it is really a weighty matter, and by calling yourself a Christian you have professed to own and avow what they then did; but I would remind you of what may have been more personal and express. Has your heart been, even from your youth, hardened to so uncommon a degree, that you have never cried to God in any season of danger and difficulty? and did you never mingle vows with those cries? Did you never promise, that if God would hear and help you in that hour of extremity, you would forsake your sins, and serve him as long as you lived? He heard and helped you, or you had not been reading these lines; and by such deliverance did, as it were, bind down your vows upon you: and therefore your guilt in the violation of them remains before him, though you are stupid enough to forget them. Nothing is forgotten, nothing is overlooked by him; and the day will come when the record shall be laid before you too.

12. And now, O sinner, think seriously with thyself what defence thou wilt make to all this. Prepare thine apology, call thy witnesses; make thine appeal from him whom thou hast thus offended to some superior judge, if such there be. Alas, those apologies are so weak and vain, that one of thy fellow-worms may easily detect and confound them, as I will endeavour presently to show thee. But thy foreboding conscience already knows the issue. Thou art convicted convicted of the most aggravated of

fences. Thou "hast not humbled thine heart, but
lifted up thyself against the Lord of heaven," Dan
v. 22, 23; and " thy sentence shall come forth from
his presence," Psal. xvii. 2. Thou hast violated his
known laws; thou hast despised and abused his numberless mercies: thou hast affronted conscience, his
vicegerent in thy soul; thou hast resisted and grieved
his Spirit; thou hast trifled with him in all thy pretended submissions; and, in one word, and that his
own, "thou hast done evil things as thou couldst,"
Jer. iii. 5. Thousands are, no doubt, already in hell,
whose guilt never equalled thine; and it is astonishing, that God has spared thee to read this representation of the case, or to make any pause upon it. Oh
waste not so precious a moment, but enter as attentively, and as humbly as thou canst, into those reflections, which suit a case so lamentable and so terrible
as thine.

THE CONFESSION OF A SINNER, CONVINCED IN GENERAL OF HIS GUILT.

Oh God! thou injured Sovereign, thou all penetrating and almighty Judge! what shall I say to this
charge? Shall I pretend I am wronged by it, and
stand on the defence in thy presence? I dare not do
it; for "thou knowest my foolishness, and none of
my sins are hid from thee," Psal. lxix. 5. My conscience tells me, that a denial of my crimes would
only increase them, and add new fuel to the fire of
thy deserved wrath. " If I justify myself, mine own
mouth will condemn me; if I say I am perfect, it will
also prove me perverse," Job ix. 20. For " innumerable evils have compassed me about: mine iniquities
have taken hold upon me, so that I am not able to
look up: they are," as I have been told in thy name,
" more than the hairs of my head, and therefore my
heart faileth me," Psal. xl. 12. I am more guilty
than it is possible for another to declare or represent.
My heart speaks more than any other accuser. And
thou, O Lord, art much "greater than my heart, and
knowest all things," 1 John iii. 20.

What has my life been but a course of rebellion against thee? It is not this or that particular action alone I have to lament. Nothing has been right in its principal views and ends. My whole soul has been disordered; all my thoughts, my affections, my desires, my pursuits, have been wretchedly alienated from thee. I have acted as if I had hated thee, who art infinitely the loveliest of all beings; as if I had been contriving how I might tempt thee to the uttermost, and weary out thy patience, marvellous as it is. My actions have been evil; my words yet more evil than they; and, O blessed God, my heart how much more corrupt than either! What an inexhausted fountain of sin has there been in it? " a fountain of original corruption," which mingled its bitter streams with the days of early childhood; and which, alas! flows on even to this day beyond what actions or words could express. I see this to have been the case, with regard to what I can particularly survey; but, oh, how many months and years have I forgotten, concerning which I only know this in the general, that they are much like those I can remember, except it be that I have been growing worse and worse, and provoking thy patience more and more, though every new exercise of it was more and more wonderful.

And how am I astonished that thy forbearance is still continued! It is, " because thou art God, and not man," Hos. xi. 9. Had I, a sinful worm, been thus injured, I could not have endured it. Had I been a prince, I had long since done justice on any rebel, whose crimes had borne but a distant resemblance to mine. Had I been a parent, I had long since cast off the ungrateful child, who had made me such a return as I have all my life long been making to thee, O thou Father of my spirit! The flame of natural affection would have been extinguished, and his sight, and his very name, would have become hateful to me. Why then, O Lord, am I not " cast out from thy presence," Jer. hi. 3; why am I not sealed up under an irreversible sentence of destruction? That I live, I owe to thine indulgence. **But,** oh, if there be yet any way of deliverance, if there be yet any hope for so guilty a creature, may it be opened upon me by thy gospel and thy grace. And if any further alarm, humiliation, or terror, be necessary to my security and salvation, may I meet them, and bear them all. Wound mine heart, O Lord, so that thou wilt but afterwards heal it; and break it in pieces, if thou wilt but at length condescend to bind 't up, Hos. vi. 1.

CHAPTER V.

THE SINNER STRIPPED OF HIS VAIN PLEAS.

The vanity of those pleas, which sinners may secretly confide in, is so apparent, that they will be ashamed at last to mention them before God, 1, 2. Such as, (1.) That they descended from pious parents, 3. (2.) That they had attended to the speculative part of religion, 4. (3.) That they had entertained sound notions, 5. (4.) That they had expressed a zealous regard to religion, and attended the outward forms of worship with those they apprehended the purest churches, 6, 7. (5.) That they had been free from gross immoralities, 8. (6.) That they did not think the consequence of neglecting religion would have been so fatal, 9. (7.) That they could not do otherwise than they did, 10. Conclusion, 11. With the meditation of a convinced sinner, giving up his vain pleas before God.

1. My last discourse left the sinner in very alarming and very pitiable circumstances; a criminal convicted at the bar of God, disarmed of all pretences to perfect innocence and sinless obedience, and consequently obnoxious to the sentence of a holy law, which can make no allowance for any transgression, no, not for the least; but pronounces death and a curse against every act of disobedience: how much more, then, against those numberless and aggravated acts of rebellion, of which, O sinner, thy conscience has condemned thee before God! I would hope some of my readers will ingenuously fall under the conviction, and not think of making any apology· for, sure

I am, that humbly to plead guilty at the divine bar, is the most decent, and, all things considered, the most prudent thing that can be done in such unhappy circumstances. Yet I know the treachery and the self-flattery of a sinful and a corrupted heart. I know what excuses it makes; and how, when it is driven from one refuge it flies to another, to fortify itself against full conviction, and to persuade, not merely another, but itself, " That, if it has been in some instances to blame, it is not quite so criminal as was represented; that there are at least considerations that plead in its favour, which, if they cannot justify, will, in some degree, excuse." A secret reserve of this kind, sometimes perhaps scarce formed into a distinct reflection, breaks the force of conviction, and often prevents that deep humiliation before God, which is the happiest token of an approaching deliverance. I will, therefore, examine into some of these particulars; and for that purpose would seriously ask thee, O sinner, what thou hast to offer in arrest of judgment, what plea thou canst urge for thyself why the sentence of God should not go forth against thee, and why thou shouldst not fall into the hands of his justice?

2. But this I must premise, that the question is not, how thou wouldst answer to me, a weak sinful worm like thyself, who am shortly to stand with thee at the same bar: ("the Lord grant that I may find mercy of the Lord in that day," 2 Tim. i. 18;) but, what wilt thou reply to thy Judge? What couldst thou plead if thou wast now actually before his tribunal; where to multiply vain words, and to frame idle apologies, would be but to increase thy guilt and provocation? Surely the very thought of his presence must supersede a thousand of those trifling excuses which now sometimes impose on " a generation that are pure in their own eyes, though they are not washed from their filthiness," Prov. xxx. 12; or, while they are conscious of their own impurities, trust in words that cannot profit, Jer. vii. 8, and " lean upon broken reeds " Isa. xxxvi. 6.

3. You will not, to be sure, in such circumstances plead "That you are descended from pious parents. That was, indeed, your privilege, and wo be to you that you have abused it, and "forsaken the God of your fathers," 2 Chron. vii. 22. Ishmael was imme_ diately descended from Abraham, the friend of God; and Esau was the son of Isaac, who was born according to the promise; yet, you know, they were both cut off from the blessing, to which they apprehended they had a kind of hereditary claim. You may remember that our Lord does not only speak of one who could call Abraham father, who was "tormented in flames," Luke xvi. 24, but expressly declares, that "many of the children of the kingdom shall be shut out of it;" and, when others come from the most distant parts to sit down in it, shall be distinguished from their companions in misery only by louder accents of lamentation, and more furious "gnashing of the teeth," Matt. viii. 11, 12.

4. Nor will you then presume to plead, "That you had exercised your thoughts about the specula_ tive part of religion:" for to what end can this serve but to increase your condemnation? Since you have broken God's law, since you have contradicted the most obvious and apparent obligations of religion, to have inquired into it, and argued upon it, is a circumstance that proves your guilt more audacious. What! did you think religion was merely an exercise of men's wit, and the amusement of their curiosity? If you argued about it on the principles of common sense, you must have judged and proved it to be a practical thing: and, if it was so, why did you not practise accordingly? You knew the particular branches of it; and why then did you not attend to every one of them? To have pleaded an unavoidable ignorance would have been the happiest plea that could have remained for you: nay, an actual, though faulty, ignorance would have been some little allay of your guilt. But if, by your own confession, you have "known your Master's will, and have not done it," you bear witness against yourself, that

you deserve to be " beaten with many stripes,' Luke xii. 47.

5. Nor yet again. will it suffice to say, " That you have had right notions, both of the doctrines and the precepts of religion." Your advantage for practising it was therefore the greater: but understanding and acting right can never go for the same thing in the judgment of God or of man. In " believing there is one God" you have done well; but " the devils also believe, and tremble," James i . 19. In acknowledging Christ to be the Son of God, and the Holy One, you have done well too; but, you know, the unclean spirits made this very orthodox confession, Luke iv. 34, 41, and yet they are " reserved in everlasting chains, under darkness, unto the judgment of the great day." Jude ver. 6. And will you place any secret confidence in that which might be pleaded by the infernal spirits as well as by you?

6. But, perhaps, you may think of pleading, " That you have actually done something in religion." Having judged what faith was the soundest, and what worship the purest, you entered yourselves into those societies where such articles of faith were professed, and such forms of worship were practised; and, amongst these, you have signalized yourselves, by the exactness of your attendance, by the zeal with which you have espoused their cause, and by the earnestness with which you have contended for such principles and practices.—O sinner, I much fear that this zeal of thine about the circumstantials of religion will swell thine account, rather than be allowed in abatement of it. He that searches thine heart knows from whence it arose, and how far it extended. Perhaps he sees that it was all hypocrisy; an artful veil, under which thou wast carrying on thy mean designs for this world; while the sacred names of God and religion were profaned and prostituted in the basest manner; and, if so, thou art cursed with a distinguished curse for so daring an insult on the divine omniscience, as well as justice Or, perhaps, the earnestness with which you ha' e been " contending

for the faith" and worship " which was once deliver
ed to the saints," Jude ver. 3, or which it is possible
you may rashly have concluded to be that, might be
mere pride and bitterness of spirit: and all the zea
you have expressed might possibly arise from a con
fidence in your own judgment, from an impatience
of contradiction, or from a secret malignity of spirit,
which delighted itself in condemning, and even in
worrying others: yea, which, if I may be allowea
the expression, fiercely preyed upon religion, as the
tiger upon the lamb, to turn it into a nature most
contrary to its own. And shall this screen you before the great tribunal? Shall it not rather awaken
the displeasure it is pleaded to avert?

7. But say that this your zeal for notions and forms
has been ever so well intended, and, so far as it has
gone, ever so well conducted too; what will that avail
towards vindicating thee in so many instances of negligence and disobedience as are recorded against thee
" in the book of God's remembrance?" Were the
revealed doctrines of the gospel to be earnestly maintained, (as indeed they ought,) and was the great
practical purpose for which they were revealed to be
forgot? Was the very mint, and anise, and cummin,
to be tithed, and were " the weightier matters of the
law to be omitted," Matt. xxiii. 23, and even that
love to God, which is its " first and great command,"
Matt. xxii. 38. Oh, how wilt thou be able to vindicate even the justest sentence thou hast passed on
others for their infidelity, or for their disobedience,
without being " condemned out of thine own mouth,"
Luke xix. 22.

8. Will you then plead " your fair moral character,
your works of righteousness arrd of mercy?" Had
your obedience to the law of God been complete, the
plea might be allowed as important and valid; but I
have supposed and proved above, that conscience
testifies to the contrary; and you will not now dare
to contradict it. I add further, had these works of
yours, which you now urge, proceeded from a sincere
love to God, and a genuine faith in the Lord Jesus

Christ, you would not have thought of pleading them any otherwise than as an evidence of your interest in the gospel covenant, and in the blessings of it, procured by the righteousness and blood of the Redeemer: and that faith, had it been sincere, would have been attended with such deep humility, and with such solemn apprehensions of the divine holiness and glory; that, instead of pleading any works of your own before God, you would rather have implored his pardon for the mixture of sinful imperfection attending the very best of them. Now, as you are a stranger to this humbling and sanctifying principle (as here, in this address, I suppose my reader to be) it is absolutely necessary you should be plainly and faithfully told, that neither sobriety, nor honesty, nor humanity, will justify you before the tribunal of God, when he "lays judgment to the line, and righteousness to the plummet," Isa. xxviii. 17, and examines all your actions, and all your thoughts with the strictest severity. You have not been a drunkard, an adulterer, or a robber. So far it is well. You stand before a righteous God, who will do you ample justice; and therefore will not condemn you for drunkenness, adultery, or robbery. But you have forgotten him, your Parent and your Benefactor; you have "cast off fear and restrained prayer before him," Job xv. 4, you have despised the blood of his Son, and all the immortal blessings which he purchased with it. For this, therefore, you are judged, and condemned. And as for any thing that has looked like virtue and humanity in your temper and conduct, the exercise of it has, in a great measure, been its own reward, if there were any thing more than form and artifice in it; and the various bounties of divine Providence to you amidst all your numberless provocations, have been a thousand times more than an equivalent for such defective and imperfect virtues as these. You remain, therefore, chargeable with the guilt of a thousand offences, for which you have no excuse at all; though there are some other instances in which you did not grossly offend. And those good works, in which you have been so ready to trust, will no more vindicate you in his awful presence, than a man's kindness to his poor neighbours would be allowed as a plea in arrest of judgment, when he stood convicted of high treason against his prince.

9. But you will, perhaps, be ready to say, "You did not expect all this: you did not think the consequences of neglecting religion would have been so fatal." And why did you not think it? Why did you not examine more attentively and more impartially? why did you suffer the pride and folly of your vain heart to take up with such superficial appearances, and trust the light suggestions of your own prejudiced mind against the express declaration of the word of God? Had you reflected on his character, as the supreme Governor of the world, you would have seen the necessity of such a day of retribution as we are now referring to. Had you regarded the Scripture, the divine authority of which you professed to believe, every page might have taught you to expect it. "You did not think of religion?" and of what were you thinking when you forgot or neglected it? Had you too much employment of another kind? of what kind, I beseech you? What end could you propose by any thing else of equal moment? Nay, with all your engagements, conscience will tell you that there have been seasons when, for want of thought, time and life have been a burden to you: yet you guarded against thought as against an enemy, and cast up, as it were, an intrenchment of inconsideration around you on every side, as if it had been to defend you from the most dangerous invasion. God knew you were thoughtless; and therefore he sent you "line upon line, and precept upon precept," Isa. xxviii. 10, in such plain language that it needed no genius or study to understand it. He tried you too with afflictions as well as with mercies, to awaken you out of your fatal lethargy; and yet, when awakened, you would lie down again upon the bed of sloth. And now, pleasing as your dreams

might be, "you must lie down in sorrow," Isa. l. 11. Reflection has at last overtaken you, and must be heard as a tormentor, since it might not be heard as a friend.

10. But some may, perhaps, imagine, that one important apology is yet unheard, and that there may be room to say, "You were, by the necessity of your nature, impelled to those things which are now charged upon you as crimes; whereas it was not in your power to have avoided them in the circumstances in which you were placed." If this will do any thing, it indeed promises to do much; so much, that it will amount to nothing. If I were disposed to answer you upon the folly and madness of your own principles, I might say, that the same consideration which proves it was necessary for you to offend, proves also that it is necessary for God to punish you: and that, indeed, he cannot but do it: and I might further say, with an excellent writer, "That the same principles which destroy the injustice of sins, destroy the injustice of punishments too." But, if you cannot admit this, if you should still reply in spite of principle, That it must be unjust to punish you for an action utterly and absolutely unavoidable; I really think you would answer right. But in that answer you will contradict your own scheme, (as I observed above:) and I leave your conscience to judge what sort of a scheme that must be which would make all kind of punishment unjust; for the argument will, on the whole, be the same whether with regard to human punishment or divine. It is a scheme full of confusion and horror. You would not, I am sure, take it from a servant who had robbed you, and then fired your house; you would never inwardly believe that he could not have helped it, or think that he had fairly excused himself by such a plea. And I am persuaded, you would be so far from presuming to offer it to God at the great day, that you would not venture to turn it into a prayer even now. Imagine you saw a malefactor dying

with such words as these: " O God, it is true, I did
indeed rob and murder my fellow-creature; but thou
knowest that, as my circumstances were ordered, I
could not do otherwise: my will was irresistibly determined by the motives which thou didst set before
me; and I could as well have shaken the foundations
of the earth, or darkened the sun in the firmament,
as have resisted the impulse which bore me on." I
put it to your conscience, whether you would not
look on such a speech as this with detestation, as one
enormity added to another. Yet, if the excuse would
have any weight in your mouth, it would have equal
weight in his, or would be equally applicable to any
the most shocking occasion. But, indeed, it is so
contrary to the plainest principles of common reason,
that I can hardly persuade myself any one could
seriously and thoroughly believe it; and should imagine my time very ill employed here, if I were to set
myself to combat those pretences to argument, by
which the wantonness of human wit has attempted
to varnish it over.

11. You see, then, on the whole, the vanity of all
your pleas, and how easily the most plausible of them
might be silenced by a mortal man like yourself; how
much more, then, by Him who searches all hearts,
and can, in a moment, flash in upon the conscience
a most powerful and irresistible conviction? What
then can you do while you stand convicted in the
presence of God? what should you do but hold your
peace under an inward sense of your inexcusable
guilt, and prepare yourself to hear the sentence which
his law pronounces against you? You must feel the
execution of it, if the gospel does not at length deliver you; and you must feel something of the terror
of it before you can be excited to seek to that gospel
for deliverance.

THE MEDITATION OF A CONVINCED SINNER GIVING UP HIS VAIN PLEAS BEFORE GOD.

Deplorable condition to which I am indeed reduced! "I have sinned;" and "what shall I say unto
thee, O thou preserver of men," Job vii. 20. What
shall I dare to say? Fool that I was, to amuse myself with such trifling excuses as these, and to imagine they could have any weight in thy tremendous
presence; or that I should be able so much as to mention them there. I cannot presume to do it; I am
silent and confounded. My hopes, alas, are slain,
and my soul itself is ready to die too, so far as an
immortal soul can die, and I am almost ready to say,
Oh that I could die entirely! I am indeed a criminal
in the hand of Justice, quite disarmed, and stripped
of the weapons in which I trusted. Dissimulation
can only add provocation to provocation. I will
therefore plainly and freely own it. I have acted as
if I "thought God was altogether such a one as myself: but," he has said, "I will reprove thee: I will
set thy sins in order before thine eyes, Psal. l. 21,
will marshal them in battle array." And oh, what
a terrible kind of host do they appear, and how do
they surround me beyond all possibility of escape!
O my soul, they have, as it were, taken thee prison-
er; and they are bearing thee away to the divine
tribunal.

Thou must appear before it; thou must see the
awful eternal Judge, who tries the very reins, Jer.
xvii. 10, and who needs no other evidence, for he
has himself been witness, Jer. xxix. 23, to all thy
rebellion; thou must see him, O my soul, sitting in
judgment upon thee; and when he is strict to mark
iniquity, Psal. cxxx. 3, how wilt thou "answer him
for one of a thousand?" Job ix. 3. And if thou canst
not answer him, in what language will he speak to
thee? Lord, as things at present stand, I can expect
no other language than that of condemnation. And
what a condemnation is it! Let me reflect upon it;

let me read my sentence before I hear t finally and irreversibly passed. I know he has recorded it in his word; and I know in the general, that the represcutation is made with a gracious design. I know that he would have us alarmed, that we may not be destroyed. Speak to me, therefore, O God, while thou speakest not for the last time, and in circumstances when thou wilt hear me no more. Speak in the language of effectual terror, so that it be not to speak me into final despair; and let thy word, however painful in its operation, be " quick and powerful, and sharper than any two-edged sword," Heb. iv. 12. Let me not vainly flatter myself; let me not be left a wretched prey to those who would " prophesy smooth things to me," Isa. xxx. 10, till I am sealed up under wrath, and feel thy justice piercing my soul, and " the poison of thine arrows drinking up all my spirits," Job vi. 4.

Before I enter upon the particular view, I know, in the general, that " it is a fearful thing to fall into the hands of the living God," Heb. x. 31. O thou living God, in one sense, I am already fallen into thine hands. I am become obnoxious to thy displeasure, justly obnoxious to it; and whatever thy sentence may be, when it " comes forth from thy presence," Psal. xvii. 2, I must condemn myself, and justify thee. Thou canst not treat me with more severity than mine iniquities have deserved; and how bitter soever that " cup of trembling" may be, Isa. li. 17, which thou shalt appoint for me, I give judgment against myself, that I deserve " to wring out the very dregs of it," Psal. lxxv. 8.

CHAPTER VI.

THE SINNER SENTENCED.

1. HEAR, O sinner, "and I will speak," Job xlii. 4, yet once more, as in the name of God; of God, thine almighty Judge, who, if thou dost not attend to his servants, will, ere long, speak unto thee in a more immediate manner, with an energy and terror which thou shalt not be able to resist.

2. Thou hast been convicted as in his presence Thy pleas have been overruled, or rather they have been silenced. It appears before God, it appears to thine own conscience, that thou hast nothing more to offer in arrest of judgment; therefore hear thy sentence, and summon up, if thou canst, all the powers of thy soul to bear the execution of it: "It is indeed a very small thing to be judged of man's judgment, but he that now judgeth thee is the Lord," 1 Cor. iv. 3, 4. Hear therefore, and tremble, while I tell thee how he will speak to thee; or rather while I show thee, from express scripture, how he does even now speak, and what is the authentic and recorded sentence of his word, even of his word who has said, "Heaven and earth shall pass away; but not one tittle of my word shall ever pass away," Matt. v. 18.

3. The law of God speaks, not to thee alone, O sinner, nor to thee by any particular address: but in a most universal language it speaks to all transgressors, and levels its terrors against all offences, great or small, without any exception; and this is its lan-

guage, " Cursed is every one that contir ueth not in all things which are written in the book of the law to do them," Gal. iii. 10. This is its voice to the whole world; and this it speaks to thee. Its awful contents are thy personal concern, O reader, and thy conscience knows it. Far from "continuing in al. things that are written therein to do them," thou canst not but be sensible, that "innumerable evils have compassed thee about," Psal. xl. 12. It is then manifest "thou art the man" whom it condemns; thou art even now, "cursed with a curse," Mal. iii. 9, as God emphatically speaks, "with the curse" of the most high God; yea, "all the curses which are written in the book of the law, are pointed against .hee," Deut. xxix. 20. God may righteously execute any of them upon thee in a moment; and though thou at present feelest none of them, yet, if infinite mercy does not prevent, it is but a little while, and they will "come into thy bowels like water," till thou art burst asunder with them, and shall penetrate "like oil into thy bones," Psalm cix. 18.

4. Thus saith the Lord, "The soul that sinneth shall die," Ezek. xviii. 4. But thou hast sinned, and therefore thou art under a sentence of death: and, oh, unhappy creature, of what a death! what will the end of these things be? That the agonies of dissolving nature shall seize thee; that thy soul shall be torn away from thy languishing body, and thou "return to the dust from whence thou wast taken," Psalm civ. 29, this is indeed one awful effect of sin. In these affecting characters has God, through all nations, and all ages of men, written the awful register and memorial of his holy abhorrence of it, and righteous displeasure against it. But alas! all this solemn pomp and horror of dying is but the opening of a dreadful scene. It is but a rough kind of stroke, by which the fetters are knocked off, when the criminal is led out to torture and execution.

5. Thus saith the Lord, "the wicked shall be turned into hell, even all the nations that forget God," Psalm ix. 17. Though there be whc le nations of

them, their multitudes and their power shall be no defence to them. They shall be driven into hell together, into that flaming prison which divine vengeance has prepared; into Tophet, which is ordained of old, even for royal sinners as well as for others, so little can any human distinction protect. " He hath made it deep and large, the pile thereof is fire and much wood; the breath of the Lord, like a stream of brimstone, shall kindle it," Isaiah xxx. 33, and the flaming torrent shall flow in upon it so fast, that it shall be turned into a sea of liquid fire; or, as the Scripture also expresses it, " A lake burning with fire and brimstone for ever and ever," Rev. xxi. 8, this is the second death, and the death to which thou, O sinner, by the word of God, art doomed.

6. And shall this sentence stand upon record in vain? shall the law speak it, and the gospel speak it? and shall it never be pronounced more audibly? and will God never require and execute the punishment? He will, O sinner, require it, and he will execute it, though he may seem for a while to delay. For well dost thou know that " he hath appointed a day in the which he will judge the whole world in righteousness, by that Man whom he hath ordained, of which he hath given assurance in having raised him from the dead," Acts xvii. 31. And when God judgeth the world, O reader, whoever thou art, he will judge thee: and while I remind thee of it, I would also remember that he will judge me: and " knowing the terror of the Lord," 2 Cor. v. 11, that I may " deliver my own soul," Ezek. xxxiii. 9, I would with all plainness and sincerity labour to deliver thine.

7. I, therefore, repeat the solemn warning: Thou, O sinner, shalt " stand before the judgment-seat of Christ," 2 Cor. v. 10. Thou shalt see that pompous appearance, the description of which is grown so familiar to thee, that the repetition of it makes no impression on thy mind: but surely, stupid as thou now art, the shrill trumpet of the archangel shall shake thy very soul: and if nothing else can awaken and

alarm thee, the convulsions and flames of a dissolving world shall do it.

8. Dost thou really think that the intent of Christ's final appearance is only to recover his people from the grave, and to raise them to glory and happiness? Whatever assurance thou hast that there shall be a resurrection of the just, thou hast the same that there shall also be a resurrection of the unjust, Acts xxiv. 15, that he shall separate the rising dead one from another, "as a shepherd divideth the sheep from the goats," Matt. xxv. 32, with equal certainty, and with infinitely greater ease. Or can you imagine that he will only make an example of some flagrant and notorious sinners, when it is said, that "all the dead, both small and great, shall stand before God," Rev. xx. 12, and that even he who knew not his master's will, and, consequently, seems of all others to have had the fairest excuse for his omission to obey it, yet even he, for that very omission shall be beaten, though with fewer stripes? Luke xii. 48. Or, can you think that a sentence to be delivered with so much pomp and majesty, a sentence by which the righteous judgment of God is to be revealed, and to have its most conspicuous and final triumph, will be inconsiderable, or the punishment to which it shall consign the sinner be slight or tolerable? There would have been little reason to apprehend that, even if we had been left barely to our own conjectures, what that sentence should be: but this is far from being the case. Our Lord Jesus Christ, in his infinite condescension and compassion, has been pleased to give us a copy of the sentence, and, no doubt, a most exact copy; and the words which contain it are worthy of being inscribed on every heart. The King, amidst all the splendour and dignity in which he shall then appear, shall say unto "those on his right hand, Come, ye blessed of my Father, inherit the kingdom prepared for you from the foundation of the world," Matt. xxv. 54, and where the word of a King is, there is power indeed. Eccles. viii. 4. And these words have a power

which may justly animate the heart of the humble Christian under the most overwhelming sorrow; and may fill him with "joy unspeakable and full of glory," 1 Pet. i. 8. To be pronounced the blessed of the Lord! to be called to a kingdom! to the immediate, the everlasting inheritance of it! and of such a kingdom! so well prepared, so glorious, so complete, so exquisitely fitted for the delight and entertainment of such creatures so formed and so renewed, that it shall appear worthy the eternal counsels of God to have contrived it, worthy his eternal love to have prepared it, and to have delighted himself with the views of bestowing it upon his people! Behold, a blessed hope indeed! a lively glorious hope, to which we are begotten again by the resurrection of Christ from the dead, 1 Pet. i. 3, and formed by the sanctifying influence of the Spirit of God upon our minds! But it is a hope, from which thou, O sinner, art at present excluded: and methinks that it might be grievous, to reflect, "These gracious words shall Christ speak to some, to multitudes, but not to me; on me there is no blessedness pronounced: for me there is no kingdom prepared." But is that all? Alas! sinner, our Lord has given thee a dreadful counterpart to this: he has told us what he will say to thee, if thou continuest what thou art; to thee, and all the nations of the impenitent and unbelieving world, be they ever so numerous, be the rank of particular criminals ever so great. He shall say to the kings of the earth, who have been rebels against him, to "the great and rich men, and the chief captains, and the mighty men, as well as to every bondman, and every freeman" of inferior rank, Rev. vi. 15, " DEPART FROM ME, YE CURSED, INTO EVERLASTING FIRE, PREPARED FOR THE DEVIL AND HIS ANGELS," Matt. xxv. 41. Oh, pause upon these weighty words, that thou mayest enter into something of the importance of them!

9. He will say, *Depart;* you shall be driven from his presence with disgrace and infamy; from Him, the source of life and blessedness, in a nearness to whom all the inhabitants of heaven continually re-

joice: you shall depart *accursed;* you have broken God's law, and its curse falls upon you, and you are and shall be under that curse, that abiding curse, from that day forward you shall be regarded by God, and all his creatures, as an accursed and abominable thing; as the most detestable and the most miserable part of the creation: you shall go into *fire;* and, oh, consider into what fire. Is it merely into one fierce blaze, which shall consume you in a moment, though with exquisite pain? that were terrible: but, oh, such terrors are not to be named with these: thine, sinner, is *everlasting fire;* it is that which our Lord has in such awful terms described as prevailing there, " where their worm dieth not, and the fire is not quenched;" and then says a second time, " Where their worm dieth not, and the fire is not quenched;" and again, in wonderful compassion, a third time, " where their worm dieth not, and the fire is not quenched," Mark ix. 44, 46, 48. Nor was it originally prepared, or principally intended for you; it was *prepared for the devil and his angels:* for those first grand rebels who were, immediately upon their fall, doomed to it; and since you have taken part with them in their apostasy, you must sink with them in that flaming ruin; and sink so much the deeper, as you have despised a Saviour who was never offered to them. These must be your companions, and your tormentors, with whom you must dwell for ever. And is it I that say this? or say not the law and the gospel the same? Does not the Lord Jesus Christ expressly say it, " who is the faithful and true witness," Rev. iii. 14, even he who himself is to pronounce the sentence?

10. And when it is thus pronounced, and pronounced by him, shall it not also be executed? Who could imagine the contrary? who could imagine there should be all this pompous declaration to fill the mind only with vain terror, and that this sentence should vanish into smoke? You may easily apprehend that this would be a greater reproach to the divine administration, than if sentence were never to be pass-

ed; and, therefore, we might easily have inferred the execution of it from the process of the preceding judgment. But lest the treacherous heart of a sinner should deceive him with so vain a hope, the assurance of that execution is immediately added in very memorable terms: It shall be done; it shall immediately be done. Then, on that very day, while the sound of it is yet in their ears, " the wicked shall go away into everlasting punishment," Matt. xxv. 46; and thou, O reader, whoever thou art, being found in their number, shalt go away with them; shalt be driven on among all these wretched multitudes, and plunged with them into eternal ruin. The wide gates of hell shall be open to receive thee; they shall be shut upon thee for ever to inclose thee, and be fast barred by the almighty hand of divine justice, to prevent all hope, all possibility of escape for ever.

11. And now prepare thyself " to meet the Lord thy God," Amos iv. 12; summon up all the resolution of thy mind to endure such a sentence, such an execution as this: for " he will not meet thee as a man," Isa. xlvii. 3, whose heart may sometimes fail him, when about to exert a needful act of severity so that compassion may prevail against reason and justice. No, he will meet thee as a God, whose schemes and purposes are as immovable as his throne I, therefore, testify to thee in his name this day, that, if God be true, he will thus speak; and that if he be able, he will thus act. And, on supposition of thy continuance in thine impenitency and unbelief, thou art brought into this miserable case, that if God be not either false or weak, thou art undone, thou art eternally undone.

THE REFLECTION OF A SINNER, STRUCK WITH THE TERROR OF HIS SENTENCE.

Wretch that I am! what shall I do? or whither shall I flee? " I am weighed in the balance, and am found wanting," Dan. v. 27. This is, indeed, my doom, the doom I am to expect from the mouth of

Christ himself, from the mouth of him that died for the redemption and salvation of men. Dreadful sentence! and so much the more dreadful when considered in that view. To what shall I look to save me from it; to whom shall I call? Shall I say to the "rocks, fall upon me, and to the hills, cover me?" Luke xxiii. 30. What should I gain by that? Were I, indeed, overwhelmed with rocks and mountains, they could not conceal me from the notice of his eye; and his hand could reach me with as much ease there as any where else.

Wretch indeed that I am! Oh that I had never been born! Oh that I had never known the dignity and prerogative of the rational nature! Fatal prerogative, indeed, that renders me obnoxious to condemnation and wrath! Oh that I had never been instructed in the will of God at all, rather than that, being thus instructed, I should have disregarded and transgressed it! Would to God I had been allied to the meanest of the human race, to them that come nearest to the state of the brutes, rather than that I should have had my lot in cultivated life, amidst so many of the improvements of reason, and (dreadful reflection) amidst so many of the advantages of religion too, and thus to have perverted all to my own destruction. Oh that God would take away this rational soul! But, alas! it will live for ever, will live to feel the agonies of eternal death. Why have I seen the beauties and glories of a world like this, to exchange it for that flaming prison? why have I tasted so many of my Creator's bounties, to wring out at last the dregs of his wrath? why have I known the delights of social life and friendly converse, to exchange them for the horrid company of devils and damned spirits in Tophet? Oh, "who can dwell with them in devouring flames! who can lie down with them in everlasting, everlasting, everlasting burnings!" Isa. xxxiii. 14.

But whom have I to blame in all this but myself? what have I to accuse but my own stupid incorrigible folly? On what is all this terrible ruin to be charged, but on this one fatal cursed cause, that, having broken God's law, I rejected his gospel too?

Yet stay, O my soul, in the midst of all these doleful, foreboding complaints. Can I say that I have finally rejected the gospel? Am I not, to this day, under the sound of it? The sentence is not yet gone forth against me in so determined a manner, as to be utterly irreversible. Through all this gloomy prospect one ray of hope breaks in, and it is possible I may yet be delivered.

Reviving thought! rejoice in it, O my soul, though it be with trembling; and turn immediately to that God who, though provoked by ten thousand offences, has not yet " sworn in his wrath, that thou shalt never" be permitted to hold further intercourse with him, or to " enter into his rest," Psal. xcv. 11.

I do then, O blessed Lord prostrate myself in the dust before thee. I own   am a condemned and miserable creature; but my language is that of the humble publican, " God be i rciful to me a sinner," Luke xviii. 13. Some gener. and confused apprehensions I have of a way by which I may possibly escape. O God, whatever that way is, show it me, I beseech thee. Point it out so plainly, that I may not be able to mistake it. And oh, reconcile my heart to it, be it ever so humbling, be it ever so painful.

Surely, Lord, I have much to learn; but be thou my teacher. Stay for a little thine uplifted hand; and, in thine infinite compassion, delay the stroke, till I inquire a little further how I may finally avoid it

CHAPTER VII.

THE HELPLESS STATE OF THE SINNER UNDER CONDEMNA
TION.

The sinner urged to consider how he can be saved from this im
pending ruin, 1, 2. (1.) Not by any thing he can offer, 3. (2.)
Nor by any thing he can endure, 4. (3.) Nor by any thing he
can do in the course of future duty, 5. (4.) Nor by any alliance
with fellow-sinners on earth, or in hell, 6—8. (5.) Nor by any
interposition or intercession of angels or saints in his favour, 9
Hint of the only method, to be afterwards more largely explained,
ib. The lamentation of a sinner in this miserable condition.

1. SINNER, thou hast heard the sentence of God, as
it stands upon record in his sacred and immutable
word.   And wilt thou lie down under it in everlasting despair? wilt thou make no attempt to be delivered from it, when it speaks nothing less than *eternal death* to thy soul?   If a criminal, condemned by
human laws, has but the least shadow of hope that
he may possibly escape, he is all attention to it.   If
there be a friend who he thinks can help him, with
what strong importunity does he entreat the interposition of that friend?   And, even while he is before
the judge, how difficult is it often to force him away
from the bar, while the cry of Mercy, mercy, mercy,
may be heard, though it be never so unreasonable?
A mere possibility that it may make some impression,
makes him eager in it, and unwilling to be silenced
and removed.

2. Wilt thou not then, O sinner, ere yet execution
's done, that execution which may, perhaps, be done
this very day, wilt thou not cast about in thy thoughts
what measures may be taken for deliverance?   Yet
what measures can be taken?   Consider attentively:
for it is an affair of moment.   Thy wisdom, thy
power, thy eloquence, or thine interest, can never be
exerted on a greater occasion.   If thou canst help
thyself, do.   If thou hast any secret source of relief,
go not out of thyself for other assistance.   If thou

hast any sa, rifice to offer, if thou hast any strength
to exert, yea, if thou hast any allies on earth, or in
the invisible world, who can defend and deliver thee,
take thine own way, so that thou mayest but be delivered at all, and we may not see thy ruin. But say,
O sinner, in the presence of God, what sacrifice thou
wilt present, what strength thou wilt exert, what
allies thou wilt have recourse to, on so urgent, so
hopeless an occasion: for, hopeless I must indeed
pronounce it, if such methods are taken.

3. The justice of God is injured: hast thou any
atonement to make to it? If thou wast brought to an
inquiry and proposal, like that of the awakened sinner, " Wherewith shall I come before the Lord, and
bow myself before the high God? Shall I come before him with burnt-offerings, with calves of a year
old? Will the Lord be pleased with thousands of
rams, or with ten thousands of rivers of oil?" Micah
vi. 6, 7. Alas! wert thou as great a prince as Solomon himself, and couldst thou indeed purchase such
sacrifices as these, there would be no room to mention them, " Lebanon would not be sufficient to burn,
nor all the beasts thereof for a burnt-offering," Isa.
xl. 16. Even under that dispensation, which admitted and required sacrifices in some cases, the blood
of bulls and of goats, though it exempted the offender from further temporal punishment, could not take
away sin, Heb. x. 4, nor prevail by any means to
purge the conscience in the sight of God. And that
soul that had done aught presumptuously, was not
allowed to bring any sin-offering, or trespass-offering
at all, but was condemned to " die without mercy."
Num. xv. 30. Now God and thy own conscience
know that thine offences have not been merely the
errors of ignorance and inadvertency, but that thou
hast sinned with an high hand, in repeated aggravated instances, as thou hast acknowledged already.—
Shouldst thou add, with the wretched sinner described
above, " Shall I give my first-born for my transgression, the fruit of my body for the sin of my soul?"
Micah vi. 7: what could the blood of a beloved

child do in such a case, but dye thy crimes so much
the deeper, and add a yet unknown horror to them?
Thou hast offended a Being of infinite majesty; and
if that offence is to be expiated by blood, it must be
by another kind of blood than that which flows in
the veins of thy children, or in thine own.

4. Wilt thou then suffer thyself, till thou hast made
full satisfaction? But how shall that satisfaction be
made? Shall it be by any calamities to be endured
in this mortal momentary life? Is the justice of God
then esteemed so little a thing, that the sorrows of a
few days should suffice to answer its demands? Or
dost thou think of future sufferings in the invisible
world? If thou dost, that is not deliverance: and,
with regard to that, I may venture to say, when thou
hast made full satisfaction, thou wilt be released:
when thou hast paid the utmost farthing of that debt,
thy prison-doors shall be opened. In the mean time,
thou must "make thy bed in hell," Psal. cxxxix. 8,
and, O unhappy man, wilt thou lie down there with
a secret hope that the moment will come when the
rigour of divine justice will not be able to inflict any
thing more than thou hast endured, and when thou
mayest claim thy discharge as a matter of right? It
would indeed be well for thee if thou couldest carry
down with thee such a hope, false and flattering as it
is: but, alas! thou wilt see things in so just a light,
that to have no comfort but this will be eternal despair. That one word of thy sentence, *everlasting
fire;* that one declaration, "The worm dieth not,
and the fire is not quenched;" will be sufficient to
strike such a thought into black confusion, and to
overwhelm thee with hopeless agony and horror.

5. Or do you think that your future reformation
and diligence in duty for the time to come will pro-
cure your discharge from this sentence? Take heed,
sinner, what kind of obedience thou thinkest of offering to an holy God. That must be spotless and complete, which his infinite sanctity can approve and accept, if he consider thee in thyself alone; there must
be no inconstancy, no forgetfulness no mixture of sin

attending it. And wilt thou, enfeebled as thou art, by so much original corruption, and so many sinful habits contracted by innumerable actual transgressions, under⁺ake to render such an obedience and that for all the remainder of thy life? In vain wouldst thou attempt it even but for one day. New guilt would immediately plunge thee into new ruin; but if it did not; if from this moment to the very end of thy life all were as complete obedience as the law of God required from Adam in paradise, would that be sufficient to cancel past guilt? would it discharge an old debt, that thou hadst not contracted a new one? Offer this to thy neighbour, and see if he will accept it for payment; and if he will not, wilt thou presume to offer it to thy God?

6. But I will not multiply words on so plain a subject. While I speak thus, time is passing away, death presses on, and judgment is approaching. And what can save thee from these awful scenes, or what can protect thee in them? Can the world save thee? that vain delusive idol of thy wishes and pursuits, to which thou art sacrificing thine eternal hopes? Well dost thou know that it will utterly forsake thee when thou needest it most; and that not one of its enjoyments can be carried along with thee into the invisible state; no, not so much as a trifle to remember it by, if thou couldst desire to remember so inconstant and so treacherous a friend as the world has been.

7. And when you are dead, or when you are dying, can your sinful companions save you? Is there any one of them, if he were ever so desirous of doing it, that " can give unto God a ransom for you," Psa. xlix. 7, to deliver you from going down to the grave, or from going down to hell? Alas! you will probabably be so sensible of this, that when you lie on the borders of the grave, you will be unwilling to see or to converse with those that were once your favourite companions. They will afflict you rather than relieve you, even then; how much less can they relieve you before the bar of God, when they are overwhelm ed with their own condemnation?

8. As for the powers of darkness, you are sure
they will be far from any ability or inclination to help
you. Satan has been watching and labouring for
your destruction, and he will triumph in it. But if
there could be any thing of an amicable confederacy
between you, what would that be but an association
in ruin? For the day of judgment of ungodly men
will also be the judgment of these rebellious spirits;
and the fire into which thou, O sinner, must depart,
is that which was " prepared for the devil and his
angels." Matt. xxv. 41.

9. Will the celestial spirits then save thee? will
they interpose their power or their prayers in thy favour? An interposition of power, when sentence is
gone forth against thee, were an act of rebellion
against Heaven, which these holy and excellent creatures would abhor. And when the final pleasure of
the Judge is known, instead of interceding, in vain,
for the wretched criminal, they would rather, with
ardent zeal for the glory of their Lord, and cordial
acquiescence in the determination of his wisdom and
justice, prepare to execute it. Yea, difficult as it may
at present be to conceive it, it is a certain truth, that
the servants of Christ who now most tenderly love
you, and most affectionately seek your salvation, not
excepting those who are allied to you in the nearest
bonds of nature, or of friendship, even they shall put
their *Amen* to it. Now, indeed, their bowels yearn
over you, and their eye poureth out tears on your
account; now they expostulate with you, and plead
with God for you, if by any means, while yet there
is hope, you may be " plucked as a firebrand out of
the burning," Amos iv. 11; but, alas! their remonstrances you will not regard; and as for their prayers,
what should they ask for you? what but this, that
you may see yourselves to be undone? and that utterly despairing of any help from yourselves, or from
any created power, you may lie before God in hu
mility and brokenness of heart; and submitting yourselves to his righteous judgment, and in an utter renunciation of all self-dependence, and of all creature-

dependence, you may lift up an humble look towards him, as almost from the depths of hell, if peradventure he may have compassion upon you, and may himself direct you to that only method of rescue which, while things continue as in present circumstances they are, neither earth, nor hell, nor heaven, can afford you.

THE LAMENTATION OF A SINNER IN THIS MISERABLE CONDITION.

Oh doleful, uncomfortable, helpless state! O wretch that I am, to have reduced myself to it! Poor, empty, miserable, abandoned creature! Where is my pride, and the haughtiness of my heart? Where are my idol deities, "whom I have loved and served, after whom I have walked, and whom I have sought," Jer. viii. 2, whilst I have been multiplying my transgressions against the Majesty of heaven? Is there no heart to have compassion upon me? is there no hand to save me? "Have pity upon me, have pity upon me, O my friends; for the hand of God hath touched me," Job xix. 21; has seized me. I feel it pressing me hard, and what shall I do? Perhaps they have pity upon me; but, alas, how feeble a compassion! Only if there be any where in the whole compass of nature any help, tell me where it may be found. O point it out; direct me towards it; or rather, confounded and astonished as my mind is, take me by the hand and lead me to it.

O ye ministers of the Lord, whose office it is to guide and comfort distressed souls, take pity upon me. I fear I am a pattern of many other helpless creatures, who have the like need of your assistance. Lay aside your other cares to care for my soul; to care for this precious soul of mine, which lies as it were bleeding to death, (if that expression may be used,) while you, perhaps, hardly afford me a look: or, glancing an eye upon me, "pass over to the other side," Luke x. 32. Yet, alas! in a case like mine, what can your interposition avail, if it be alone?

" If the Lord do not help me, how can ye help me."
2 Kings vi. 27.

Oh God of the spirits of all flesh, Num. xvi. 2,
I lift up mine eyes unto thee, and " cry unto thee, as
out of the belly of hell," Jonah ii. 2; I cry unto thee
at least from the borders of it. Yet while I lie before
thee in this infinite distress, I know that thine almighty power and boundless grace can still find out
a way for my recovery.

Thou art he whom I have most of all injured and
affronted; and yet from thee alone must I now seek
redress. " Against thee, thee only, have I sinned,
and done evil in thy sight," Psal. li. 4; so that " thou
mightest be justified when thou speakest, and be
clear when thou judgest," though thou shouldst this
moment adjudge me to eternal misery. And yet I
find something that secretly draws me to thee, as if
I might find rescue there where I have deserved the
most aggravated destruction. Blessed God, " I have
destroyed myself; but in thee is my help," Hos. xiii.
9, if there can be help at all.

I know, in the general, that " thy ways are not as
our ways, nor thy thoughts as our thoughts;" but
are as " high above them as the heavens are above
the earth," Isa. lv. 8, 9. " Have mercy," therefore,
" upon me, O God, according to thy loving kindness,
according to the multitude of thy tender mercies,"
Psal. li. 1. O point out the path to the city of refuge! O lead me thyself " in the way everlasting,"
Psal. cxxxix. 24. I know, in the general, that thy
gospel is the only remedy. O teach thy servants to
administer it! O prepare mine heart to receive it,
and suffer not, as in many instances, that malignity
which has spread itself through all my nature, to turn
that noble medicine into poison.

CHAPTER VIII.

NEWS OF SALVATION BY CHRIST, BROUGHT TO THE CON-
VINCED AND CONDEMNED SINNER.

The awful things which have hitherto been said, intended not to
grieve, but to help, 1. After some reflection on the pleasure with
which a minister of the gospel may deliver the message with
which he is charged, 2; and some reasons for the repetition of
what is in speculation so generally known, 3; the author proceeds
briefly to declare the substance of these glad tidings, viz: That
God having, in his infinite compassion, sent his Son to die for
sinners, is now reconcilable through him, 4—6: so that the most
heinous transgressions shall be entirely pardoned to believers, and
they made completely and eternally happy, 7, 8. The sinner's
reflection on this good news.

1. My dear reader, it is the great design of the gospel, and, wherever it is cordially received, it is the
glorious effect of it, to fill the heart with sentiments
of love; to teach us to abhor all unnecessary rigour
and severity, and to delight, not in the grief, but in
the happiness of our fellow-creatures. I can hardly
apprehend how he can be a Christian, who takes
pleasure in the distress which appears even in a
brute, much less in that of a human mind; and, especially, in such distress as the thoughts I have been
proposing must give, if there be any due attention to
their weight and energy. I have often felt a tender
regret while I have been representing these things;
and I could have wished from mine heart, that it had
not been necessary to have placed them in so severe
and so painful a light. But now I am addressing
myself to a part of my work, which I undertake with
unutterable pleasure; and to that which indeed I had
in view, in all those awful things which I have already been laying before you. I have been show-
ing you, that, if you hitherto have lived in a state of
impenitence and sin, you are condemned by God's
righteous judgment, and have in yourself no spring
of hope and no possibility of deliverance. But I
mean not to leave you under this sad apprehension,

to lie down and die in despair, complaining of that cruel zeal which has " tormented you before the time," Matt. viii. 29.

2. Arise, O thou dejected soul, that art prostrate in the dust before God, and trembling under the terrors of his righteous sentence: for I am commissioned to tell thee, that though " thou hast destroyed thyself, in God is thine help," Hosea xiii. 9.   I bring thee " good tidings of great joy," Luke ii. 10, which delight my own heart while I proclaim them, and will, I hope, reach and revive thine; even the tidings of salvation by the blood and righteousness of the Redeemer.   And I give it thee, for thy greater security, in the words of a gracious and forgiving God, that " he is in Christ reconciling the world unto himself, and not imputing to them their trespasses," 2 Cor. v. 19.

3. This is the best news that ever was heard; the most important message which God ever sent to his creatures; and though I doubt not at all, but living, as you have done, in a Christian country, you have heard it often, perhaps a thousand and a thousand times, I will, with all simplicity and plainness, repeat it to you again, and repeat it as if you had never heard it before.   If thou, O sinner, shouldst now, for the first time, feel it, then will it be as a new gospel unto thee, though so familiar to thine ear; nor shall it be grievous for me to speak what is so common, since to you it is safe and necessary, Phil. iii. 1. They who are most deeply and intimately acquainted with it, instead of being cloyed and satiated, will hear it with distinguished pleasure; and as for those who have hitherto slighted it, I am sure they had need to hear it again.   Nor is it absolutely impossible that some one soul, at least, may read these lines, who has never been clearly and fully instructed in this important doctrine, though his everlasting all depends on knowing and receiving it.   I will therefore take care that such a one shall not have it to plead at the bar of God, that though he lived in a Christian country, he was never plainly and faithfully taught

the doctrine of salvation by Jesus Christ, " the way, the truth, and the life, by whom alone we come unto the Father," John xiv. 6.

4. I do therefore testify unto you this day, that the holy and gracious Majesty of heaven and earth, fore-seeing the fatal apostasy into which the whole hu-man race would fall, did not determine to deal in a way of strict and rigorous severity with us, so as to consign us over to universal ruin and inevitable dam-nation; but, on the contrary, he determined to enter into a treaty of peace and reconciliation, and to pub-lish to all, whom the gospel should reach, the express offers of life and glory, in a certain method, which his infinite wisdom judged suitable to the purity of his nature, and the honour of his government. This method was indeed a most astonishing one, which, familiar as it is to our thoughts and our tongues, I cannot recollect and mention without great amaze-ment. He determined to send his own Son into the world, " the brightness of his glory, and the express image of his person," Heb. i. 3, partaker of his own divine perfections and honours, to be not merely a teacher of righteousness, and a messenger of grace, but also a sacrifice for the sins of men; and would consent to his saving them on no other condition but this, that he should not only labour, but die in the cause.

5. Accordingly, at such a period of time as infinite Wisdom saw most convenient, the Lord Jesus Christ appeared in human flesh; and after he had gone through incessant and long continued fatigues, and borne all the preceding injuries which the ingratitude and malice of men could inflict, he voluntarily " sub-mitted himself to death, even the death of the cross," Phil. ii. 8, and having been "delivered for our of-fences, was raised again for our justification," Rom. iv. 25. After his resurrection he continued long enough on earth to give his followers most convincing evidences of it, and then "ascended into heaven in their sight," Acts i. 9—11, and sent down his Spi-rit from thence upon his apostles, to enable them, in

the most persuasive and authoritative manner, to
" preach the gospel," Luke xxiv. 40, and he has giver
it in charge to them, and to those who, in every age,
succeed them in this part of their office, that it should
be published " to every creature," Mark xvi. 15, that
all who believe in it may be saved, by virtue of its
abiding energy, and the immutable power and grace
of its divine author, who is " the same yesterday, to-
day, and for ever," Heb. xiii. 8.

6. This gospel do I therefore now preach, and proclaim unto thee, O reader, with the sincerest desire
that, through divine grace, it may this very day be
" salvation to thy soul," Luke xix. 9.   Know therefore, and consider it, whosoever thou art, that as
surely as these words are now before thine eyes, so
sure it is that the incarnate Son of God " was made
a spectacle to the " world, and to angels, and to men,"
1 Cor. iv. 9, his back torn with scourges, his head
with thorns, his limbs stretched out as on a rack, and
nailed to the accursed tree; and in this miserable
condition he was hung up by his hands and his feet,
as an object of public infamy and contempt.   Thus
did he die, in the midst of all the taunts and insults
of his cruel enemies who thirsted for his blood; and
which was the saddest circumstance of all, in the
midst of these agonies with which he closed the most
innocent, perfect, and useful life that ever was spent
upon earth, he had not those supports of the divine
presence which sinful men have often experienced,
when they have been suffering for the testimony of
their conscience.   They have often burst out into
transports of joy and songs of praise while their ex-
ecutioners have been glutting their hellish malice,
and more than savage barbarity, by making their
torments artificially grievous; but the crucified Jesus
cried out, in the distress of his spotless and holy soul,
" My God, my God, why hast thou forsaken me?"
Matt. xxvii. 46.

7. Look upon our dear Redeemer!   Look up to
this mournful, dreadful, yet, in one view, delightful
spectacle, and then ask thine own heart, Do I be-

iieve that Jesus suffered and died thus? and why did he suffer and die? Let me answer in God's own words, " He was wounded for our transgressions, he was bruised for our iniquities, and the chastisement of our peace was upon him, that by his stripes we might be healed: it pleased the Lord to bruise him, and to put him to grief, when he made his soul an offering for sin;" for the Lord " laid on him the 'niquity of us all," Isa. liii. 5, 6, 10. So that I may address you in the words of the Apostle, " Be it known unto you therefore, that through this man is preached unto you the forgiveness of sin," Acts xiii. 38, as it was his command, just after he arose from the dead, that " repentance and remission of sins should be preached in his name unto all nations, beginning at Jerusalem," Luke xxiv. 47, the very place where his blood had so lately been shed in so cruel a manner. I do therefore testify unto you, in the words of another inspired writer, that " Christ was made sin," that is, a sin-offering, " for us, though he knew no sin, that we might be made the righteousness of God in him," 2 Cor. v. 21, that is, that through the righteousness he has fulfilled, and the atonement he has made, we might be accepted by God as righteous, and be not only pardoned, but received into his favour. " To you is the word of this salvation sent," Acts xiii. 26. and to you, O reader, are the blessings of it even now offered by God; sincerely offered; so that, after all I have said under the former heads, it is not your having broken the law of God that shall prove your ruin, if you do not also reject his gospel. It is not all those legions of sins which rise up in battle array against you that shall be able to destroy you, if unbelief do not lead them on, and final impenitence do not bring up the rear. I know that guilt is a timorous thing: I will therefore speak in the words of God himself; nor can any be more comfortable: " He that believeth on the Son hath everlasting life, John iii. 36 ; and he shall never come into condemnation, John v. 24: there is therefore now no condemnation," no kind or deg.ee of it, to them, to any one

of them, " who are in Christ Jesus, who walk not
after the flesh, but after the Spirit," Rom. viii. 1. You
have indeed been a very great sinner, and your offences have truly been attended with most heinous
aggravations; nevertheless, you may rejoice in the
assurance, that " where sin hath abounded, there
shall grace much more abound," Rom. v. 20; that
" where sin hath reigned unto death," where it has
had its most unlimited sway, and most unresisted triumph, there shall " righteousness reign to eternal life
through Jesus Christ our Lord," Rom. v. 21. That
righteousness to which, on believing on him, thou
wilt be entitled, shall not only break those chains by
which sin is (as it were,) dragging thee at its chariot
wheels with a furious pace to eternal ruin, but it shall
clothe thee with the robes of salvation, shall fix thee
on a throne of glory, where thou shalt live and reign
for ever among the princes of heaven; shalt reign in
immortal beauty and joy, without one remaining scar
of divine displeasure upon thee, without any single
mark by which it could be known that thou hadst ever
been obnoxious to wrath and a curse; except it be
an anthem of praise, to " the Lamb that was slain,
and has washed thee from thy sins in his own blood,"
Rev. i. 5.

8. Nor is it necessary, in order to thy being released from guilt, and entitled to this high and complete felicity, that thou shouldst, before thou wilt venture to apply to Jesus, bring any good works of thine
own to recommend thee to his acceptance.   It is indeed true, that if thy faith be sincere, it will certainly
produce them: but I have the authority of the word
of God to tell thee, that if thou this day sincerely be-
lievest in the name of the Son of God, thou shalt this
day be taken under his care, and be numbered among
those of his sheep, to whom he has graciously declared that " he will give eternal life;" and, that they
shall " never perish," John x. 28. Thou hast no
need therefore to say, " Who shall go up into heaven? or, who shall descend into the deep". for me?
" For the word is nigh thee, in thy mouth, and in

thine heart," Rom. x. 6, 7, 8. With this joyful message " I leave thee; with this faithful saying. ' indeed worthy of all acceptation, 1 Tim. i. 15; with
this gospel, O sinner, which is my life, and which, if
thou dost not reject it, will be thine too.

THE SINNER'S REFLECTION ON THIS GOOD NEWS.

Oh my soul, how astonishing is the message which
thou hast this day received! I have indeed often
neard it before, and it is grown so common to me
that the surprise is not sensible: but reflect, O my
soul, what it is thou hast heard; and say, whether
the name of the Saviour, whose message it is, may
not well be called " Wonderful, Counsellor," Isa. ix.
6, when he displays before thee such wonders of love,
and proposes to thee such counsels of peace.

Blessed Jesus, is it indeed thus? Is it not the
fiction of the human mind? Surely it is not! What
human mind could have invented or conceived it?
It is a plain certain fact, that thou didst leave the
magnificence and joy of the heavenly world in compassion to such a wretch as I ! Oh, hadst thou
from that height of dignity and felicity only looked
down upon me for a moment, and sent some gracious
word to me for my direction and comfort, even by
the least of thy servants, justly then might I have
prostrated myself in grateful admira.'on, and have
kissed the very footsteps of him that published the
salvation, Isa. lii. 7. But didst thou condescend to be
thyself the messenger? What grace had that been,
though thou hadst but once in person made the
declaration, and immediately returned back to the
throne, from whence divine compassion brought thee
down? But this is not all the triumph of thine illustrious grace; it not only brought thee down to earth,
but kept thee here in a frail and wretched tabernacle
for long successive years, and at length it cost thee
thy life, and stretched thee out as a malefactor upon
the cross, after thou hadst borne insult and cruelty,

which it may justly wound my heart so much as to think of; and thus thou hast atoned injured justice and " redeemed me to God with thine own blood," Rev. v. 9.

What shall I say? " Lord, I believe, help thou mine unbelief," Mark ix. 24. It seems to put faith to the stretch, to admit what it indeed exceeds the utmost stretch of imagination to conceive. Blessed, for ever blessed be thy name, O thou Father of mercies, that thou hast contrived the way. Eternal thanks to the Lamb that was slain, and to that kind Providence that sent the word of this salvation to me. O let me not for ten thousand worlds, " receive this grace of God in vain!" 2 Cor. vi. 1. O impress this gospel upon my soul, till its saving virtue be diffused over every faculty! Let it not only be heard, and acknowledged, and professed, but felt! Make it thy power to my eternal salvation, Rom. i. 16, and raise me to that humble tender gratitude, to that active unwearied zeal in thy service, which becomes one " to whom so much is forgiven," Luke vii. 47, and forgiven upon such terms as these.

I feel a sudden glow in mine heart while these tidings are sounding in mine ears; but, oh, let it not be a slight superficial transport! O let not this which I would fain call my Christian joy be as that foolish laughter with which I have been so madly enchanted, " like the crackling blaze of thorns under a pot," Eccles. vii. 6. O teach me to secure this mighty blessing, this glorious hope, in the method which thou hast appointed, and preserve me from mistaking the joy of nature, while it catches a glimpse of its rescue from destruction, for that consent of grace which embraces and insures the deliverance.

CHAPTER IX.

◆ MORE PARTICULAR ACCOUNT OF THE WAY BY WHICH THIS SALVATION IS TO BE OBTAINED.

An inquiry into the way of salvation by Christ being supposed, 1. The sinner is in general directed to repentance and faith, 2; and urged to give up all self-dependence, 3; and to seek salvation by free grace, 4. A summary of more particular directions is proposed, 5. (1.) That the sinner should apply to Christ, 6; with deep abhorrence of his former sins, 7; and a firm resolution of forsaking them, 8. (2.) That he solemnly commit his soul into the hands of Christ, the great vital act of faith, 9; which is exemplified at large, 10. (3.) That he make it in fact the governing care of his future life to obey and imitate Christ, 11. This is the only method of obtaining gospel salvation, 12. The sinner deliberating on the expediency of accepting it.

1 I now consider you, my dear reader, as coming to me with the inquiry which the Jews once addressed to our Lord, " What shall we do that we may work the works of God?" John vi. 28; what method shall I take to secure that redemption and salvation which I am told Christ has procured for his people? I would answer it as seriously and carefully as possible, as one that knows of what importance it is to you to be rightly informed; and that knows also how strictly he is to answer to God for the sincerity and care with which the reply is made. May I be enabled to " speak as his oracle," 1 Pet. iv. 11; that is, in such a manner as faithfully to echo back what the sacred oracles teach.

2. And here, that I may be sure to follow the safest guides, and the fairest examples, I must preach salvation to you, in the way of " repentance toward God, and of faith in our Lord Jesus Christ," Acts xx. 21; that good old doctrine which the apostles preached, and which no man can pretend to change, but at the peril of his own soul and of theirs who attend to him.

3. I suppose that you are by this time convinced of your guilt and condemnation, and of your own

!nability to recover yourself. Let me, nevertheless, urge you to feel that conviction yet more deeply, and to impress it with yet greater weight upon your soul; that you have " undone yourself," and that " in yourself is not your help found," Hosea xiii. 9. Be persuaded, therefore, expressly and solemnly, and sincerely, to give up all self-dependence, which, if you do not guard against it, will be ready to return secretly, before it is observed, and will lead you to attempt building up what you have just been destroying.

4. Be assured, that if ever you are saved, you must ascribe that salvation entirely to the free grace of God. If, guilty and miserable as you are, you are not only accepted, but crowned, you must " lay down your crown," with all humble acknowledgment, before the throne, Rev. iv. 10. " No flesh must glory in his presence; but he that glorieth must glory in the Lord; for of him are we in Christ Jesus, who of God is made unto us wisdom, and righteousness, and sanctification, and redemption," 1 Cor. i. 29—31; and you must be sensible you are in such a state, as having none of these in yourself, to need them in another. You must therefore be sensible that you are ignorant and guilty, polluted, and enslaved; or, as our Lord expresses it, (with regard to some that were under a Christian profession,) that, as a sinner, " you are wretched, and miserable, and poor, and blind, and naked," Rev. iii. 17.

5. If these views be deeply impressed upon your mind, you will be prepared to receive what I am now to say. Hear, therefore, in a few words, your duty, your remedy, and your safety, which consists in this: " that you must apply to Christ with a deep abhorrence of your former sins, and a firm resolution of forsaking them; forming that resolution in the strength of his grace, and fixing your dependence on him for your acceptance with God, even while you are purposing to do your very best; and when you have actually done the best you ever will do in consequence of that purpose."

6. The first and most important advice that I can give you in the present circumstances is, that " you look to Christ, and apply yourself to him." And here, " say not in your heart, who shall ascend into heaven, to bring him down to me?" Rom. x. 6; or, who shall raise me up thither to present me before him? The blessed Jesus, " by whom all things consist," Col. i. 17, by whom the whole system of them is supported, forgotten as he is by most that bear his name, " is not far from any of us," Acts xvii. 27; nor could he have promised to have been, " wherever two or three are met together in his name," Matt. xviii. 20, but in consequence of those truly divine perfections by which he is every where present. Would you therefore, O sinner, desire to be saved? go to the Saviour: would you desire to be delivered? look to that great Deliverer; and though you should be so overwhelmed with guilt, and shame, and fear, and horror, that you should be incapable of speaking to him, fall down in this speechless confusion at his feet, and " behold him, as the Lamb of God, that taketh away the sin of the world," John i. 29.

7. Behold him, therefore, with an attentive eye, and say whether the sight does not touch, and even melt, thy very heart? Dost thou not feel what a foolish and what a wretched creature thou hast been, that for the sake of such low and sordid gratifications and interests as those which thou hast been pursuing thou shouldst thus " kill the Prince of life?" Acts iii. 15. Behold the deep wounds which he bore for thee. Look on him whom thou hast pierced, and surely thou must mourn, Zech. xii. 10, unless thine heart be hardened into stone. Which of thy past sins canst thou reflect upon, and say, " For this it was worth my while thus to have injured my Saviour, and to have exposed the Son of God to such sufferings!" And what future temptations can arise so considerable, that thou shouldst say, " For the sake of this I will crucify my Lord again?" Heb. vi. 6. Sinner, thou must repent; thou must repent of every sin, and must forsake it; but if thou dost it to any pur-

pose, I well know it must be at the foot o. the cross
Thou must sacrifice every lust, even the dearest
though it should be like a right hand, or a right eye,
Matt. v. 29, 30: and therefore, that thou mayest, if
possible, be animated to it, I have led thee to that
altar, on which " Christ himself was sacrificed for
thee, an offering of a sweet-smelling savour," Eph.
v. 2. Thou must " yield up thyself to God, as one
alive from the dead," Rom. vi. 13, and therefore I
have showed thee at what price he purchased thee:
" For thou wast not redeemed with corruptible things,
as silver and gold, but with the precious blood of the
Son of God, that Lamb without blemish and without
spot," 1 Pet. i. 18, 19. And now I would ask thee,
as before the Lord, what does thine own heart say
to it? Art thou grieved for thy former offences? art
thou willing to forsake thy sins? art thou willing to
become the cheerful, thankful servant of him " who
hath purchased thee with his own blood?"

8. I will suppose such a purpose as this rising in
thine heart: how determinate it is, and how effectual
it may be, I know not; what different views may
arise hereafter, or how soon the present sense may
wear off: but this I assuredly know, that thou wilt
never see reason to change these views; for however
thou mayest alter, the Lord " Jesus Christ is the same
yesterday, to-day, and for ever," Heb. xiii. 8; and
the reasons that now recommend repentance and
faith, as fit and as necessary, will continue invariable
as long as the perfections of the blessed God are the
same, and as long as his Son continues the same.

9. But while you have these views and these purposes, I must remind you, that this is not all that is
necessary to your salvation. You must not only
purpose, but, as God gives opportunity, you must act
as those who are convinced of the evil of sin, and of
the necessity and excellence of holiness: and that
you may be enabled to do so in other instances, you
must, in the first place, and as the first great work
of God, (as our Lord himself calls it,) " believe in
him whom God hath sent," John vi. 29. You must

confide in him; must commit your soul into the hands of Christ, to be saved by him in his own appointed method of salvation. This is the great act of saving faith; and I pray God that you may experimentally know what it means, so as to be able to say with the apostle Paul, in the near view of death itself, " I know whom I have believed, and am persuaded that he is able to keep that which I have committed to him until that day," 2 Tim. i. 12, that great decisive day, which, if we are Christians, we have always in view. To this I would urge you; and O that I could be so happy as to engage you to it while I am illustrating it in this and the following addresses! Be assured you must not apply yourself immediately to God, as absolutely or in himself considered, in the neglect of a Mediator. It will neither be acceptable to him, nor safe for you, to rush into his presence without any regard to his own Son, whom he has appointed to introduce sinners to him; and if you come otherwise, you come as one who is not a sinner: the very manner of presenting the address will be interpreted as a denial of that guilt with which he knows you are chargeable: and therefore he will not admit you, nor so much as look upon you. And accordingly, our Lord, knowing how much every man living was concerned in this, says in the most universal terms, " No man cometh unto the Father but by me," John xiv. 6.

10. Apply therefore to this glorious Redeemer, amiable, as he will appear to every believing eye, in the blood which he shed upon the cross, and in the wounds which he received there. Go to him, O sinner, this day, this moment, with all thy sins about thee. Go just as thou art; for if thou wilt never apply to him till thou art first righteous and holy, thou wilt never be righteous and holy at all; nor canst be so, on this supposition, unless there were some way of being so without him, and then there would be no occasion for applying to him for righteousness and holiness. It were indeed as if it should be said, that a sick man should defer his application to a physician

till his health be recovered.   Let me, therefore, repeat it without offence, go to him just as thou art,
and say, (O that thou mayest this moment be enabled to say it from thy very soul!) Blessed Jesus,
I am surely one of the most sinful, and one of the
most miserable creatures that ever fell prostrate before thee; nevertheless, I come because I have heard
that thou didst once say, " Come unto me, all ye that
labour, and are heavy laden, and I will give you
rest," Matt. xi. 28. I come because I have heard
that thou didst graciously say, " Him that cometh
unto me, I will in no wise cast out," John vi. 37.   O
thou Prince of peace, O thou King of glory, I am a
condemned miserable sinner.   I have ruined my own
soul, and am condemned for ever, if thou dost not
help me and save me.   I have broken thy Father's
law and thine, for thou art " one with him," John x.
30.   I have deserved condemnation and wrath, and
I am, even at this very moment, under a sentence of
everlasting destruction: a destruction which will be
aggravated by all the contempt which I have cast
upon thee, Oh thou bleeding Lamb of God: for I
cannot, and will not dissemble it before thee, that I
have wronged thee, most basely and ungratefully
wronged thee, under the character of a Saviour, as
well as of a Lord.   But now, I am willing to submit
to thee; and I have brought my poor trembling soul,
to lodge it in thine hands, if thou wilt condescend to
receive it; and if thou dost not, it must perish.   O
Lord, I lie at thy feet: stretch out " thy golden scep
tre, that I may live," Esth. iv. 11.   Yea, " if it please
the king, let the life of my soul be given me at my
petition," Esth. vii. 3.   I have no treasure, wherewith to purchase it: I have no equivalent to give
thee for it; but if that compassionate heart of thine
can find a pleasure in saving one of the most distressed creatures under heaven, that pleasure thou
mayest here find.   O Lord, I have foolishly attempted
to be mine own Saviour; but it will not do.   I am
sensible the attempt is vain; and therefore I give it
over, and look unto thee.   On thee, blessed Jesus,

who art sure and steadfast, do I desire to fix my anchor. On thee, as the only sure foundation, would I build my eternal hopes. To thy teaching, O thou unerring Prophet of the Lord, would I submit: be thy doctrines ever so mysterious, it is enough for me, that thou thyself hast said it. To thine atonement, obedience, and intercession, O thou holy and ever-acceptable High-priest would I trust. And to thy government, O thou exalted Sovereign, would I yield a willing, delightful subjection. In token of reverence and love, I "kiss the Son," Psal. ii. 12; I kiss the ground before his feet. I admit thee, O my Saviour, and welcome thee with unutterable joy, to the throne in my heart. Ascend it, and reign there for ever! Subdue mine enemies, O Lord, for they are thine; and make me thy faithful and zealous servant; faithful to death, and zealous to eternity!

11. Such as this must be the language of your very heart before the Lord. But then remember, that in consequence thereof, it must be the language of your life too. The unmeaning words of the lips would be a vain mockery. The most affectionate transport of the passions, should it be transient and ineffectual, would be but like a blaze of straw, presented instead of incense at his altar. With such humility, with such love, with such cordial self-dedication and submission of soul, must thou often prostrate thyself, in the presence of Christ; and then thou must go away, and keep him in thy view; must go away, and live unto God through him, "denying ungodliness and worldly lusts, and behaving thyself soberly, righteously, and godly, in this vain ensnaring world," Tit. ii. 12. You must make it your care, to show your love by obedience; by forming yourself as much as possible, according to the temper and manner of Jesus, in whom you believe. You must make it the great point of your ambition, (and a nobler view you cannot entertain,) to be a living image of Christ; that, so far as circumstances will allow, even those who have heard and read but little of

him, may by observing you, in some measure see
and know what kind of a life that of the blessed
Jesus was And this must be your constant care,
your prevailing character as long as you live.   You
must follow him whithersoever he leads you; must
follow, with a cross on your shoulder when he commands you to take it up, Matt. xvi. 24; and so must
" be faithful even to the death; expecting the crown
of life." Rev. ii. 10.

12. This, so far as I have been able to learn from
the word of God, is the way to safety and glory; the
surest, the only way you can take.   It is the way,
which every faithful minister of Christ has trod, and
is treading; and the way to which, as he tenders the
salvation of his own soul, he must direct others. We
cannot, we would not alter it, in favour of ourselves,
or of our dearest friends.   It is the way, in which
alone, so far as we can judge, it becomes the blessed
God to save his apostate creatures.   And therefore,
reader, I beseech and entreat you seriously to cousi-
der it; and let your own conscience answer, as in the
presence of God, whether you are willing to acquiesce
in it, or not. But know, that to reject it is thine eternal death: For as " there is no other name under
heaven given among men, whereby we can be
saved," Acts iv. 12, but this of Jesus of Nazareth,
so there is no other method but this, in which Jesus
himself will save us.

THE SINNER DELIBERATING ON THE EXPEDIENCY OF FALL-
ING IN WITH THIS METHOD OF SALVATION.

Consider, O my soul, what answer wilt thou return to such proposals as these!   Surely, if I were
to speak the first dictate of this corrupt and degene
rate heart, it would be " this is a hard saying, and
who can hear it?" John vi. 60. To be thus humbled,
thus mortified, thus subjected! To take such a yoke
upon me, and to carry it as long as I live! To give
up every darling lust, though dear to me as *a right*

eye, and seemingly necessary as *a right hand!* To submit, not only my life, but my heart, to the command and discipline of another! To have a master there, and such a master as will control many of its favourite affections, and direct them quite into another channel! A master, who himself represents his commands, by *taking up the cross, and following him!* To adhere to the strictest rules of godliness and sobriety, of righteousness and truth; not departing from them in any allowed instance, great or small, upon any temptation, for any advantage, to escape any inconvenience and evil, no, not even for the preservation of life itself; but upon a proper call of Providence, to act as if I " hated even my own life!" Luke xvi. 26. Lord, it is hard to flesh and blood; and yet I perceive and feel, there is one demand yet harder than this.

With all these precautions, with all these mortifications, the pride of my nature would find some inward resource of pleasure, might I but secretly think, that I had been my own saviour; that my own wisdom, and my own resolution, had broken the bands and chains of the enemy; and that I had drawn out of my own treasures, the price with which my redemption was purchased. But must I lie down before another, as guilty and condemned, as weak and helpless? And must the obligation be multiplied, and must a mediator have his share too? Must I go to the cross for my salvation, and seek my glory from the infamy of that? Must I be stripped of every pleasing pretence to righteousness, and stand in this respect upon a level with the vilest of men? stand at the bar among the greatest criminals, pleading guilty with them, and seeking deliverance by that very act of grace, whereby they have obtained it?

I dare not deliberately say, This method is unreasonable. My conscience testifies, that I have sinned, and cannot be justified before God, as an innocent, and obedient creature. My conscience tells me, that all these humbling circumstances are fit: that it is fit, **a** convicted criminal should be brought upon his

knees: that a captive rebel should give up the **wea**
pons of his rebellion, and bow before his sovereign
if he expects his life. Yea, my reason, as well as my
conscience, tells me, that it is fit and necessary; that
if I am saved at all, I should be saved from the power
and love of sin, as well as from the condemnation of
it; and that if sovereign Mercy gives me a new life,
after having deserved eternal death, it is most fit I
should " yield myself to God, as alive from the dead,"
Rom. vi. 13.   But, " O wretched man that I am, I
feel a law in my members, that wars against the law
of my mind," Rom. vii. 23, 24, and opposes the conviction of my reason and conscience.   Who shall deliver me from this bondage?   Who shall make me
willing to do that, which I know in my own soul to
be most expedient ?   O Lord, subdue my heart, and
let it not be drawn so strongly one way, while the
nobler powers of my mind would direct it another.
Conquer every licentious principle within, that it may
be my joy to be so wisely governed, and restrained.
Especially, subdue my pride, that lordly corruption,
which so ill suits an impoverished and condemned
creature; that thy way of salvation may be amiable
to me, in proportion to the degree in which it is hum
bling. I feel a disposition to " linger in Sodom, but
O be merciful to me, and pull me out of it," Gen.
xix. 16, before the storms of thy flaming vengeance
fall, and t ere be no more escaping!

CHAPTER X.

THE SINNER SERIOUSLY URGED AND ENTREATED TO ACCEPT OF SALVATION IN THIS WAY.

Since many who have been impressed with these things, suffer the impression to wear off in vain, 1. strongly as the case speaks for itself, sinners are to be entreated to accept this salvation, 2. Accordingly, the reader is entreated, (1.) by the majesty and mercy of God, 3. (2.) By the dying love of our Lord Jesus Christ, 4. (3.) By the regard due to our fellow-creatures, 5. (4.) By the worth of his own immortal soul, 6. The matter is solemnly left with the reader, as before God, 7. The sinner yielding to these entreaties, and declaring his acceptance of salvation by Christ.

1. THUS far have I often known convictions and impressions to arise, (if I might judge by the strongest appearances,) which after all have worn off again. Some unhappy circumstance of external temptation, ever joined by the inward reluctance of an unsanctified heart to this holy and humbling scheme of redemption, has been the ruin of multitudes. And " through the deceitfulness of sin, they have been hardened," Heb. iii. 13, till they seem to have been " utterly destroyed, and that without remedy," Prov. xxix. 1. And therefore, O thou immortal creature, who art now reading these lines, I beseech thee, that while affairs are in this critical situation, while there are these balancings of mind between accepting and rejecting that glorious gospel, which, in the integrity of my heart, I have now been laying before you, you would once more give me an attentive audience, while I plead in God's behalf, (shall I say?) or rather in your own; while " as an ambassador for Christ, and as though God did beseech you by me, I pray you in Christ's stead, that you would be reconciled to God," 2 Cor. v. 20; and would not, after these awakenings and these inquiries, by a madness which it will surely be the doleful business of a miserable eternity to lament, reject this compassionate *counsel of God towards you.*

2. One would indeed imagine, there should be no need of importunity here. One would conclude, that as soon as perishing sinners are told, that an offended God is ready to be reconciled; that he offers them a full pardon for all their aggravated sins, yea, that he is willing to adopt them into his family now, that he may at length admit them to his heavenly presence; all should with the utmost readiness and pleasure embrace so kind a message, and fall at his feet in speechless transports of astonishment, gratitude, and joy. But alas, we find it much otherwise. We see multitudes quite unmoved, and the impressions which are made on many more are feeble and transient. Lest it should be thus with you, Oh reader, let me urge the message with which I have the honour to be charged: let me *entreat you to be reconciled to God*, and to accept of pardon and salvation in the way in which it is so freely offered to you.

3. I entreat you, " by the majesty of that God, in " whose name I come;" whose voice fills all heaven with reverence and obedience. He speaks not in vain to legions of angels: but if there could be any contention among those blessed spirits, it would be, who should be first to execute his commands. O let him not speak in vain to a wretched mortal! I entreat you " by the terrors of his wrath," who could speak to you in thunder; who could, by one single act of his will, cut off this precarious life of yours, and send you down to hell. I beseech you " by his mercies, by his tender mercies;" by the bowels of his compassion, which still yearn over you, as those of a parent over a dear son, over a tender child, whom, notwithstanding his former ungrateful rebellions, " he earnestly remembers still," Jer. xxxi. 20. I beseech and entreat you, " by all this paternal goodness," that you do not (as it were) compel him to lose the cha- racter of the gentle parent, in that of the righteous Judge; so that, (as he threatens with regard to those whom he had just called *his sons and his daughters)* " a fire should be kindled in his anger, which should buru unto the lowest hell," Deut. xxxii. 19, 22.

4. I beseech you further, " by the name and love of our dying Saviour." I beseech you, by all the condescension of his incarnation; by that poverty, to which he voluntarily submitted that you might be enriched with eternal treasures; 2 Cor. viii. 9, by all the gracious invitations which he gave, which still sound in his word, and still coming (as it were) warm from his heart, are " sweeter than honey, or the honey-comb," Psal. xix. 10. I beseech you, by all his glorious works of power and of wonder, which were also works of love. I beseech you, by the memory of the most benevolent person, and the most generous friend   I beseech you, by the memory of what he suffered, as well as of what he said and did; by the agony which he endured in the garden, when his body was covered with a dew of blood, Luke xxii. 44. I beseech you, by all that tender distress which he felt, when his dearest friends " forsook him and fled," Matt. xxvi. 56, and his blood-thirsty enemies dragged him away, like the meanest of slaves, and like the vilest of criminals. I beseech you, by the blows and bruises, by the stripes and lashes, which this injured sovereign endured while in their rebellious hands; by the shame of spitting, from which he hid not that kind and venerable countenance, Isa. l. 6. I beseech you, by the purple robe, the sceptre of reed, and the crown of thorns, which this King of glory wore, that he might set us among the princes of heaven, Psal. cxiii. 8. I beseech you, by the heavy burden of the cross, under which he panted, and toiled, and fainted, in the painful way to Golgotha, John xix. 17, that he might free us from the burden of our sins. I beseech you, by the remembrance of those rude nails, that tore the veins and arteries, the nerves and tendons of his sacred *hands and feet;* and by that invincible, that triumphant goodness, which, while the iron pierced his flesh, engaged him to cry out, " Father, forgive them, for they know not what they do," Luke xxiii. 34. I beseech you, by the unutterable anguish which he bore, when lifted up upon the cross, and extended

there as on a rack, for six painful hours, that you
open your heart to those attractive influences, which
have *drawn to him* thousands and ten thousands,
John xii. 32. I beseech you, by all that insult and
derision, which the " Lord of glory bore there ;" Matt.
xxvii. 29, 44, by that parching thirst which could
hardly obtain the relief of vinegar, John xix. 28,
29, by that doleful *cry*, so astonishing in the mouth
of the *only begotten* of the Father, " My God, my
God, why hast thou forsaken me?" Matt. xxvii. 46.
I beseech you, by that grace that subdued and par-
doued a dying malefactor, Luke xxiii. 42, 43, by
that compassion for sinners, by that compassion for
vou, which wrought in his heart, long as its vital motion continued, and which ended not when he *bowed
his head*, saying, " It is finished, and gave up the
ghost," John xix. 30. I beseech you, by the triumphs
of that resurrection by which he was declared to
be the son of God with power, by the Spirit of holiness which wrought to accomplish it ; Rom. i. 4, by
that gracious tenderness which attempered all those
triumphs, when he said to her out of whom he had
cast seven devils, concerning his disciples who had
treated him so basely, "Go, tell my brethren, I ascend
unto my Father and your Father, unto my God and
your God," John xx. 17. I beseech you, by that
condescension, with which he said to Thomas, when
his unbelief had made such an unreasonable demand,
" Reach hither thy finger, and behold my hands, and
reach hither thine hand, and thrust it into my side;
and be not faithless but believing," John xx. 27. I
beseech you, by that generous and faithful care of his
people, which he carried up with him to the regions
of glory, and which engaged him to send down *his
Spirit*, in that rich profusion of miraculous gifts to
spread the progress of his saving word, Acts ii. 33.
I beseech you, by that voice of sympathy and power,
with which he said to Saul, while injuring his church,
" Saul, Saul, why persecutest thou me?" Acts ix. 4, by
that generous goodness, which spared that prostrate
enemy, when he lay trembling at his feet, and raised

nim to so high a dignity, as to be " not inferior to the very chiefest apostles," 2 Cor. xii. 11. I beseech you, by the memory of all that Christ has already done, by the expectation of all he will further do for his people. I beseech you, at once, by the sceptre of his grace, and by that sword of his justice, with which his incorrigible enemies shall be slain before him, Luke xix. 27, that you do not trifle away these precions moments, while his Spirit is thus breathing upon you; that you do not lose an opportunity which may never return, and on the improvement of which your eternity depends.

5. I beseech you, " by all the bowels of compassion which you owe to the faithful ministers of Christ," who are studying and labouring, preaching and praying, wearing out their time, exhausting their strength, and, very probably, shortening their lives, for the salvation of your soul, and of souls like yours. I beseech you, by the affection, with which *all that love our Lord Jesus Christ in sincerity,* long to see you brought back to him. I beseech you, by the friendship of the living, and by the memory of the dead; by the ruin of those who have trifled away their days, and perished in their sins, and by the happiness of those who have embraced the gospel, anu are saved by it. I beseech you, by the great expec-tation of that important day, " when the Lord Jesus shall be revealed from heaven," 2 Thess. i. 7, by the terrors of a dissolving world, 2 Pet. iii. 10, by " the sound of the archangel's trumpet," 1 Thess. iv. 16, and of that infinitely more awful sentence, "Come, ye blessed, and, Depart ye cursed," Matt. xxv. 34, 41, with which that grand solemnity shall close.

6. I beseech you finally, " by your own precious and immortal soul," by the sure prospect of a dying bed, or of a sudden surprise into the invisible state; and as you would feel one spark of comfort, in your departing spirit when *your flesh and your heart are failing.* I beseech you, by your own personal appearance before the tribunal of Christ, (for a personal appearance it must be, even to them who now sit on

thrones of their own;) by all the transports of the blessed, and by all the agonies of the damned, the one or the other of which must be your everlasting portion. I affectionately entreat and beseech you, in the strength of all these united considerations, as you will answer it to me, who may in that day be summoued to testify against you; and, which is unspeakably more, as you will answer it to your own conscience, as you will answer it to the eternal Judge; that you dismiss not these thoughts, these meditations, and these cares, till you have brought matters to a happy issue; till you have made a resolute choice of Christ, and his appointed way of salvation, and till you have solemnly devoted yourself to God in the bonds of an everlasting covenant.

7. And thus I leave the matter before you, and before the Lord. I have told you my errand: I have discharged my embassy. Stronger arguments I cannot use; more endearing and more awful considerations I cannot suggest. Choose therefore, whether you will go out, as it were, clothed in sackcloth, to cast yourself at the feet of him who now sends you these equitable and gracious terms of peace and pardon; or, whether you will hold it out till he appears sword in hand, to reckon with you for your treasons and your crimes, and for this neglected embassy among the rest of them. Fain would I hope the best; nor can I believe, that *this labour of love* shall be so entirely unsuccessful, that not one soul shall be brought to the foot of Christ, in cordial submission and humble faith. " Take with you therefore words and turn unto the Lord," Hos. xiv. 2, and O that those which might follow, in effect at least, be the genuine language of every one that reads them!

THE SINNER YIELDING TO THESE ENTREATIES, AND DE-
CLARING HIS ACCEPTANCE OF SALVATION BY CHRIST.

Blessed Lord, it is enough! It is too much! Surely there needs not this variety of arguments, this impor-tunity of persuasion, to court me to be happy, to pre-vail upon me to accept of pardon, of life, of eternal glory. Compassionate Saviour, my soul is subdued, so that I trust, the language of thy grief is become that of my penitence, and I may say, " My heart is melted like wax in the midst of my bowels," Psal. xxii. 14.

O gracious Redeemer! I have already neglected thee too long. I have too often injured thee; have crucified thee afresh by my guilt and impenitence, as if I had taken pleasure in " putting thee to an open shame," Heb. vi. 6. But my heart now bows itself before thee, in humble unfeigned submission. I desire to make no terms with thee but these—that I may be entirely thine. I cheerfully present thee with a blank, entreating thee, that thou wilt do me the honour to signify upon it, what is thy pleasure Teach me, O Lord, *what thou wouldst have me to do!* For I desire to learn the lesson, and to learn it that I may practise it. If it be more than my feeble powers can answer, thou wilt, I hope, give me more strength; and in that strength I will serve thee. O receive a soul, which thou hast made willing to be thine!

No more, O blessed Jesus, no more is it necessary to beseech and entreat me. Permit me rather to address myself to thee with all the importunity of a perishing sinner, that at length sees and knows " there is salvation in no other," Acts iv. 12. Permit me now, Lord, to come, and throw myself at thy feet, like a helpless outcast, that has no shelter but in thy generous compassion; like one pursued by the avenger of blood, and seeking earnestly an admittance into the city of refuge, Josh. xx. 2. 3.

" I wait for the Lord, my soul doth wait; and in thy word do I hope," Psal. cxxx. 5, that thou " wilt receive me graciously," Hos. xiv. 2. My soul confides in thy goodness, and adores it. I adore the patience which has borne with me so long; and the grace that now makes me heartily willing to be thine; to be thine on thine own terms, thine on any terms. O secure this treacherous heart to thyself! O unite me to thee in such inseparable bonds, that none of

tne allurements of flesh and blood, none of the vani
ties of an ensnaring world, none of the solicitations ot
sinful companions, may draw me back from thee, and
plunge me into new guilt and ruin. " Be surety, O
Lord, for thy servant for good," Psal. cxix. 122, that
I may still keep my hold on thee, and so on eterna.
life; till at length I know more fully, by joyful and
everlasting experience, how complete a Saviour thou
art. Amen.

CHAPTER XI.

A SOLEMN ADDRESS TO THOSE WHO WILL NOT BE PERSUADED TO FALL IN WITH THE DESIGN OF THE GOSPEL.

Universal success not to be expected, 1. Yet as unwilling absolutely to give up any, the author addresses, (1.) those who doubt
of the truth of Christianity, urging an inquiry into its evidence,
and directing to proper methods for that purpose, 2—4. (2.)
Those who determine to give it up without further examination,
5; and presume to set themselves to oppose it, 6. (3.) Those
who speculatively assent to Christianity as true, and yet will sit
down without any practical regard to its most important and
acknowledged truths. Such are dismissed with a representation
of the absurdity of their conduct on their own principles, 7, 8;
with a solemn warning of its fatal consequences, 9, 10; and a
compassionate prayer, 11; which concludes the chapter, and this
part of the work.

1. I WOULD humbly hope, that the preceding chapters
will be the means of awakening some stupid and
insensible sinners; the means of convincing them of
their need of gospel salvation, and of engaging some
cordially to accept it. Yet I cannot flatter myself so
far, as to hope this should be the case with regard to
all into whose hands this book shall come. " What
am I, alas, better than my fathers," 1 Kings xix. 4,
or better than my brethren, who have in all ages
been repeating their complaint, with regard to multitudes, that they " have stretched out their hands all
the day long to a disobedient and gainsaying people?"

Rom. x. 21. Many such may, perhaps, be found, in the number of my readers: many, on whom, neither considerations of terror, nor of love, will make any deep and lasting impression: many, who, as our Lord learned by experience to express it, " when we pipe to them, will not dance, and when we mourn unto them, will not lament," Matt. xi. 17. I can say no more to persuade them, if they make light of what I have already said. Here, therefore, we must part; in this chapter I must take my leave of them; and, O, that I could do it in such a manner as to fix, at parting, some convictions upon their hearts; that, though I seem to leave them for a little while, and send them back to review again the former chapters, as those in which alone they have any present concern, they might soon, as it were, overtake me again, and find a suitableness in the remaining part of this discourse, which at present they cannot possibly find. Unhappy creatures! I quit you, as a physician quits a patient whom he loves, and is just about to give over as incurable; he returns again and again, and re-examines the several symptoms, to observe whether there be not some one of them more favourable than the rest, which may encourage a renewed application.

2. So would I once more return to you. You do not find in yourself any disposition to embrace the gospel, to apply yourself to Christ, to give yourself up to the service of God, and to make religion the business of your life. But if I cannot prevail upon you to do this, let me engage you at least to answer me, or rather to answer your own conscience, " Why will you not do it?" Is it owing to any secret disbelief of the great principles of religion? If it be, the case is different from what I have yet considered, and the cure must be different. This is not a place to combat with the scruples of infidelity. Nevertheless, I would desire you seriously to inquire how far those scruples extend. Do they affect only some particular doctrines of the gospel on which my argument has turned? or do they affect the whole Chris-

tian revelation? or do they reach yet further, and extend themselves to natural religion as well as re. vealed, so that it should be a doubt with you whether there be any God, and Providence, and future state, or not? As these cases are all different, so it will be of great importance to distinguish the one from the other, that you may know on what principle to build as certain, in the examination of those concerning which you are yet in doubt. But whatever these doubts are, I would further ask you, how long have they continued, and what method have you taken to get them resolved? Do you imagine that in matters of such moment, it will be an allowable case for you to trifle on, neglecting to inquire into the evidence of these things, and then plead your not being satisfied in that evidence, as an excuse for not acting accord. ing to them? Must not the principles of common sense assure you that, if these things be true, (as when you talk of doubting about them, you acknow. ledge it at least possible they may be,) they are of infinitely greater importance than any of the affairs of life, whether of business or pleasure, for the sake of which you neglect them? Why then do you continue indolent and unconcerned, from week to week, and from month to month, which, probably, conscience tells you is the case?

3. Do you ask what method you should take to be resolved? It is no hard question. Open your eyes; set yourself to think: let conscience speak, and verily do I believe that, if it be not seared in an uncommon degree, you will find shrewd forebodings of the certainty both of natural and revealed religion, and of the absolute necessity of repentance, faith, and holiness, to a life of future felicity. If you are a person of any learning, you cannot but know by what writers, and in what treatises, these great truths are defended. And, if you are not, you may find, in almost every town and neighbourhood, persons capa ole of informing you in the main evidences of Christianity, and of answering such scruples against it as unlearned minds may have met with. Set yourself,

hen, in the name of God, immediately to consider the matter. If you study at all, bend your studies close this way; and trifle not with mathematics, or poetry, or history, or law, or physic, (which are all comparatively light as a feather,) while you neglect this. Study the arguments as for your life; for much more than life depends on it. See how far you are satisfied, and why that satisfaction reaches no further. Compare evidences on both sides. And above all, consider the design and tendency of the New Testament, to what it would lead you, and all them that cordially obey it; and then say whether it be not good. And consider how naturally its truth is connected with its goodness. Trace the characters and sentiments of its authors, whose living image (if I may be allowed the expression) is still preserved in their writings; and then ask your own heart, Can you think this was a forgery, an impious cruel forgery? For such it must have been if it were a forgery at all, a scheme to mock God, and to ruin men, even the best of men, such as reverenced conscience, and would abide all extremities for what they apprehend to be truth. Put the question to your own heart, Can I in my conscience believe it to be such an imposture? Can I look up to an omniscient God, and say, " O Lord, thou knowest that it is in reverence to thee, and in love to truth and virtue, that I reject this book, and the method to happiness here laid down?"

4. But there are difficulties in the way. And what then? Have those difficulties never been cleared? Go to the living advocates for Christianity, to those of whose abilities, candour, and piety, you have the best opinion, if your prejudices will give you leave to have a good opinion of any such: tell them your difficulties; hear their solutions; weigh them seriously, as those who know they must answer it to God; and, while doubts continue, follow the truth as far as it will lead you, and take heed that you do not " imprison it in unrighteousness," Rom. i. 18.

Nothing appears more inconsistent and absurd

10

than for a man solemnly to pretend dissatisfaction in the evidence of the gospel, as a reason why he can. not in conscience be a thorough Christian; when yet at the same time he violates the most apparent dic- tates of reason and conscience, and lives in vices con- . demned even by the heathen. Oh, sirs, Christ has judged concerning such; and judged most righteous- ly and most wisely; " They do evil, and therefore they hate the light, neither come they to the light, lest their deeds should be made manifest, and be re- proved," John iii. 20. But there is a light that will make manifest and reprove their works, to which they shall be compelled to come, and the painful scrutiny of which they shall be forced to abide.

5. In the mean time, if you are determined to in- quire no further into the matter now, give me leave at least, from a sincere concern, that you may not heap upon your head more aggravated ruin, to entreat you that you would be cautious how you expose yourself to yet greater danger by what you must yourself own to be unnecessary, I mean at- tempts to pervert others from believing the truth of the gospel. Leave them, for God's sake, and for your own, in possession of those pleasures, and those hopes, which nothing but Christianity can give them, and act not as if you were solicitous to add to the guilt of an infidel the tenfold damnation, which they who have been the perverters and destroyers of the souls of others must expect to meet, if that gospel, which they have so adventurously opposed, should prove, as it certainly will, a serious, and to them a dreadful truth.

6. If I cannot prevail here, but the pride of dis- playing a superiority of understanding should bear on such a reader, even in opposition to his own favourite maxims of the innocence of error, and the equality of all religions consistent with social virtue, to do his utmost to trample down the gospel with contempt, I would, however, dismiss him with one proposal, which I think the importance of the affair. may fully justify. · If you have done with your

examination into Christianity, and determine to live and conduct yourself as if it were assuredly false, sit down then and make a memorandum of that determination. Write it down: " On such a day of such a year, I deliberately resolved that I would live and die rejecting Christianity myself, and doing all I could to overthrow it. This day I determined not only to renounce all subjection to, and expectation from Jesus of Nazʌreth, but also to make it a serious part of the business of my life to destroy, as far as I possibly can, all regard to him in the minds of others, and to exert my most vigorous efforts in the way of reasoning, or of ridicule, to sink the credit of his religion, and if it be possible, to root it out of the world; in calm steady defiance of that day, when his followers say, Hə shall appear in so much majesty and terror, to execute the vengeance threatened to his enemies." Dare you write this and sign it? I firmly believe that many a man, who would be thought a deist, and endeavours to increase the number, would not: and if you in particular dare not to do it, whence does that small remainder of caution arise? the cause is plain. There is in your conscience some secret apprehension that this rejected, this opposed, this derided gospel may, after all, prove true; and if there be such an apprehension, then let conscience do its office, and convict you of the impious madness of acting as if it were most certainly and demonstrably false. Let it tell you at large how possible it is that " haply you may be found fighting against God," Acts v. 39; that, bold as you are, in defying the terrors of the Lord, you may possibly fall into his hands, may chance to hear that despised sentence, which, when you hear it from the mouth of the eterʌal Judge, you will not be able to despise: I will repeat it again in spite of all your scorn, you may hear the King say to you, " Depart, accursed, into everlasting fire, prepared for the devil and his an gels," Matt. xxv. 41. And now go and pervert and burlesque the Scripture, go and lampoon the character of its heroᵉˢ, and ridicule the sublime discourses of its prophets and its apostles, as some have done who have left little behind them but the short-lived monuments of their ignorance, their profaneness, and their malice: go and spread like them the banners of infidelity, and pride thyself in the number of credu lous creatures listed under them. But take heed lest the insulted Galilean direct a secret arrow to thine heart, and stop thy licentious breath before it has finished the next sentence thou wouldst utter against him.

7. I will now turn myself from the deist or the sceptic, and direct my address to the nominal Chris-tian; if he may upon any terms be called a Christian, who feels not, after all I have pleaded, a disposition to subject himself to the government and the grace of that Saviour whose name he bears. O sinner, thou art turning away from my Lord, in whose cause I speak; but let me earnestly entreat thee, seriously to consider why thou art turning away, "and to whom thou wilt go" from him, whom thou acknowledgest "to have the words of eternal life," John vi. 68. You call yourself a Christian, and yet will not by any means be persuaded to seek salva-tion in good earnest from and through Jesus Christ, whom you call your Master and your Lord. How do you for a moment excuse this negligence to your own conscience? If I had urged you on any contro-verted point, it might have altered the case. If I had laboured hard to make you the disciple of any par-ticular party of Christians, your delay might have been more reasonable: nay, perhaps, your refusing to acquiesce might have been an act of apprehended duty to our common Master. But is it matter of controversy among Christians, whether there be a great, holy, and righteous God? and whether such a being, whom we agree to own, should be reverenced and loved, or neglected and dishonoured? Is it mat-ter of controversy whether a sinner should deeply and seriously repent of his sins, or whether he should go on in them? Is it a disputed point amongst us whether Jesus became incarnate, and died upon the

cross fr the redemption of sinners or no?   And if it
be not, can it be disputed by them who believe him
to be the Son of God, and the Saviour of men, whether a sinner should seek to him or neglect him? or
whether one who professes to be a Christian should
depart from iniquity, or give himself up to the practice of it?   Are the precepts of our great Mastel
written so obscurely in his word, that there should
be room seriously to question whether he require a
devout, holy, humble, spiritual, watchful, self-denying life, or whether he allow the contrary?   Has
Christ, after all his pretensions of bringing life and
immortality to light, left it more uncertain than he
found it, whether there be any future state of happiness and misery, or for whom these states are respec-
tively intended?   Is it matter of controversy whether
God will or will not " bring every work into judgment, with every secret thing, whether it be good, or
whether it be evil?" Eccl. xii. 14; or whether at the
conclusion of that judgment, " the wicked shall go
away into everlasting punishment, and the righteous
into life eternal?" Matt. xxv. 46.   You will not, I
am sure, for very shame, pretend any doubt about
those things, and yet call yourself a Christian.   Why
then will you not be persuaded to lay them to heart,
and to act as duty and interest so evidently require?
O sinner, the cause is too obvious; a cause, indeed,
quite unworthy of being called a reason.   It is because thou art blinded and besotted with thy vanities
and thy lusts.   It is because thou hast some perishing trifle, which charms thy imagination and thy
senses, so that it is dearer to thee than God and
Christ, than thy own soul and its salvation.   It is,
in a word, because thou art still under the influence
of that carnal mind, which, whatever pious forms
it may sometimes admit and pretend, " is enmity
against God, and is not subject to the law of God,
neither indeed can be," Rom. viii. 7.   And therefore
thou art in the very case of those wretches, concerning whom our Lord said, in the days of his flesh,
" Ye will not come unto me that ye might have life,"

John v. 40; and therefore "ye shall die in your sins,
John viii. 24.

8. In this case I see not what it can signify to renew those expostulations and addresses, which I have
made in the former chapters. As our blessed Redeemer says of those who rejected his gospel, "Ye
have both seen and hated both me and my Father;"
John xv. 24, so may I truly say with regard to you,
I have endeavoured to show you in the plainest and
clearest words, both Christ and the Father; I have
urged the obligations you are under to both; I have
laid before you your guilt, and your condemnation;
I have pointed out the only remedy; I have pointed
out the Rock on which I have built my own eternal
hopes, and the way in which alone I expect salvation; I have recommended those things to you, which,
if God gives me an opportunity, I will, with my dying
breath, earnestly and affectionately recommend to my
own children, and to all the dearest friends that I have
upon earth who may then be near me; esteeming it
the highest token of my friendship, the surest proof
of my love to them: and if believing the gospel to
be true, you resolve to reject it, I have nothing further to say, but that you must abide by the couse-
quence—Yet as Moses, when he went out from the
presence of Pharaoh for the last time, finding his
heart yet more hardened by all the judgments and
deliverances with which he had formerly been exercised, denounced upon him God's passing through
the land in terror to smite the first-born with death,
and warned him of that great and lamentable cry
which the sword of the destroying angel should raise
throughout all his realm; Exod. ix. 4—6, so will I,
sinner, now when I am quitting thee, speak to thee
yet again, "whether thou wilt hear or whether thou
wilt forbear," Ezek. ii. 7, and denounce that much
more terrible judgment, which the sword of divine
vengeance already whetted and drawn and bathed as
it were in heaven, Isa. xxxiv. 5, is preparing against
thee; which shall end in a much more doleful cry;
though thou wert greater and more obstinate than

that haughty monarch. Yes, sinner, that I may, with the apostle Paul, when, " turning to others," who are more like to hear me, " shake my raiment, and say, I am pure from your blood," Acts xviii. 6, I will once more tell you what the end of these things will be; and, oh, that I could speak to purpose! Oh that I could thunder in thine ear such a peal of ter rors as might awaken thee, and be too loud to be. drowned in all ti.o noise of carnal mirth, or to be deadened by those dangerous opiates, with which thou art contriving so stupefy thy conscience!

9. Seek what amusements and entertainments thou wilt, O sinner, I tell thee, if thou wert equal in dignity, and power, and magnificence, to the great monarch of Babylon, " thy pomp shall be brought down to the grave, and all the sound of thy viols; the worm shall be spread under thee, and the worm shall cover thee," Isa. xiv. 11. Yes, sinner, " the end of these things is death," Rom. vi. 21, death in its most terrible sense to thee, if this continue thy governing temper. Thou canst not avoid it; and if it be possible for any thing that I can say to prevent, thou shalt not forget it. Your " strength is not the strength of stones, nor is your flesh of brass," Job vi. 12. You are accessible to diseases as well as others; and if some sudden accident do not prevent it, we shall soon see how heroically you will behave yourself on a dying bed, and in the near views of eternity. You that now despise Christ, and trifle with his gospel, we shall see you droop and languish; shall see all your relish for your carnal recreations, and your vain companions, lost. And if perhaps one and another of them bolt in upon you, and is brutish and desperate enough to attempt to entertain a dying man with a gay story, or a profane jest, we shall see how you will relish it. We shall see what comfort you will have in reflecting on what is past, or what hope in looking forward to what is to come. Perhaps, trembling and astonished, you will then be inquiring, in a wild kind of consternation, " what you shall do to be saved;" :alli ig for the ministers of Christ, whom

you now despise for the earnestness with which they would labour to save your soul; and, it may be, falling into a delirium, or dying convulsions, before they can come.   Or perhaps we may see you flattering yourself, through a long lingering illness, that you shall still recover, and putting off any serious reflection and conversation, for fear it should overset your spirits; and the cruel kindness of friends and physicians, as if they were in league with Satan to make the destruction of your soul as sure as possible, may perhaps abet this fatal deceit.

10. And if any of these probable cases happen, that is, in short, unless a miracle of grace snatch you "as a brand out of the burning," when the flames have as it were already taken hold of you, all these gloomy circumstances, which pass in the chambers of illness, and the bed of death, are but the forerunners of infinitely more dreadful things, Oh, who can describe them! who can imagine them! when surviving friends are tenderly mourning over the breathless corpse, and taking a fond farewell of it before it is laid to consume away in the dark and silent grave, into what hands, O sinner, will thy soul be fallen! what scenes will open upon thy separate spirit, even before thy deserted flesh be cold, or thy sightless eyes are closed! it shall then know what it is to return to God to be rejected by him, as having rejected his gospel and his Son, and despised the only treaty of reconciliation; and that such a one so amazingly condescending and gracious.   Thou shalt know what it is to be disowned by Christ, whom thou hast refused to entertain; and what it is, as the certain and immediate consequence of that, to be left in the hands of the malignant spirits of hell.   There will be no more friendship then; none to comfort, none to alleviate thy agony and distress; but on the contrary, all around thee labouring to aggravate and increase them.   Thou shalt pass away the intermediate years of the separate state in dreadful expectation, and bitter outcries of horror and remorse; and then thou shalt hear the trumpet of the archangel, in whatever cavern of that

gloomy world thou art lodged. Its sound shall penetrate thy prison, where, doleful and horrible as it is,
thou shalt nevertheless wish that thou mightest still
be allowed to hide thy guilty head, rather than show
it before the face of that awful Judge, before whom
" heaven and earth are flying away," Rev. xx. 11.
But thou must come forth, and be reunited to a
body, now formed for ever to endure agonies, which
in this mortal state would have dissolved it in a moment. You would not be persuaded to come to Christ
before: you would stupidly neglect him, in spite of
reason, in spite of conscience, in spite of all the ten-
derest solicitations of the gospel, and the repeated
admonitions of its most faithful ministers: but now,
sinner, you shall have an interview with him; if that
may be called an interview, in which you will not
dare to lift up your head to view the face of your
tremendous Judge.   There, at least, how distant soever the time of our life, and the place of our abode,
may have been, there shall we see how courageously
your hearts will endure, and how " strong your hands
will be, when the Lord doth this," Ezek. xxii. 14.
There shall I see thee, O reader, whoever thou art
that goest on in thine impenitency, among thousands
and ten thousands of despairing wretches, trembling
and confounded. There shall I hear thy cries among
the rest, rending the very heavens in vain. The Judge
will rise from the tribunal with majestic composure,
and leave thee to be hurried down to those everlasting burnings to which his righteous vengeance hath
doomed thee because thou wouldst not be saved from
them.   Hell shall shut its mouth upon thee for ever,
and the sad echo of thy groans and outcries shall be
lost amidst the hallelujahs of heaven to all that find
mercy of the Lord in that day.

11. This will most assuredly be the end of these
things and thou, as a Christian, professest to know
and to believe it.   It moves my heart at least, if it
moves not thine.   I firmly believe that every one
who himself obtains salvation and glory, will bear
so much of his Saviour's image in wisdom and good

ness, in zeal for God and a steady regard to the happiness of the whole creation, that he will behold this
sad scene with calm approbation, and without any
painful commotion of mind.   But as yet I am flesh
and blood; and therefore my bowels are troubled,
and mine eyes often overflow with grief, to think that
wretched sinners will have no more compassion upon
their own souls; to think that in spite of all admonition, they will obstinately run upon final everlasting
destruction. It would signify nothing to add a prayer
here, or a meditation for your use. Poor creature! you
will not meditate! you will not pray! Yet, as I have
often poured out my heart in prayer over a dying
friend, when the force of his distemper has rendered
him incapable of joining with me, so will I now apply
myself to God for you, O unhappy creature!   And
if you disdain so much as to read what my compassion dictates, yet I hope they who have felt the power
of the gospel on their own souls, as they cannot but
pity such as you, will join with me in such cordial,
though broken petitions as these:

A PRAYER IN BEHALF OF AN IMPENITENT SINNER, IN THE CASE DESCRIBED ABOVE.

Almighty God! " with thee all things are possible,"
Matt. xix. 26; to thee, therefore, do I humbly apply
myself in behalf of this dear immortal soul, which
thou here seest perishing in its sins, and hardening
itself against that everlasting gospel, which has been
the power of God to the salvation of so many thousands and millions.   Thou art witness, O blessed
God, thou art witness to the plainness and seriousness with which the message has been delivered.   It
is in thy presence that these awful words have been
written, and in thy presence have they been read.
Be pleased, therefore, to record it in the book of thy
remembrance, that so, if this wicked man dies in his
iniquity, after the warning has been so plainly and
so solemnly given him, his blood may not be required

at my hand, Ezek. xxxiii. 8, 9 ; nor at the hand of that
Christian friend, whoever he is, by whom this book
has been put into his, with a sincere desire for the
salvation of his soul. Be witness, O blessed Jesus,
" in the day in which thou shalt judge the secrets of
all hearts," Rom. ii. 16, that thy gospel has been
preached to this hardened wretch, and salvation by
thy blood has been offered him, though he continue
to despise it. And may thine unworthy messenger
be unto God a sweet savour in Christ, in this very
soul, even though it should at last perish, 2 Cor. ii.
15.

But, O that, after all his hardness and impeni
tence, thou wouldst still be pleased, by the sovereign
power of thine efficacious grace, to awaken and convert him! Well do we know, O thou Lord of universal nature, that He who made the soul can cause
the sword of conviction to come near and enter into
it. O that, in thine infinite wisdom and love, thou
wouldst find out a way to interpose, and save this
sinner from death, from eternal death! O that, if it
be thy blessed will, thou wouldst immediately do it!
Thou knowest, O God, he is a dying creature: thou
knowest that if any thing be done for him, it must
be done quickly: thou seest, in the book of thy wise
and gracious decrees, a moment marked, which must
seal him up in an unchangeable state: O that thou
wouldst lay hold on him, while he is yet " joined to
the living," and " hath hope!" Eccl. ix. 4. Thy immutable laws, in the dispensation of grace, forbid that
a soul should be converted and renewed after its entrance on the invisible world: O let thy sacred Spirit
work, while he is yet as it were within the sphere of
his operations! Work, O God, by whatever method
thou pleasest, only have mercy upon him! O Lord,
have mercy upon him, that he sink not into those
depths of damnation and ruin, on the very brink of
which he so evidently appears! O that thou wouldst
bring him, if that be necessary, and seem to thee
most expedient, into any depths of calamity and distress! O that, with Manasseh, he may be " taken in

the thorns, and laden with the fetters of affliction," if that may but cause him " to seek the God of his fathers," 2 Cor. xxxiii. 11, 12.

But I prescribe not to thine infinite wisdom. Thou hast displayed thy power in glorious and astonishing instances; which I thank thee that I have so circum- stantially known, and by the knowledge of them have been fortified against the rash confidence of those who weakly and arrogantly pronounce that to be impossible which is actually done.   Thou hast, I know, done that by a single thought in retirement, when the happy man reclaimed by it has been far from means, and far from ordinances, which neither the most awful admonitions, nor the most tender en- treaties, nor the most terrible afflictions, nor the most wonderful deliverances, had been able to effect.

Glorify thy name, O Lord, and glorify thy grace, in the method which to thine infinite wisdom shall seem most expedient!   Only grant, I beseech thee, with all humble submission to thy will, that this sin ner may be saved; or if not, that the labour of this part may not be altogether in vain; but that, if some reject it to their aggravated ruin, others may hearken and live: that those thy servants, who have labour- ed for their deliverance and happiness, may view them in the regions of glory, as the spoils which thou hast honoured them as the instruments of recovering; and may join with them in the hallelujahs of heaven, " to him who hath loved us, and washed us from our sins in his own blood, and hath made us" of con- demned rebels, and accursed polluted sinners, " kings and priests unto God; to him be glory and dominion for ever and ever," Amen. Rev. i. 5, 6.

CHAPTER XII.

AN ADDRESS TO A SOUL SO OVERWHELMED WITH A SENSE OF THE GREAT-
NESS OF ITS SINS, THAT IT DARES NOT APPLY ITSELF TO CHRIST WITH
ANY HOPE OF SALVATION.

The case described at large, 1—4, as it frequently occurs, 5. Grant-
ing all that the dejected soul charges on itself, 6. The invitations
and promises of Christ give hope, 7. The reader urged, under
all his burdens and fears, to an humble application to him, 8.
Which is accordingly exemplified in the concluding reflection and
prayer.

1. I HAVE now done with those unhappy creatures who despise the gospel, and with those who neglect it. With pleasure do I now turn myself to those who will hear me with more regard. Among the various cases which now present themselves to my thoughts, and demand my tender, affectionate, respectful care, there is none more worthy of compassion than that which I have mentioned in the title of this chapter; none which requires a more immediate attempt of relief.

2. It is very possible, some afflicted creature may be ready to cry out, It is enough: aggravate my grief and my distress no more. The sentence you have been so awfully describing, as what shall be passed and executed on the impenitent and unbelieving, is my sentence: and the terrors of it are my terrors. For " mine iniquities are gone up into the heavens," Rev. xviii. 5, and my transgressions have reached unto the clouds. My case is quite singular. Surely there never was so great a sinner as I. I have received so many mercies, I have enjoyed so many advantages, I have heard so many invitations of gospel grace; and yet my heart has been so hard, and my nature is so exceeding sinful, and the number and aggravating circumstances of my provocations have been such, that I dare not hope. It is enough that God has supported me thus long; it is enough that, after so many years of wickedness, I am yet out of

hell. Every day's reprieve is a mercy at which ɪ am astonished. I lie down and wonder that deatl. and damnation have not seized me in my walks the day past. I arise and wonder that my bed has not oeen my grave; wonder that my soul is not separa. ted from my flesh, and surrounded with devils and damned spirits.

3. I have indeed heard the message of salvation; but, alas, it seems no message of salvation to me. There are happy souls that have hope; and their hope is indeed in Christ, and the grace of God manifested in him. But then they feel in their hearts an encouragement to apply to him; whereas I dare not do it. Christ and grace are things in which I fear I have no part, and must expect none. There are exceeding rich and precious promises in the word of God; but they are to me as a sealed book, and are hid from me as to any personal use. I know Christ is able to save; I know he is willing to save some; but that he should be willing to save me, such a polluted, such a provoking creature, as, God knows, and as conscience knows, I have been, and to this day am; this I know not how to believe; and the utmost that I can do towards believing it is to acknowledge that it is not absolutely impossible, and that I do not yet lie down in complete despair; though, alas! I seem upon the very borders of it, and expect every day and hour to fall into it.

4. I should not, perhaps, have entered so fully into this case if I had not seen many in it; and I will add, reader, for your encouragement, if it be your case, several who are now in the number of the most established, cheerful, and useful Christians. And I hope divine grace will add you to the rest, if " out of these depths" you be enabled to " cry unto God," Psal. cxxx. 1, and though, like Jonah, you may seem to be " cast out from his presence," yet still with Jonah, you " look towards his holy temple," Jonah ii. 4.

5. Let it not be imagined that it is in any neglect of that blessed Spirit, whose office it is to be the great Comforter, that I now attempt to reason you out of

this disconsolate frame; for it is as the great source of reason that he deals with rational creatures, and it is in the use of rational means and considerations that he may most justly be expected to operate. Give me leave, therefore, to address myself calmly to you, and to ask you what reason you have for all these passionate complaints and accusations against yourself? what reason have you to suggest that your case is singular when so many have told you they have felt the same? what reason have you to conclude so hardly against yourself, when the gospel speaks in such favourable terms? or what reason to imagine that the gracious things it says are not intended for you? You know indeed more of the corruptions of your own heart than you know of the hearts of others; and you make a thousand charitable excuses for their visible failings and infirmities which you make not for your own; and it may be some of those, whom you admire as eminent saints when compared with you, are on their part, humbling themselves in the dust as unworthy to be numbered among the least of God's people, and wishing themselves like you, in whom they think they see much more good, and much less of evil, than in themselves.

6. But to suppose the worst: what if you were really the vilest sinner that ever lived upon the face of the earth? what " if your iniquities had gone up unto the heavens," Rev. xviii. 5, every day, and your transgressions had reached unto the clouds, reached thither with such horrid aggravations, that earth and heaven should have had reason to detest you as a monster of impiety? Admitting all this, " is any thing too hard for the Lord?" Gen. xviii. 14; are any sins of which a sinner can repent of so deep a dye that the blood of Christ cannot wash them away? Nay though it would be daring wickedness and monstrous folly for any " to sin that grace might abound." Rom. vi. 1, yet had you indeed raised your account beyond all that divine grace has ever yet pardoned, who should " limit the holy one of Israel?" Psal. lxxviii. 41, or who should pretend to say that it was impos-

sible that God might, for your very wretchedness choose you out from others, to make you a monument of mercy, and a trophy of hitherto unparalleled grace! The apostle Paul strongly intimates this to have been the case with regard to himself; and why might not you likewise, if indeed " the chief of sinners, obtain mercy, that in you, as the chief, Jesus Christ might show forth all long suffering, for a pattern to them who shall hereafter believe?" 1 Tim. i. 15, 16.

7. Gloomy as your apprehensions are, I would ask you plainly, Do you in your conscience think that Christ is not able to save you? What, is he not " able to save, even to the uttermost, them that come unto God by him," Heb. vii. 25. Yes, you will say, abundantly able to do it; but I dare not imagine that he will do it. And how do you know that he will not? He has helped the very greatest sinners of all, that have yet applied themselves to him; and he has made thee offers of grace and salvation in the most engaging and encouraging terms: " if any man thirst, let him come unto me and drink:" John vii. 37. Let him that is athirst come; and whosoever will, let him take of the water of life freely:" Rev. xxii. 17. Come unto me all ye that labour and are heavy laden, and I will give you rest," Matt. ix. 28, and, once more, " Him that cometh unto me, I will in no wise cast out," John vi. 37. True, you will say, none that are given him by the Father: could I know I was of that number I could then apply cheerfully to him. But, dear reader, let me entreat you to look into the text itself, and see whether that limitation be expressly added there. Do you there read, " None of them whom the Father hath given me shall be cast out?" The words are in a much more encouraging form: and why should you frustrate his wisdom and goodness by such an addition of your own? " Add not to his words, lest he reprove thee:" Prov. xxx. 6, take them as they stand, and drink in the consolation of them. Our Lord knew into what perplexity some serious minds might possibly be thrown by what he

had before been saying, "All that the Father hath given me shall come unto me;" and therefore as it were on purpose to balance it, he adds those gracious words, "Him that cometh unto me, I will in no wise" by no means, on no consideration whatever, "cast out."

8. If therefore you are already discouraged and terrified at the greatness of your sins, do not add to their weight and number that one greater and worse than all the rest, a distrust of the faithfulness and grace of the blessed Redeemer. Do not, so far as in you lies, oppose all the purposes of his love to you. O distressed soul, whom dost thou dread? to whom dost thou tremble to approach? Is there any thing so terrible in a crucified Redeemer, in "the Lamb that was slain?" If thou carriest thy soul, almost sinking under the burden of its guilt, to lay it down at his feet, what dost thou offer him but the spoil which he bled and died to recover and possess? and did he purchase it so dearly that he might reject it with disdain? Go to him directly, and fall down in his presence, and plead that misery of thine which thou hast now been pleading in a contrary view, as an engagement to your own soul to make the application, and as an argument with the compassionate Saviour to receive you: go, and be assured, " that where sin hath abounded, there grace shall much more abound," Rom. v. 20. Be assured, that if one sinner can promise himself a more certain welcome than another, it is not he that is least guilty and miserable, but he that is most deeply humbled before God, under a sense of that misery and guilt, and lies the lowest in the apprehension of it.

REFLECTION ON THESE ENCOURAGEMENTS, ENDING IN AN HUMBLE AND EARNEST APPLICATION TO CHRIST FOR MERCY.

O my soul, what sayest thou to these things? Is there not at least a possibility of help from Christ? and is there a possibility of help any other way? Is

" any other name given under heaven whereby we may be saved?" Acts iv. 12. I know there is none. I must then say, like the lepers of Israel, 2 Kings vii. 4: If I sit here I perish, and if I make my application in vain, I can but die. But peradventure he may save my soul alive. I will therefore arise, ana go unto him; or rather, believing him here by his spiritual presence, sinful and miserable as I am, I will this moment fall down on my face before him, ana pour out my soul unto him.

Blessed Jesus, I present myself unto thee as a wretched creature, driven indeed by necessity to do it. For, surely were not that necessity urgent and absolute, I should not dare for very shame to appear in thine holy and majestic presence. I am fully convinced that my sins and my follies have been inexcusably great, more than I can express, more than I can conceive. I feel a source of sin in my corrupt and degenerate nature, which pours out iniquity as a fountain sends out its water, and makes me a burden and a terror to myself. Such aggravations have attended my transgressions, that it looks like presumption so much as to ask pardon of them; and yet would it not be greater presumption to say, that they exceed thy mercy, and the efficacy of thy blood? to say that thou hast power and grace enough to pardon and save only sinners of a lower order, while such as I lie out of thy reach? Preserve me from that blasphemous imagination! Preserve me from that unreasonable suspicion! Lord, thou canst do all things, " neither is there any thought of mine heart withholden from thee," Job xiii. 2. Thou art indeed as thy word declares, " able to save unto the uttermost," Heb. vii. 25, and therefore breaking through all the oppositions of shame and fear that would keep me from thee, I come and lie down as in the dust before thee. " Thou knowest, O Lord, all my sins, and all my follies," Psal. lxix. 5. I cannot, and I hope I may say, I would not disguise them before thee, or set myself to find out plausible excuses. Accuse me, Lord, as thou pleasest; and I will ingenuously plead guilty to all thine accusations. I will own myself as great a sinner as thou callest me; but I am still a sinner that comes unto thee for pardon. If I must die, it shall be submitting, and owning the justice of the fatal stroke. If I perish, it shall be " laying hold," as it were " on the horns of the altar;" laying myself down at thy footstool, though I have been such a rebel against thy throne. Many have received a full pardon there, have met with favour even beyond their hopes. And are all thy compassions, O blessed Jesus, exhausted? and wilt thou now begin to reject an humble creature who flies to thee for life, and pleads nothing but mercy and free grace? " Have mercy upon me," O most gracious Redeemer, "have mercy upon me," and " let my life be precious in thy sight!" 2 Kings i. 14. O, do not resolve to send me down to that state of final misery and despair, from which it was thy gracious purpose to deliver and save so many!

Spurn me not away, O Lord, from thy presence, nor be offended when I presume to lay hold on thy royal robe, and say that I cannot and " will not let thee go till my suit is granted," Gen. xxxii. 26. Oh, remember, that my eternity is at stake! Remember, O Lord, that all my hopes of obtaining eternal happiness, and avoiding everlasting, helpless, hopeless destruction, are anchored upon thee: they hang upon thy smiles, or drop at thy frown. Oh, have mercy upon me, for the sake of this immortal soul of mine; or, if not for the sake of mine alone, for the sake of many others, who may, on the one hand, be encouraged by thy mercy to me, or on the other, may be greatly wounded and discouraged by my helpless despair. I beseech thee, O Lord, for thine own sake, and for the display of thy Father's rich and sovereign grace; I beseech thee by the blood thou didst shed on the cross; I beseech thee by the covenant of grace and peace, into which the Father did enter with thee for the salvation of believing and repenting sinners. save me. Save me, O Lord, who earnestly desire to repent and believe! I am indeed a sinner, in whose final and everlasting destruction thy justice might be greatly glorified: but, oh, if thou wilt pardon me, it will be a monument raised to the honour of thy grace, and the efficacy of thy blood, in proportion to the degree in which the wretch, to whom thy mercy is extended, was mean and miserable without it. Speak, Lord, by thy blessed Spirit, and banish my fears. Look unto me with love and grace in thy countenance, and say to me as in the days of thy flesh thou didst to many an humble supplicant, " Thy sins are forgiven thee, go in peace."

CHAPTER XIII.

THE DOUBTING SOUL MORE PARTICULARLY ASSISTED IN ITS INQUIRIES AS TO THE SINCERITY OF ITS FAITH AND REPENTANCE.

Transient impressions liable to be mistaken for conversion, which would be a fatal error, 1. General scheme for self-examination, 2. Particular inquiries; (1.) What views there have been of sin? 3. (2.) What views there have been of Christ? 4; as to the need the soul has of him, 5; and its willingness to receive him with a due surrender of heart to his service, 6. Nothing short of this sufficient, 7; the soul submitting to divine examination, the sincerity of its faith and repentance.

1. In consequence of all the serious things which have been said in the former chapters, I hope it will be no false presumption to imagine that some religious impressions may be made on hearts which had never felt them before; or may be revived where they have formerly grown cold and languid. Yet I am very sensible, and I desire that you may be so, how great danger there is of self-flattery on this important head; and how necessary it is to caution men against too hasty a conclusion that they are really converted, because they have felt some warm emotion on their minds, and have reformed the gross irre gularities of their former conduct. A mistake here might be infinitely fatal; it may prove the occasion

of that false peace, which shall lead a man to bless himself in his own heart, and to conclude himself se- cure, while all the threatenings and curses of God's law are sounding in his ears, and lie indeed directly against him, Deut. xxix. 19, 20; while in the mean time he applies to himself a thousand promises, in which he has no share; which may prove, therefore, like generous wine to a man in a high fever, or strong opiates to one in a lethargy. The stony ground re- ceived the word with joy, and a promising harvest seemed to be springing up: yet it soon withered away, Matt. xiii. 5, 6, and no reaper filled his arms with it. Now, that this may not be the case with you, that all my labours and yours hitherto may not be lost, and that a vain dream of security and happi- ness may not plunge you deeper in misery and ruin, give me leave to lead you into a serious inquiry into your own heart; that so you may be better able to judge of your case, and to distinguish between what is at most being only near the kingdom of heaven, and becoming indeed a member of it.

2. Now this depends upon the sincerity of your faith in Christ, when faith is taken in its largest ex- tent, as explained above; that is as comprehending repentance, and that steady purpose of new and uni- versal obedience, of which, wherever it is real, faith will assuredly be the vital principle. Therefore, to assist you in judging of your state, give me leave to ask you, or rather to entreat you to ask yourself, what views you have had, and now have of sin, and of Christ, and what your future purposes are with regard to your conduct in the remainder of life that may lie before you. I shall not reason largely upon the several particulars I suggest under these heads, but rather refer you to your own reading and obser- vation, to judge how agreeable they are to the word of God, the great rule by which our characters must quickly be tried, and our eternal state unalterably determined.

3. Inquire seriously, in the first place, what views you have had of sin, and what sentiments you have

felt in your soul with regard to it. There was a time when it wore a flattering aspect, and made a fair enchanting appearance, so that all your heart was charmed with it, and it was the very business of your life to practise it. But you have since been unde-ceived: you have felt it "bite like a serpent, and sting like an adder," Prov. xxiii. 32; you have beheld it with an abhorrence far greater than the delight which it ever gave you. So far it is well. It is thus with every true penitent, and with some I fear who are not of that number. Let me, therefore, inquire further, whence arose this abhorrence? Was it merely from a principle of self-love? was it merely because you had been wounded by it? was it merely because you had thereby brought condemnation and ruin upon your own soul? Was there no sense of its deformity, of its baseness, of its malignity, as com-mitted against the blessed God, considered as a glo-rious, a bountiful, and a merciful being? Were you never pierced by an apprehension of its vile ingrati-tude? And as for those purposes which have arisen in your heart against it, let me beseech you to reflect how they have been formed, and how they have hitherto been executed. Have they been universal? have they been resolute? and yet, amidst all that resolution, have they been humble? When you declared war with sin, was it with every sin? and is it an irreconcilable war which you determine by divine grace to push on, till you have entirely con quered it, or die in the attempt? And are you ac-cordingly active in your endeavours to subdue and destroy it? If so, what are "the fruits worthy of repentance which you bring forth?" Luke iii. 8. It does not, I hope, all flow away in floods of grief: have you ceased to do evil? are you learning to do well? Isa. i. 16, 17. Does your reformation show that you repent of your sins? or do your renewed relapses into sin prove that you repent even of what you call your repentance? Have you an inward abhorrence of all sin, and an unfeigned zeal against ? And does that produce a care to guard against the occasions of it, and temptations to it? Do you watch against the circumstances that have ensnared you? And do you particularly double your guard against "that sin which does most easily beset you?" Heb xii. 1. Is that laid aside, that the Christian race may be run: laid aside, with a firm determination that you will return to it no more, that you will hold no more parley with it, that you will never take another step towards it?

4 Permit me also further to inquire, what your views of Christ have been, what you think of him, and of your concern with him. Have you been fully convinced that there must be a correspondence settled between him and your soul; and do you see and feel, that you are not only to pay him a kind of distant homage, and transient compliment, as a very wise, benevolent, and excellent person, whose name and memory you have a reverence for; but that, as he lives and reigns, as he is ever near you, and always observing you, so you must look to him, must approach him, must humbly transact business with him, and that, business of the highest import- ance, on which your salvation depends?

5. You have been brought to inquire, " wherewith shall I come before the Lord, and bow myself before the most high God?" Micah vi. 6. And once, per- haps, you were thinking of sacrifices, which your own stores might have been sufficient to furnish out. Are you now convinced they will not suffice, and that you must have recourse to the Lamb which God has provided? Have you had a view of Jesus, as "taking away the sin of the world?" John i. 29; as " made a sin-offering for us, though he knew no sin, that we might be made the righteousness of God in him?" 2 Cor. v. 21. Have you viewed him as per fectly righteous in himself? and, despairing of being justified by any righteousness of your own, have you " submitted to the righteousness of God?" Rom. x. 3 Has your heart ever been brought to a deep convic tion of this important truth, that if ever you are saved at all, it must be through Christ; that if ever God

extend mercy to you at all, it must be for his sake, that if ever you are fixed in the temple of God above, you must stand there as an everlasting trophy of that victory which Christ has gained over the powers of hell, who would otherwise have triumphed over you?

6. Our Lord says, "Look unto me, and be ye saved," Isa. xlv. 22; he says, "If I be lifted up, I will draw all men unto me," John xii. 32. Have you looked to him as the only Saviour? have you been drawn unto him by that sacred magnet, the attractive influence of his dying love? Do you know what it is to come to Christ as a poor, "weary, and heavy laden sinner, that you may find rest?" Matt. xi. 28. Do you know what it is in a spiritual sense, to "eat the flesh and drink the blood of the Son of man?" John vi. 53; that is, to look upon Christ crucified as the great support of your soul, and to feel a desire after him, earnest as the appetite of nature after its necessary food. Have you known what it is cordially to surrender yourself to Christ, as a poor creature whom love has made his property? Have you committed your immortal soul to him, that he may purify and save it; that he may govern it by the dictates of his word, and the influences of his Spirit; that he may use it for his glory; that he may appoint it to what exercise and discipline he pleases, while it dwells here in flesh? and that he may receive it at death, and fix it among those spirits, who, with perpetual songs of praise, surround his throne, and are his servants for ever! Have you heartily consented to this? and do you, on this account of the matter, renew your consent? do you renew it deliberately and determinately, and feel your whole soul, as it were, saying, *Amen*, while you read this? If this be the case, then I can with great pleasure give you, as it were, the right hand of fellowship, and salute and embrace you as a sincere disciple of the Lord Jesus Christ, as one who is "delivered from the power of darkness, and is translated into the kingdom of the Son of God," Col. i. 13. I can then salute you in the Lord, as one to whom, as a minister of

Jesus, I am commissioned and charged to speak comfortably, and to tell you, not that I absolve you from
your sins, for it is a small matter to be judged of
man's judgment, but that the blessed God himself
absolves you; that you are one to whom he has said
in his gospel, and is continually saying, " Your sins
are forgiven you," Luke vii. 48; therefore go in
peace, and take the comfort of it.

7. But if you are a stranger to these experiences,
and to this temper which I have now described, the
great work is yet undone; you are an impenitent and
unbelieving sinner, and " the wrath of God abideth
on you," John iii. 36. However you may have
been awakened and alarmed, whatever resolutions
you may have formed for amending your life, how
right soever your notions may be, how pure soever
your forms of worship, how ardent soever your zeal,
how severe soever your mortification, how humane
soever your temper, how inoffensive soever your life
may be, I can speak no comfort to you. Vain are
all your religious hopes, if there has not been a cordial humiliation before the presence of God for all
your sins; if there has not been this avowed war
declared against every thing displeasing to God ; if
there has not been this sense of your need of Christ,
and of your ruin without him; if there has not been
this earnest application to him, this surrender of your
soul into his hands by faith ; this renunciation of
yourself, that you might fix on him the anchor of
your hope; if there has not been this unreserved
dedication of yourself to be at all times, and in all
respects, the faithful servant of God through him;
and if you do not with all this acknowledge that
you are an unprofitable servant, who have no other
expectation of acceptance or of pardon, but only
through his righteousness and blood, and through the
riches of divine grace in him; I repeat it again, that
all your hopes are vain, and you are building on the
sand, Matt. vii. 26. The house you have already
raised must be thrown down to the ground, and the
foundation be removed and laid anew, or you and

all your hopes will shortly be swept away with it, and buried under it in everlasting ruin.

THE SOUL SUBMITTING TO DIVINE EXAMINATION THE SINCERITY OF ITS REPENTANCE AND FAITH.

O Lord God, thou "searchest all hearts, and triest the reins of the children of men," Jer. xvii. 10. "Search me, O Lord, and know my heart; try me, and know my thoughts; and see if there be any wicked way in me, and lead me in the way everlasting," Psal. cxxxix. 23, 24. Does not my conscience, O Lord, testify in thy presence, that my repentance and faith are such as have been described, or at least, that it is my earnest prayer that they may be so? Come, therefore, O thou blessed Spirit, who art the Author of all grace and consolation, and work this temper more fully in my soul. O represent sin to mine eyes in all its most odious colours, that I may feel a mortal and irreconcilable hatred to it! O represent the majesty and mercy of the blessed God in such a manner, that my heart may be alarmed, and that it may be melted! "Smite the rock, that the waters may flow," Psal. lxxviii. 20, waters of genuine, undissembled, and filial repentance. "Convince me." O thou blessed Spirit, "of sin, of righteousness, and of judgment," John xvi. 8. Show me that I have undone myself, "but that my help is found in God alone," Hos. xiii. 9, in God through Christ, in whom alone he will extend compassion and help to me. According to thy peculiar office, "take of Christ, and show it unto me," John xvi. 15. Show me his power to save. Show me his willingness to exert that power. Teach my faith to behold him, as extended on the cross, with open arms, and with a pierced bleeding side; and so telling me, in the most forcible language, what room there is in his very heart for me; may I know what it is to have my whole heart subdued by love! so subdued, as to be "crucified with him," Rom. vi. 6, to be dead to sin, and dead to the world, "but alive unto God through Jesus Christ," Rom. vi. 11. In his power and love may I confide! To him may I, without any reserve, commit my spirit! His image may I bear! His laws may I observe; his service may I pursue! And may I remain through time and eternity, a monument of the efficacy of his gospel, and a trophy of his victorious grace!

O blessed God, if there be any thing wanting towards constituting me a sincere Christian, discover it to me, and work it in me! Beat down, I beseech thee, every false and presumptuous hope, how costly soever that building may have been which is thus laid in ruins, and how proud soever I may have been of its vain ornaments. Let me know the worst of my case, be that knowledge ever so distressful; and if there be remaining danger, O let my heart be fully sensible of it, sensible while yet there is remedy.

If there be any secret sin yet lurking in my soul, which I have not sincerely renounced, discover it to me, and rend it out of my heart, though it should have shot its roots ever so deep, and should have wrapped them all around it, so that every nerve should be pained by the separation. Tear it away, O Lord, by a hand graciously severe! and by degrees, yea, Lord, by speedy advances, go on, I beseech thee, to perfect what is still lacking in my faith, 1 Thess. iii. 10. Accomplish in me " all the good pleasure of thy goodness," 2 Thess. i. 11. Enrich me, O heavenly Father, with all the graces of thy Spirit; form me to the complete image of thy dear Son: and then, for his sake, come unto me, and manifest thy gracious presence in my soul, John xiv. 21, 23, till it is ripened for that state of glory, for which all these operations are intended to prepare it. Amen.

CHAPTER XIV.

1. WHEN I consider the infinite importance of eternity, I find it exceedingly difficult to satisfy myself in
any thing which I can say to men, where their eternal interests are concerned. I have given you a view,
I hope I may truly say, a just as well as faithul view,
of a truly Christian temper already. Yet, for your
further assistance, I would offer it to your consideration in various points of light, that you may be assist
ed in judging of what you are, and of what you
ought to be. And in this I aim, not only at your
conviction, if you are yet a stranger to real religion,
but at your further edification, if by the grace of God
you are by this time experimentally acquainted with

---

* N. B. This chapter is almost an abridgment of that excellent
book of Dr. Evans, entit ed, " The Christian Temper," so far as it
relates to the description of it. For particular arguments, to enforce
each part of this temper, I must refer the reader to the book itself.

it. Happy will you be, happy beyond expression, if, as you go on from one article to another, you can say, " This is my temper and character." Happy in no inconsiderable degree, if you can say, " This is what I desire, what I pray for, and what I pursue, in preference to every opposite view, though it be not what I have as yet attained."

2. Search then, and try, " what manner of spirit you are of," Luke ix. 55. And may " he that searcheth all hearts" direct the inquiry; and enable you so to judge yourself, that you may not be condemned of the Lord, 1 Cor. xi. 31, 32.

3. Know, in the general, that if you are " a Christian indeed," you have been " renewed in the spirit of your mind," Eph. iv. 23, so renewed as to be regenerate " and born again." It is not enough to have assumed a new name, to have been brought under some new restraints, or to have made a partial change in some particulars of your conduct. The change must be great and universal. Inquire then, whether you have entertained new apprehensions of things, have formed a practical judgment different from what you formerly did: whether the ends you propose, the affections, which you feel working in your heart, and the course of action to which, by those affections, you are directed, be on the whole new or old.— Again, if you are a Christian indeed, you are " partaker of a divine nature," 2 Pet. i. 4, divine in its original, its tendency, and its resemblance. Inquire therefore whether God hath implanted a principle in your heart which tends to him, and which makes you like him. Search your soul attentively, to see if you have really the image there of God's moral perfections, of his holiness and righteousness, his goodness and fidelity; for " the new man is after God created in righteousness and true holiness," Eph. iv. 24, and " is renewed in knowledge after the image of him that created him," Col. iii. 10.

4. For your further assistance, inquire whether " the same mind be in you which was also in Christ,"

Phil. ii. 5; whether you bear the image of God's incarnate Son, the brightest and the fairest resemblance of the Father, which earth or heaven has ever beheld? The blessed Jesus designed himself to be a model for all his followers; and he is certainly a model most fit for our imitation; an example in our nature, and in circumstances adapted to general use; an example recommended to us at once by its spotless perfection, and by the endearing relation in which he stands to us, as our Master, our friend, and our head, as the person by whom our everlasting state is to be fixed, and in a resemblance to whom our final happiness is to consist, if ever we are happy at all. Look then into the life and temper of Christ, as described and illustrated in the gospel, and search whether you can find any thing like it in your own life. Have you any thing of his devotion, love, and resignation to God? Any thing of his humility, meekness, and benevolence to men? Any thing of his purity and wisdom, his contempt of the world, his patience, his fortitude, his zeal? And indeed, all the other branches of the Christian temper, which do not imply previous guilt in the person, by whom they are exercised, may be called in to illustrate and assist your inquiries under this head.

5. Let me add, if you are a Christian, you are in the main " spiritually minded, as knowing that is life and peace; whereas to be carnally minded is death," Rom. viii. 6. Though you "live in the flesh, you will not war after it," 2 Cor. x. 3, you will not take your orders and your commands from it. You will indeed attend to its necessary interests as matter of duty, but it will still be with regard to another and a nobler interest, that of the rational and immortal spirit. Your thoughts, your affections, your pursuits, your choice, will be determined by a regard to things spiritual rather than carnal.—In a word "you will walk by faith, and not by sight," 2 Cor. v. 7. Future, invisible, and, in some degree, incomprehensible objects, will take up your mind. Your faith will act on

the being of God, his perfections, his providences, his precepts, his threatenings, and his promises. It will act upon Christ, whom having not seen, you will love and honour, 1 Pet. i. 8. It will act on that un-seen world, which it knows to be eternal, and there-fore infinitely more worthy of your affectionate re-gard, than any of "those things which are seen, and are temporal," 2 Cor. iv. 13.

6. These are general views of the Christian tem-per, on which I would entreat you to examine your-self. And now I would go on to lead you into a survey of the grand branches of it, as relating to God, our neighbour, and ourselves: and of those qualifica-tions which must attend each of these branches; such as sincerity, constancy, tenderness, zeal and prudence. And I beg your diligent attention, while I lay before you a few hints with regard to each, by which you may judge the better both of your state and of your duty.

7. Examine, then, I entreat you, " the temper of your heart, with regard to the blessed God." Do you find there a reverential fear, and a supreme love and veneration for his incomparable excellencies, a desire after him as the highest good, and a cordial gratitude towards him as your supreme benefactor? Can you trust his care? Can you credit his testimony? Do you desire to pay an unreserved obedience to all that he commands, and an humble submission to all the disposals of his providence? Do you design his glory as your noblest end, and make it the great business of your life to approve yourself to him? Is it your governing care to imitate him, and to " serve him in spirit and in truth?" John iv. 24.

8. Faith in Christ I have already described at large; and therefore shall say nothing further, either of that persuasion of his power and grace, which is the great foundation of it; or of that acceptance of Christ under all his characters, or that surrender of the soul into his hands, in which its peculiar and distinguishing nature consists.

9. If this faith in Christ be sincere, " it will un doubtedly produce a love to him;" which will ex

press itself in affectionate thoughts of him: in strict fidelity to him; in a careful observation of his charge; in a regard to his Spirit, to his friends, and to his interests; in a reverence to the memorials of his dying love, which he has instituted; and in an ardent desire after that heavenly world where he dwells, and where he will at length " have all his people to dwell with him," John xvii. 24.

10. I may add, agreeably to the word of God, that thus believing in Christ, and loving him, you will " also rejoice in him;" in his glorious design, and in his complete fitness to accomplish it; in the promises of his word, and in the privileges of his people. It will be matter of joy to you that such a Redeemer has appeared in this world of ours; and your joy for yourself will be proportionable to the degree of clearness with which you discern your interest in him, and relation to him.

11. Let me further lead you into some reflections on the temper of your heart towards the blessed Spirit. If we " have not the Spirit of Christ, we are none of his," Rom. viii. 9. If we are not " led by the Spirit of God, we are not the children of God," Rom. viii. 14. You will then, if you are a real Christian, desire that you may " be filled with the Spirit," Eph v. 18, that you may have every power of your soul subject to his authority; that his agency on your heart may be more constant, more operative, and more delightful. And to cherish these sacred influences, you will often have recourse to serious consideration and meditation: you will abstain from those sins which tend to grieve him: you will improve the tender seasons in which he seems to breathe upon your soul; you will strive earnestly with God in prayer, that you may have him " shed on you" still more " abundantly through Jesus Christ," Tit. iii. 6. and you will be desirous to fall in with the great end of his mission, which was to " glorify Christ," John xvi. 14, and to establish his kingdom. You will desire his influences, as the Spirit of adoption, to render your acts of worship free and affectionate; your sor-

row for sin overflowing and tender; your resignation meek, and your love ardent: in a word, to carry you through life and death with the temper of a child who delights in his father, and who longs for his more immediate presence.

12. Once more. If you are a Christian indeed, you will be desirous to obtain the spirit of courage. Amidst all that humility of soul to which you will be formed, you will wish to commence a hero in the cause of Christ, opposing with a vigorous resolution, the strongest efforts of the power of darkness, the inward corruption of your own heart, and all the outward difficulties you may meet with in the way of your duty, while in the cause and in the strength of Christ you go on " conquering and to conquer."

13. All these things may be considered as branches of godliness; of that godliness which is " profitable for all things," and hath the " promise of the life which now is, and of that which is to come," 1 Tim. iv. 8.

14. Let me now further lay before you some branches of the Christian temper, which relate more immediately to ourselves. And here, if you are a Christian indeed, you will undoubtedly " prefer the soul to the body, and things eternal to those things that are temporal." Conscious of the dignity and value of your immortal part, you will come to a firm resolution to secure its happiness, whatever is to be resigned, whatever is to be endured in that view. If you are a real Christian, you will be also " clothed with humility," 1 Pet. v. 5. You will have a deep sense of your own imperfections, both natural and moral; of the short extent of your knowledge, of the uncertainty and weakness of your resolutions, and of your continual dependence upon God, and upon almost every thing about you. And especially, you will be deeply sensible of your guilt; the remembrance of which will fill you with shame and confusion, even when you have some reason to hope it is forgiven. This will forbid all haughtiness and insolence in your behaviour to your fellow-creatures. It

will teach you under afflictive providences, with all
holy submission to " bear the indignation of the
Lord," as those that know they have sinned against
him," Micah vii. 9. Again, if you are a Christian indeed, you will labour after "purity of soul," and maintain a fixed abhorrence of all prohibited sensual indulgence.   A recollection of past impurities will fill
you with shame and grief; and you will endeavour
for the future to guard your thoughts and desires, as
well as your words and actions, and to abstain not
only from the commission of evil, but from the distant appearance and probable occasions of it, 1 Thes.
v. 22, as conscious of the perfect holiness of that God
with whom you converse, and of the purifying nature of that hope, 1 John iii. 3, which, by his gospel
he has taught you to entertain.

15. With this is nearly allied that " amiable virtue of temperance," which will teach you to guard
against such a use of meats and drinks as indisposes
the body for the service of the soul; or such an indulgence in either, as will rob you of that precious jewel,
your time, or occasion an expense beyond what your
circumstances will admit, and beyond what will consist with what you owe to the cause of Christ, and
those liberalities to the poor, which your relation and
theirs to God and each other will require.   In short,
you will guard against whatever has a tendency
to increase a sensual disposition; against whatever
would alienate the soul from communion with God,
and would diminish its zeal and activity in his service.

16. The divine philosophy of the blessed Jesus will
also teach you " a contented temper."   It will moderate your desires of those worldly enjoyments, after
which many feel such an insatiable thirst, ever growing with indulgence and success.   You will guard
against an immoderate care about those things which
would lead you into a forgetfulness of your heavenly
inheritance.   If Providence disappoint your under-
takings you will submit.   If others be more prosperous, you will not envy them; but rather will be
thankful for what God is pleased to bestow upon

them, as well as for what he gives you. No unlawful methods will be used to alter your present condition; and whatever it is, you will endeavour to make the best of it; remembering it is what infinite Wisdom and Goodness have appointed you, and that it is beyond all comparison better than you have deserved; yea, that the very deficiencies and inconveniences of it may conduce to the improvement of your future and complete happiness.

17. With contentment, if you are a disciple of Christ, "You will join patience too," and "in patience will possess your soul." Luke xxi. 19. You cannot indeed be quite insensible either of afflictions or of injuries; but your mind will be calm and composed under them, and steady in the prosecution of proper duty, though afflictions press, and though your hopes, your dearest hopes and prospects be delayed. Patience will prevent hasty and rash conclusions, and fortify you against seeking irregular methods of relief; disposing you, in the mean time, till God shall be pleased to appear for you, to go on steadily in the way of your duty; " committing yourself to him in well-doing," 1 Pet. iv. 19. You will also be careful, that " patience may have its perfect work," James i. 4, and prevail in proportion to those circumstances which demand its peculiar exercise. For instance, when the successions of evil are long and various, so that deep calls to deep, and all God's waves and billows seem to be going over you one after another; Psal. xlii. 7; when God touches you in the most tender part; when the reasons of his conduct to you are quite unaccountable; when your natural spirits are weak and decayed; when unlawful methods of redress seem near and easy; still your reverence for the will of your heavenly Father will carry it against all, and keep you waiting quietly for deliverance in his own time and way.

18. I have thus led you into a brief review of the Christian temper, with respect to God and ourselves: permit me now to add, That the gospel will teach you another set of very important lessons with re-

spect to your fellow-creatures. They are all summed up in this: "Thou shalt love thy neighbour as thy self." Rom. xiii. 9; and " whatsoever thou wouldst" (that is, whatsoever thou couldst in an exchange of circumstances fairly and reasonably desire,) " that others should do unto thee, do thou likewise the same unto them," Matt. vii. 12.   The religion of the blessed Jesus, when it triumphs in your soul, will conquer the predominancy of an irregular self-love, and will teach you candidly and tenderly to look upon your neighbour as another self.   As you are sensible of your own rights, you will be sensible of his; as you support your own character, you will support his.   You will desire his welfare, and be ready to relieve his necessity, as you would have your own consulted by another.   You will put the kindest construction upon his most dubious words and actions: you will take pleasure in his happiness: you will feel his distress, in some measure, as your own.   And most happy will you be, when this obvious rule is familiar to your mind, when this golden law is written upon your heart; and when it is habitually and impartially consulted by you upon every occasion, whether great or small.

19. The gospel will also teach you, " to put on meekness," Col. iii. 12; not only with respect to God, submitting to the authority of his word, and the disposal of his Providence, as was urged before, but also with regard to your brethren of mankind.   Its gentle instructions will form you to calmness of temper under injuries and provocations, so that you may not be angry without or beyond just cause.   It will engage you to guard your words, lest you provoke and exasperate those you should rather study by love to gain, and by tenderness to heal.   Meekness will render you slow in using any rough and violent methods, if they can by any means be lawfully avoided; and ready to admit, and even to propose, a reconciliation, after they have been entered into, if there yet may be hope of succeeding.   So far as this branch of the Christian temper prevails in your heart, you will take

care to avoid every thing which might give unnecessary offence to others; you will behave yourself in a
modest manner, according to your station; and it will
work, both with regard to superiors and inferiors;
teaching you duly to honour the one, and not to
overbear or oppress the other. And in religion itself,
it will restrain all immoderate sallies and harsh censures; and will command down that wrath of man,
which, instead of working, so often opposes, the
righteousness of God, James i. 20, and shames and
wounds that good cause in which it is boisterously
and furiously engaged.

20. With this is naturally connected " a peaceful
disposition." If you are a Christian indeed, you will
have such a value and esteem for peace, as to endeavour to obtain and preserve it " as much as lieth in
you," Rom. xii. 18, as much as you fairly and honourably can. This will have such an influence upon
your conduct, as to make you not only cautious of
giving offence, and slow in taking it, but earnestly
desirous to regain peace as soon as may be, when it
is in any measure broken; that the wound may be
healed while it is green, and before it begins to ran-
kle and fester. And more especially this disposition
will engage you " to keep the unity of the Spirit in
the bond of peace," Eph. iv. 3, with all that in " every
place call on the name of the Lord Jesus Christ," 1
Cor. i. 2; whom, if you truly love, you will also love
all those whom you have reason to believe to be his
disciples and servants.

21. If you be yourself indeed of that number,
you will also " put on bowels of mercy," Col. iii. 12.
The mercies of God, and those of the blessed Redeemer, will work on your heart, to mould it to sentiments
of compassion and generosity, so that you will feel
the wants and sorrows of others; you will desire to
relieve their necessities, and, as you have opportunity, you will do good both to their bodies and their
souls; expressing your kind affections in suitable actions, which may both evidence their sincerity and
render them effectual.

13

22. As a Christian, you will also maintain truth inviolable, not only in your solemn testimonies, when confirmed by an oath, but likewise in common conversation. You will remember, too, that your promises bring an obligation upon you, which you are by no means at liberty to break through. On the whole, you will be careful to keep a strict correspondence between your words and your actions, in such a manner as becomes a servant of the God of truth.

23. Once more, as amidst the strictest care to observe all the divine precepts you will still find many imperfections, on account of which you will be obliged to pray that "God would not enter into strict judgment with you," as well knowing "that in his sight you cannot be justified," Psal. cxliii. 2; you will be careful not to judge others in such a manner as should awaken the severity of his judgment against yourself, Matt. vii. 1, 2. You will not, therefore, judge them pragmatically, that is, when you have nothing to do with their actions; nor rashly, without inquiring into circumstances; nor partially, without weighing them attentively and fairly; nor uncharitably, putting the worst construction upon things in their own nature dubious, deciding upon intentions as evil, further than they certainly appear to be so, pronouncing on the state of men, or on the whole of their character, from any particular action, and involving the innocent with the guilty. There is a moderation contrary to all these extremes, which the gospel recommends; and if you receive the gospel in good earnest into your heart, it will lay the axe to the root of such evils as these.

24. Having thus briefly illustrated the principal branches of the Christian temper and character, I shall conclude the representation with reminding you of some general qualifications, which must be mingled with all, and give a tincture to each of them; such as sincerity, constancy, tenderness, zeal and prudence.

25. Always remember, "that sincerity is the very soul of true religion." A single intention to please

God, and to approve ourselves to him, must animate and govern all that we do in it. Under the influence of this principle you will impartially inquire into every intimation of duty, and apply to the practice of it so far as it is known to you. Your heart will be engaged in all you do. Your conduct in private and in secret will be agreeable to your most public behaviour. A sense of the divine authority will teach you to "esteem all God's precepts concerning all things to be right, and to hate every false way," Psal. cxix. 128.

26. Thus are you "in simplicity and godly sincerity to have your conversation in the world," 2 Cor. i. 12. And you are also to charge it upon your soul to be "steadfast and immovable, always abounding in the work of the Lord," 1 Cor. xv. 58. There must not only be some sudden fits and starts of devotion, or of something which looks like it, but religion must be an habitual and permanent thing. There must be a purpose to adhere to it at all times. It must be made the stated and ordinary business of life. Deliberate and presumptuous sins must be carefully avoided; a guard must be maintained against the common infirmities of life; and falls of one kind or of another must be matter of proportionate humiliation before God, and must occasion renewed resolution for his service. And thus you are to go on to the end of your life, not discouraged by the length and difficulty of the way, nor allured on the one hand, or terrified on the other, by all the various temptations which may surround and assault you. Your soul must be fixed on this basis, and you are still to behave yourself as one who knows he serves an unchangeable God, and who expects from him a kingdom which cannot be removed, Heb. xii. 28.

27. Again, so far as the gospel prevails in youi heart, "your spirit will be tender, and the stone will be transformed into flesh." You will desire that your apprehensions of divine things may be quick, your affections ready to take proper impressions, your conscience always easily touched, and, on the

whole, your resolutions pliant to the divine authority and cordially willing to be, and to do, whatever God shall appoint.   You will have a tender regard to the word of God, a tender caution against sin, a tender guard against the snares of prosperity, a tender submission to God's afflicting hand: in a word, you will be tender wherever the divine honour is concerned: and careful neither to do any thing yourself, nor to allow any thing in another, so far as you can influence, by which God should be offended, or religion reproached.

28. Nay, more than all this, you will, so far as true Christianity governs in your mind, " exert a holy zeal in the service of your Redeemer and your Father."   You will be zealously affected in every good thing, Gal. iv. 18, in proportion to its apprehended goodness and importance.   You will be zealous especially to correct what is irregular in yourself, and to act to the uttermost of your ability for the cause of God.   Nor will you be able to look with an indifferent eye on the conduct of others in this view; but, as far as charity, meekness, and prudence will admit, you will testify your disapprobation of every thing in it which is dishonourable to God and injurious to men.   And you will labour not only to reclaim men from such courses, but to engage them to religion, and to quicken them in it.

29. And, once more, you will desire " to use the prudence which God hath given you," in judging what is, in present circumstances, your duty to God, your neighbour and yourself; what will be, on the whole, the most acceptable manner of discharging it, and how far it may be most advantageously pursued; as remembering, that he is indeed the wisest and the happiest man, who, by constant attention of thought, discovers the greatest opportunities of doing good, and with ardent and animated resolution breaks through every opposition that he may improve those opportunities.

30. This is such a view of the Christian temper as could conveniently be thrown within such narrow

limits; and, I hope it may assist many in the great and important work of self-examination. Let your own conscience answer how far you have already attained it, and how far you desire it; and let the principal topics here touched upon be fixed in your memory and in your heart, that you may be mentioning them before God in your daily addresses to the throne of grace, in order to receive from him all necessary assistance for bringing them into practice.

A PRAYER, CHIEFLY IN SCRIPTURAL LANGUAGE, IN WHICH THE SEVE-
RAL BRANCHES OF THE CHRISTIAN TEMPER ARE MORE BRIEFLY ENUME-
RATED, IN THE ORDER LAID DOWN ABOVE.

Blessed God, I humbly adore thee, as the great " Father of lights, and the giver of every good and every perfect gift," James i. 7. From thee, therefore, I seek every blessing, and especially those which may lead me to thyself, and prepare me for the eternal enjoyment of thee. I adore thee as " the God who searches the heart, and tries the reins of the children of men," Jer. xvii. 10. " Search me, O God, and know my heart; try me, and know my thoughts: see if there be any wicked way in me, and lead me in the way everlasting," Psal. cxxxix. 23, 24. May I know " what manner of spirit I am of," Luke ix. 55, and be preserved from mistaking where the error might be infinitely fatal!

May I, O Lord, " be renewed in the spirit of my mind!" Eph. iv. 23. " A new heart do thou give me, and a new spirit do thou put within me! Ezek. xxxvi. 26. " Make me partaker of divine nature;" 2 Pet. i. 4, and " as he who hath called me is holy, may I be holy in all manner of conversation!" 1 Pet. i. 15. May " the same mind be in me that was also in Christ Jesus;" Phil. ii. 5; may I " so walk even as he walked!" 1 John ii. 6. " Deliver me from being carnally-minded, which is death; and make me spiritually-minded, since that is life and peace!" Rom. viii. 6 And may I, while I pass through this world of sin, " walk by faith and not by sight; 2 Cor. v. 7, and be strong in faith, giving glory to God!" Rom. iv. 20

May "thy grace, O Lord, which hath appeared
unto all men," and appeared to me with such glorious evidence and lustre, "effectually teach me to
deny ungodliness and worldly lusts, and to live soberly, righteously, and godly!" Tit. ii. 11, 12.   Work
in mine heart that "godliness which is profitable unto
all things:" 1 Tim. iv. 8, and teach me, by the influences of thy blessed Spirit, to love thee the Lord my
God with all my heart, and with all my soul, and
with all my mind, and with all my strength! Mark
xii. 30.   May I yield myself unto thee as alive from
the dead; Rom. vi. 13, and "present my body a living sacrifice, holy and acceptable in thy sight, which
is my most reasonable service," Rom. xii. 1.   May I
entertain the most faithful and affectionate regard to
the blessed Jesus, thine incarnate Son, "the brightness of thy glory, and the express image of thy person!" Heb. i. 3.   Though I have not seen him, may
I love him; and in "him, though now I see him not,
yet believing, may I rejoice with joy unspeakable
and full of glory:" 1 Pet. i. 8.   And may "the life
which I live in the flesh," be daily "by the faith of
the Son of God!" Gal. ii. 20.   May I "be filled with
the Spirit; Eph. v. 18, and may I be led by it;" Rom.
viii. 14, and so may it be evident to others, and especially to my own soul, that I am a child of God, and
an heir of glory.   May I "not receive the spirit of
bondage unto fear, but the spirit of adoption, whereby I may be enabled to cry, Abba, Father!" Rom.
viii. 15.   May he work in me as "the spirit of love,
and of power, and of a sound mind," 2 Tim. i. 7, that
so I may "add to my faith virtue!" 2 Pet. i. 5.   May
I be strong and very courageous, Josh. i. 7, and quit
myself like a man, 1 Cor. xvi. 13, and like a Christian, in the work to which I am called, and in that
warfare which I had in view when I listed under the
banner of the great Captain of my salvation.

Teach me, O Lord, seriously to consider the nature
of my own soul, and to set a suitable value upon it!
May I "labour not only," or chiefly, "for the meat
that perisheth, but for that which endureth to eter

nal life!" John vi. 27. May I " humble myself under thy mighty hand," and be "clothed with humility; 1 Pet. v. 5, 6, decked with the ornament of a meek and quiet spirit, which, in the sight of God, is of great price!" 1 Pet. iii. 4. May I be "pure in heart, that I may see God," Matt. v. 8; mortifying my members which are on the earth," Col. iii. 5, so that if a right eye offend me, I may pluck it out; and if a right hand offend me, I may cut it off!" Matt. v. 29, 30. "May I be temperate in all things, 1 Cor. ix. 25, content with such things as I have, Heb. xiii. 5, and instructed to be so in whatsoever state I am!" Phil. iv. 11. May " patience also have its perfect work in me, that I may be in that respect complete, and wanting nothing!" James i. 4.

Form me, O Lord, I beseech thee, to a " proper temper toward my fellow-creatures." May I love "my neighbour as myself; Gal. v. 14; and whatsoever I would that others should do unto me, may I also do the same unto them." Matt. vii. 12. May I " put on meekness," Col. iii. 12, under the greatest injuries and provocations; "and, if it be possible, as much as lieth in me, may I live peaceably with all men." Rom. xii. 18. May I be " merciful, as my Father in heaven is merciful." Luke vi. 36. May I speak the "truth from my heart," Psal. xv. 2; and may I speak "it in love," Eph. iv. 15; guarding against every instance of a censorious and malignant disposition; and taking care not "to judge" severely, as I would not " be judged," Matt. iii. 1, with a severity which thou, Lord, knowest, and which my own conscience knows, I should not be ab'e to support.

I entreat thee, O Lord, to work in me ' all those qualifications of the Christian temper," which may render it peculiarly acceptable to thee, and may prove ornamental to my profession in the world. Renew, " I beseech thee, a right spirit within me;" Psal. li. 10, make me an Israelite indeed, in whom there is no allowed guile! John i. 47. And while I feast on " Christ, as my passover sacrificed for me, may I keep the feast with the unleavened bread of sincerity and truth." 1 Cor. v. 7, 8. Make me, I beseech thee, O thou Almighty and unchangeable God, " steadfast and immovable, always abounding in thy work, as knowing my labour in the Lord will not be" finally " in vain." 1 Cor. xv. 58. May my heart be tender, 2 Kings xxii. 19, easily impressed with thy word and providences, touched with an affectionate concern for thy glory, and sensible of every impulse of thy Spirit. May I be " zealous for my God," Num. xxv. 13, with a " zeal according to knowledge, Rom. x. 2, and charity, 1 Cor. xvi. 14; and teach me in thy service, to join the wisdom of the serpent," Matt. x. 16, with the boldness of the lion, and " the innocence of the dove!" Thus render me, by thy grace, a shining image of my dear Redeemer; and at length bring me to wear the bright resemblance of his holiness and his glory in that world where he dwells; that I may ascribe everlasting honours to him, and to thee, O thou Father of mercies, whose invaluable gift he is, and to thine Holy Spirit, through whose gracious influences I would humbly hope I may call thee my Father, and Jesus my Saviour. Amen.

CHAPTER XV.

THE READER REMINDED HOW MUCH HE NEEDS THE ASSISTANCE OF THE SPIRIT OF GOD, TO FORM HIM TO THE TEMPER DESCRIBED ABOVE, AND WHAT ENCOURAGEMENT HE HAS TO EXPECT IT.

Forward resolutions may prove ineffectual, 1. Yet religion is not to be given up in despair, but divine grace sought, 2. A general view of its reality and necessity, from reason, 3, and Scripture, 4. The Spirit to be sought as the Spirit of Christ, 5; and in that view, the great strength of the soul, 6. The encouragement there is to hope for the communication of it, 7. A concluding exhortation to pray for it, 8. And an humble address to God pursuant to that exhortation.

1. I HAVE now laid before you a plan of that temper and character which the gospel requires, and which,

if you are a true Christian, you will desire and pursue. Surely there is in the very description of it, something which must powerfully strike every mind, which has any taste for what is truly beautiful and excellent. And I question not, but you, my dear reader, will feel some impression of it upon your heart. You will immediately form some lively purpose of endeavouring after it; and perhaps you may imagine you shall certainly and quickly attain to it. You see how reasonable it is, and what desirable consequences necessarily attend it, and the aspect which it bears on your present enjoyment, and your future happiness; and therefore are determined you will act accordingly. But give me leave seriously to remind you how many there have been (would to God that several such instances had not happened within the compass of my personal observation!) "whose goodness hath been like a morning cloud, and the early dew, which soon passeth away," Hos. vi. 4. There is not room, indeed, absolutely to apply the words of Joshua, taken in the most rigorous sense, when he said to Israel, (that he might humble their too hasty and sanguine resolutions,) "Ye cannot serve the Lord," Josh. xxiv. 19; but I will venture to say, you cannot easily do it. Alas! you know not the difficulties you have to break through; you know not the temptations which Satan will throw in your way; you know not how importunate your vain and sinful companions will be to draw you back into the snare you may attempt to break; and above all, you know not the subtle artifices which your own corruptions will practise upon you, in order to recover their dominion over you. You think the views you now have of things will be lasting, because the principles and objects to which they refer are so; but perhaps to-morrow may undeceive you, or rather deceive you anew. To-morrow may present some trifle in a new dress, which shal amuse you into a forgetfulness of all this, nay, per haps, before you lie down on your bed, the impressions you now feel may wear off. The corrupt de sires of your own heart, now perhaps a little charmed down, and lying as if they were dead, may spring up again with new violence, as if they had slept only to recruit their vigour; and if you are not supported by a better strength than your own, this struggle for liberty will only make your future claims the heavier, the more shameful, and the more fatal.

2. What, then, is to be done? Is the convinced sinner to lie down in despair, and say, " I am a helpless captive, and by exerting myself with violence may break my limbs sooner than my bonds, and increase the evil I would remove?" God forbid! You cannot, I am persuaded, be so little acquainted with Christianity as not to know, that the doctrine of divine assistance bears a very considerable part in it. You have often, I doubt not, read of " the law of the Spirit of life in Christ, as making us free from the law of sin and death," Rom. viii. 2; and have been told that " through the Spirit we mortify the deeds of the body," Rom. viii. 13; you have read of " doing all things through Christ who strengtheneth us," Phil. iv. 13; whose " grace is sufficient for us, and whose strength is made perfect in weakness," 2 Cor. xii. 9; permit me, therefore, now to call your attention to this, as a truth of the clearest evidence, and of the utmost importance.

3. Reason, indeed, as well as the whole tenor of Scripture, agrees with this. The whole created world has a necessary dependence on God: from him even the knowledge of natural things is derived, Psal. xciv. 10; and skill in them is to be ascribed to him, Exod. xxxi. 3. 6. Much more loudly does so great and so excellent a work, as the new-forming the human mind, bespeak its divine Author. When you consider how various the branches of the Christian temper are, and how contrary many of them also are to that temper which has prevailed in your heart, and governed your life in time past, you must really see divine influences as necessary to produce and nourish them, as the influences of the sun and rain are to call up the variety of plants and flowers, and

grain, and fruits, by which the earth is adorned, and our life supported. You will be yet more sensible of this, if you reflect on the violent opposition which this happy work must expect to meet with, which if you have not already experienced, it must be because you have but very lately begun to think of religion.

4. Accordingly, if you give yourself leave to consult Scripture on this head, (and if you would live like a Christian, you must be consulting it every day, and forming your notions and actions by it,) you will see that the whole tenor of it teaches that dependence upon God which I am now recommending. You will particularly see, that the production of religion in the soul is matter of divine promise; that when it has been effected, Scripture ascribes it to a divine agency, and that the increase of grace and piety in the heart of those who are truly regenerate, is also spoken of as the work of God, who begins and carries it on until the day of Jesus Christ, Phil. i. 6.

5. In consequence of all these views, lay it down to yourself as a most certain principle, that no attempt in religion is to be made in your own strength. If you forget this, and God purposes finally to save you, he will humble you by repeated disappointments, till he teach you better. You will be ashamed of one scheme and effort, and of another, till you settle upon the true basis. He will also probably show you, not only in the general that your strength is to be derived from heaven; but particularly, that it is the office of the blessed Spirit to purify the heart, and to invigorate holy resolutions; and also, that in all these operations he is to be considered as the Spirit of Christ, working under his directions, and as a vital communication from him, under the character of the great head of the church, the grand Treasurer and Dispenser of these holy and beneficial influences. On which account it is called the " supply of the Spirit of Jesus Christ," Phil. i. 19, who is " exalted at the right hand of the Father, to give repentance and remission of sins," Acts v. 31, in " whose grace alone we can be

strong," 2 Tim. ii. 1, "and of whose fulness we receive, even grace for grace," John i. 16.

6. Resolve, therefore, strenuously for the service of God, and for the care of your soul; but resolve modestly and humbly. "Even the youths shall faint and be weary, and the young men utterly fall; but they who wait on the Lord," are the persons who renew their strength, Isa. xl. 30, 31. When a soul is almost afraid to declare in the presence of the Lord, that it will not do this or that which has formerly offended him; when it is afraid absolutely to promise that it will perform this or that duty with vigour and constancy; but only expresses its humble and earnest desire that it may by grace be enabled to avoid the one, or pursue the other; then, so far as my observation or experience has reached, it is in the best way to learn the happy art of conquering temptations, and of discharging duty.

7. On the other hand, let not your dependence upon this Spirit, and your sense of your own weakness and insufficiency for any thing spiritually good without his continued aid, discourage you from devoting yourself to God, and engaging in a religious life, considering what abundant reason you have to hope that these gracious influences will be communicated to you.—The light of nature, at the same time that it teaches the need we have of help from God in a virtuous course, may lead us to conclude, that so benevolent a Being, who bestows on the most unworthy and careless part of mankind so many blessings will take a peculiar pleasure in communicating to such as humbly ask them, those gracious assistances which may form their deathless souls into his own resemblance, and fit them for that happiness to which their rational nature is suited, and for which it was in its first constitution intended.—The word of God will much more abundantly confirm such a hope. You there hear divine wisdom crying, even to those who had trifled with her instructions, " Turn ye my reproof, and I will pour out my spirit upon r, Prov. i. 23. You hear the Apostle saying,

· Let us come boldly to the throne of grace, that we may obtain mercy, and find grace to help in every time of need," Heb. iv. 16. Yea, you there hear our Lord himself urging, in this sweet and convincing manner, "if ye, being evil, know how to give good gifts unto your children, how much more shall your heavenly Father give his holy Spirit unto them that ask him?" Luke xi. 13. This gift and promise of the Spirit was given unto Christ, when he ascended up on high, in trust for all his true disciples. God hath "shed it abroad abundantly upon us in him," Tit. iii. 6. And I may add, that the very desire you feel after the further communication of the Spirit is the result of the first fruits of it already given: so that you may with peculiar propriety interpret it as a special call, " to open your mouth wide that he may fill it," Psal. lxxxi. 10. You thirst, and therefore you may cheerfully plead, that Jesus hath invited you to come unto him and drink; with a promise, not only that " you shall drink if ye come unto him," but also that "out of your belly shall flow," as it were, " rivers of living water," John vii. 37, 38, for the edification and refreshment of others.

8. Go forth, therefore, with humble cheerfulness, to the prosecution of all the duties of the Christian life. Go, and prosper, " in the strength of the Lord, making mention of his righteousness, and of his only," Psal. lxxi. 16.—And, as a token of further communications, may your heart be quickened to the most earnest desires after the blessings I have now been recommending to your pursuit! May you be stirred up to pour out your soul before God in such holy breathings as these; and may they be your daily language in his gracious presence.

AN HUMBLE SUPPLICATION FOR THE INFLUENCES OF DIVINE GRACE, TO FORM AND STRENGTHEN RELIGION IN THE SOUL.

Blessed God! I sincerely acknowledge before thee mine own weakness and insufficiency for any thing

that is spiritually good. I have experienced it a thou
sand times; and yet my foolish heart would again
trust itself, Prov. xxviii. 26, and form resolutions in
its own strength. But let this be the first fruits of
thy gracious influence upon it, to bring it to an humble distrust of itself, and to a repose on thee.

Abundantly do I rejoice, O Lord, in the kind as-
surances which thou givest me of thy readiness to
bestow liberally and richly so great a benefit. I do,
therefore, according to thy condescending invitation,
"come with boldness to the throne of grace, that I
may find grace to help in every time of need," Heb.
iv. 16. I mean not, O Lord God, to turn thy grace
into wantonness or perverseness, Jude ver. 4, or to
make my weakness an excuse for my negligence and
sloth. I confess thou hast already given me more
strength than I have used; and I charge it upon myself, and not on thee, that I have not long since received still more abundant supplies. I desire for the
future to be found diligent in the use of all appointed
means; in the neglect of which, I well know, that
petitions like these would be a profane mockery, and
might much more probably provoke thee to take
away what I have, than prevail upon thee to impart
more: but firmly resolving to exert myself to the
utmost, I earnestly entreat the communications of
thy grace, that I may be enabled to fulfil that resolution.

"Be surety, O Lord, unto thy servant for good,"
Psal. cxix. 122. Be pleased to shed abroad thy sancti
fying influences on my soul, to form me for every
duty thou requirest. Implant, I beseech thee, every
grace and virtue deep in mine heart; and maintain
the happy temper in the midst of those assaults, from
within and from without, to which I am continually
liable, while I am still in this world, and carry about
with me so many infirmities. Fill my breast, I beseech thee, with good affections towards thee, my
God, and towards my fellow-creatures. Remind me
always of thy presence; and may I remember, that
every secret sentiment of my soul is open to thee

May I, therefore, guard against the first risings of sin, and the first approaches to it: and that Satan may not find room for his evil suggestions, I earnestly beg that thou, Lord, wouldst fill my heart with thine Holy Spirit, and take up thy residence there. "Dwell in me, and walk with me," 2 Cor. vi. 16, "and let my body be the temple of the Holy Ghost," 1 Cor. vi. 19.

May I be so "joined to Christ Jesus my Lord, as "to be one spirit with him," 1 Cor. vi. 17, and feel his invigorating influences continually bearing me on, superior to every temptation, and to every corruption; that while the "youths shall faint and be weary, and the young men utterly fall, I may so wait upon the Lord as to renew my strength," Isa. xl. 30, 31, and may go on from one degree of faith and love, and zeal, and holiness, to another, till I appear perfect before thee in Zion," Psal. lxxxiv. 7, to drink in immortal vigour and joy from thee, as the everlasting fountain of both, through Jesus Christ, my Lord, in whom I have righteousness and strength," Isa. xlv. 24, and to whom I desire ever to ascribe the praise of all my improvements in both. Amen.

CHAPTER XVI.

THE CHRISTIAN CONVERT WARNED OF, AND ANIMATED AGAINST THOSE DISCOURAGEMENTS WHICH HE MUST EXPECT TO MEET WITH WHEN ENTERING ON A RELIGIOUS COURSE.

Christ has instructed his disciples to expect opposition and difficul ties in the way to heaven, 1. Therefore, (I.) A more particular view of them is taken, as arising (1.) From the remainders of indwelling sin, 2. (2) From the world, and especially from former sinful companions, 3. (3) from the temptations and suggestions of Satan, 4. (II.) The Christian is animated and encouraged by various considerations to oppose them; particularly, by—the presence of God,—the aids of Christ,—the example of others, who though feeble, have conquered,—and the crown of glory to be expected, 5, 6. Therefore, though apostasy would be infinitely fatal, the Christian may press on cheerfully, 7. Accordingly the soul, alarmed by these views, is represented as committing itself to God, in the prayer which concludes the chapter.

1. WITH the utmost propriety has our divine Master required us to " strive to enter in at the strait gate," Luke xiii. 24, thereby (as it seems) intimating, not only that the passage is narrow, but that it is beset with enemies; beset on the right hand and on the left with enemies cunning and formidable. And be assured, O reader, that whatever your circumstances in life are, you must meet and encounter them. It will, therefore, be your prudence to survey them attentively in your own reflections, that you may see what you are to expect; and may consider in what armour it is necessary you should be clothed, and with what weapons you must be furnished to manage the combat. You have often heard them marshalled as it were, under three great leaders, the flesh, the world, and the devil; and according to this distribution, I would call you to consider the forces of each, as setting themselves in array against you. O that you may be excited to " take to yourself the whole armour of God, and to quit yourself like a man," 1 Cor. xvi. 13, and a Christian!

2. Let your conscience answer whether you do not

carry about with you a corrupt and a degenerate nature. You will, I doubt not, feel its effects. You
will feel, in the language of the apostle, (who speaks
of it as the case of Christians themselves,) " the flesh
lusting against the spirit, so that you will not be able,"
in all instances, " to do the things that you would,"
Gal. v. 17. You brought irregular propensities into
the world along with you; and you have so often
indulged those sinful inclinations that you have greatly increased their strength, and you will find, in consequence of it, that these habits cannot be broken
through without great difficulty. You will, no doubt,
often recollect the strong figures in which the prophet
describes a case like yours; and you will own that it
is justly represented by that " of an Ethiopian changing his skin, and the leopard his spots," Jer. xiii. 23.
It is indeed possible that at first you may find such
an edge and eagerness upon your own spirits, as may
lead you to imagine, that all opposition will immediately fall before you; but, alas! I fear, that in a
little time these enemies, which seemed to be slain at
your feet, will revive and recover their weapons; and
renew the assault in one form or another. And perhaps your most painful combats may be with such
as you had thought most easy to be vanquished; and
your greatest danger may arise from some of those
enemies from whom you apprehended the least; particularly from pride, and from indolence of spirit
from a secret alienation of heart from God, and from
an indisposition for conversing with him, through an
immoderate attachment to things seen and temporal
which may be oftentimes exceeding dangerous to
your salvation, though perhaps they be not absolutely and universally prohibited. In a thousand of these
instances you must learn to deny yourself, or you
cannot be Christ's disciple, Matt. xvi. 24.

3. You must also lay your account to find great
difficulties from the world; from its manners, cus-
toms, and examples. The things of the world will
hinder you one way, and the men of the world an
other. Perhaps you may meet with much less assist

ance in religion than you are now ready to expect from good men. The present generation of them is generally so cautious to avoid every thing that looks like ostentation, and there seems something so insupportably dreadful in the charge of enthusiasm, that you will find most of your Christian brethren studying to conceal their virtue and their piety much more than others study to conceal their vices and their profaneness. But while, unless your situation be singularly happy, you meet with very little aid one way, you will, no doubt, find great opposition another. The enemies of religion will be bold and active in their assaults, while many of its friends seem unconcerned: and one sinner will probably exert himself more to corrupt you than ten Christians to secure and save you. They who have once been your companions in sin will try a thousand artful methods to allure you back again to their forsaken society; some of them perhaps with an appearance of tender fondness; and many more by the almost irresistible art of banter and ridicule; that boasted test of right and wrong, as it has been wantonly called, will be tried upon you, perhaps without any regard to decency, or even to common humanity. You will be derided and insulted by those whose esteem and affection you naturally desire: and may find much more propriety than you imagine in the expression of the Apostle, "the trial of cruel mockings," Heb. xi. 36, which some fear more than either sword or flames. This persecution of the tongue you must expect to go through, and perhaps you may be branded as a lunatic, for no other cause than that you now begin to exercise your reason to purpose, and will not join with those that are destroying their own souls in their wild career of folly and madness.

4. And it is not at all improbable, that in the mean time, Satan may be doing his utmost to discourage and distress you. He will, no doubt, raise in your imagination the most tempting idea of the gratifications, the indulgences, and the companions, you are obliged to forsake; and give you the most dis-

couraging and terrifying view of the difficulties, se-verities, and dangers, which are (as he will persuade
you) inseparable from religion. He will not fail to
represent God himself, the fountain of goodness and
happiness, as a hard master, whom it is impossible
to please. He will perhaps fill you with the most
distressing fears, and with cruel and insolent malice
glory over you as his slave, when he knows you are
the Lord's freeman. At one time he will study, by
his vile suggestions, to interrupt you in your duties,
as if they gave him an additional power over you: at
another time he will endeavour to weary you of your
devotion, by influencing you to prolong it to an im-moderate and tedious length, lest his power should
be exerted upon you when it ceases. In short, this
practised deceiver has artifices, which it would re
quire whole volumes to display, with particular cau
tions against each. And he will follow you with
malicious arts and pursuits to the very end of your
pilgrimage; and will leave no method unattempted
which may be likely to weaken your hands, and to
sadden your heart; that if, through the gracious in-terposition of God, he cannot prevent your final hap-piness, he may at least impair your peace and your
usefulness as you are passing to it.

5. This is what the people of God feel; and what
you will feel in some degree or other, if you have
your lot and your portion among them. But, after
all, be not discouraged: Christ is " the Captain of
your salvation," Heb. ii. 10. It is delightful to con-sider him under this view. When we take a survey
of these hosts of enemies, we may lift up our head
amidst them all, and say, " More and greater is he
that is with us, than all those that are against us,"
2 Kings vi. 16. Trust in the Lord, " and you will
be like Mount Zion, which cannot be moved, but
abideth for ever," Psal. cxxv. 1. When your ene-mies press upon you, remember you are to " fight
in the presence of God," Zech. x. 5. Endeavour
therefore to act a gallant and resolute part: endea-vour to " resist them steadfastly in the faith," 1 Pet

v. 9.   Remember, " he can give power to the faint, and increase strength to them that have no might," Isa. xl. 29.   He has done it in ten thousand instances already; and he will do it in ten thousand more. How many striplings have conquered their gigantic foes in all their most formidable armour, when they have gone forth against them, though but, as it were, " with a staff and a sling, in the name of the Lord God of Israel!" 1 Sam. xvii. 40, 45.   How many women and children have trodden down the force of the enemy, and " out of weakness have been made strong!" Heb. xi. 34.

6. Amidst all the opposition of earth and hell, look upward, and look forward, and you will feel your heart animated by the view.   Your General is near: he is near to aid you; he is near to reward you. When you feel the temptation press the hardest, think of him who endured even the cross itself for your rescue.   View the fortitude of your divine Leader, and endeavour to march on in his steps. Hearken to his voice, for he proclaims it aloud, " Behold I come quickly, and my reward is with me," Rev. xxii. 12.   Be thou faithful unto death, " and I will give thee a crown of life," Rev. ii. 10.   And, O how bright will it shine! and how long will its lustre last, when the gems that adorn the crowns of monarchs, and pass (instructive thought!) from one royal hand to another through succeeding centuries, are melted down in the last flame, it is " a crown of glory which fadeth not away," 1 Pet. v. 4.

7. It is indeed true, that " such as turn aside to crooked paths will be led forth with the workers of iniquity," Psal. cxxv. 5, to that terrible execution which the divine justice is preparing for them; and that it would have been " better for them not to have known the way of righteousness, than after having known it, to turn aside from the holy commandment," 2 Pet. ii. 21.   But I would, by divine grace, " hope better things of you," Heb. vi. 9.   And I make it my hearty prayer for you, my reader, that you may be " kept by the mighty power of God, kept as in a gar

ıison, on all sides, fortified in the securest manner, "through faith unto salvation," 1 Pet. ii. 5.

THE SOUL, ALARMED BY A SENSE OF THESE DIFFICULTIES, COMMITTING ITSELF TO DIVINE PROTECTION.

Blessed God it is to thine almighty power that I flee. Behold me surrounded with difficulties and dangers, and stretch out thine omnipotent arm to save me; " O thou that savest by thy right hand them that put their trust in thee, from those that rise up against them," Psal. xvii. 7. This day do I solemnly put myself under thy protection; exert thy power in my favour, and permit me to " make the shadow of thy wings my refuge," Psal. lvii. 1. Let thy grace be sufficient for me, and thy strength " be made perfeet in my weakness," 2 Cor. xii. 9. I dare not say, " I will never forsake thee; I will never deny thee," Mark xiv. 31; but I hope I can truly say, O Lord, I would not do it, and that, according to my present apprehension and purpose, death would appear to me much less terrible than in any wilful and deliberate instance to offend thee. O root out those corruptions from my heart, which in an hour of pressing temptation, might incline me to view things in a different light, and so might betray me into the hand of the enemy. Strengthen my faith, O Lord, and encourage my hope. Inspire me with an heroic resolution in opposing every thing that lies in my way to heaven; and let me " set my face like a flint," Isa. l. 7, against all the assaults of earth and hell. " If sinners entice me," let me " not consent," Prov. i. 10; if they insult me, let me not regard it; if they threaten me, let me not fear. Rather may a holy and ardent, yet prudent and well governed zeal take occasion, from that malignity of heart which they discover, to attempt their conviction and reformation. At least, let me never be ashamed to plead thy cause against the most profane deriders of religion. Make me to hear joy and gladness in my soul and I will endeavour to " teach transgressors thy ways, that sinners may be converted unto thee," Psal. li. 8. 13.   Yea, Lord, while my fears continue, though I should apprehend myself condemned, I am condemned so righteously for my own folly, that I would be thine advocate, though against myself.

Keep me, O Lord, now, and all times.   Never let me think, whatever age or station I attain, that I am strong enough to maintain the combat without thee; nor let me imagine myself, even in this infancy of religion in my soul, so weak, that thou canst not support me.   Wherever thou leadest me, there let me follow; and whatever station thou appointest me, there let me labour; there let me maintain the holy war against all the enemies of my salvation, and rather fall into it than basely abandon it.

And thou, O glorious Redeemer, the " Captain of my salvation," the great " author and finisher of my faith," Heb. xii. 2, when I am in danger of denying thee as Peter did, look upon me with that mixture of majesty and tenderness, Luke xxii. 61, which may either secure me from falling, or may speedily recover me to God and my duty again.   And teach me to take occasion, even from my miscarriages, to humble myself more deeply for all that has been amiss, and to redouble my uture diligence and caution.   Amen

CHAPTER XVII.

THE CHRISTIAN URGED TO, AND ASSISTED IN, AN EXPRESS ACT OF SELF-DEDICATION TO THE SERVICE OF GOD.

The advantages of such a surrender are briefly suggested, 1. Advices for the manner of doing it; that it be deliberate, cheerful, entire, and perpetual, 2—4; and that it be expressed with some affecting solemnity, 5. A written instrument to be signed and declared before God at some season of extraordinary devotion, proposed, 6, 7. The chapter concludes with a specimen of such an instrument, together with an abstract of it, to be used with proper and requisite alterations.

1. As I would hope, that notwithstanding all the forms of opposition which do or may arise, yet in consideration of those noble supports and motives which have been mentioned in the two preceding chapters, you are heartily determined for the service of God, I would now urge you to make a solemn surrender of yourself unto it. Do not only form such a purpose in your heart, but expressly declare it in the divine presence. Such solemnity in the manner of doing it is certainly very reasonable in the nature of things; and surely it is highly expedient, for binding to the Lord such a treacherous heart, as we know our own to be. It will be pleasant to reflect upon it, as done at such and such a time, with such and such circumstances of place and method, which may serve to strike the memory and the conscience. The sense of the vows of God which are upon you will strengthen you in an hour of temptation; and the recollection may also encourage your humble boldness and freedom in applying to him, under the character and relation of " your covenant God and Father," as future exigences may require.

2. Do it, therefore, but do it deliberately. Consider what it is you are to do: and consider how reasonable it is that it should be done, and done cordially and cheerfully; " and not by constraint, but willingly," 1 Pet. v. 2; for, in this sense, and in every

other, " God loves a cheerful giver," 2 Cor. ix. 7
Now, surely there is nothing we should do with
greater cheerfulness, or more cordial consent, thar.
making such a surrender of ourselves to the Lord;
to the God who created us, who brought us into this
pleasant and well furnished world, who supported
us in our tender infancy, who guarded us in the
thoughtless days of childhood and youth, who has
hitherto continually helped, sustained, and preserved
us.   Nothing can be more reasonable than that we
should acknowledge him as our rightful Owner and
our sovereign Ruler; than that we should devote
ourselves to him as our most gracious Benefactor,
and seek him as our supreme felicity.   Nothing can
be more apparently equitable than that we, the pro-
duct of his power, and the price of his Son's blood,
should be his, and his for ever.   If you see the
matter in its just view, it will be the grief of your
soul that you have ever alienated yourself from the
blessed God and his service; so far will you be from
wishing to continue in that state of alienation another
year, or another day.   You will rejoice to bring back
to him his revolted creature; and as you have in
times past " yielded your members, as instruments
of unrighteousness unto sin," you will delight to
yield yourself " unto God, as alive from the dead,
and to employ your members as instruments of righteousness unto God," Rom. vi. 13.

3. The surrender will also be as entire as it is
cheerful and immediate.   All you are, and all you
have, and all you can do, your time, your possessions, your influence over others, will be devoted to
him, that for the future it may be employed entirely
for him, and to his glory.   You will desire to keep
back nothing from him; but will seriously judge that
you are then in the truest and noblest sense your
own, when you are most entirely his.   You are also,
on this great occasion, to resign all that you have to
the disposal of his wise and gracious Providence, not
only owning his power, but consenting to his undoubted right, to do what he pleases with you, and

all that he has given you; and declaring a hearty approbation of all that he has done, and of all that he may further do.

4. Once more, let me remind you that this surrender must be perpetual. You must give yourself up to God in such a manner, as never more to pretend to be your own: for the rights of God are, like his nature, eternal and immutable: and with regard to his rational creatures, are " the same yesterday, to-day, and for ever."

5. I would further advise and urge, that this dedication may be made with all possible solemnity. Do it in express words. And perhaps it may be in many cases most expedient, as many pious divines have recommended, to do it in writing. Set your hand and seal to it, That on such a day of such a month and year, and at such a place, on full consideration and serious reflection, you came to this happy resolution, " that whatever others might do, you would serve the Lord," Josh. xxiv. 13.

6. Such an instrument you may, if you please, draw up for yourself; or if you rather choose to have it drawn up to your hand, you may find something of this nature below, in which you may easily make such alterations as shall suit your circumstances, where there is any thing peculiar in them. But whatever you use, weigh it well, meditate attentively upon it, that you may " not be rash with your mouth to utter any thing before God," Eccl. v. 2. And when you determine to execute this instrument, let the transaction be attended with some more than ordinary religious retirement. Make it, if you conveniently can, a day of secret fasting and prayer; and when your heart is prepared with a becoming awe of the divine majesty, with an humble confidence in his goodness, and an earnest desire of his favour, then present yourself on your knees before God, and read it over deliberately and solemnly; and when you have signed it, lay it by in some secure place, where you may review it whenever you please; and make it a rule with yourself to review

it, if possible, at certain seasons of the year, that you
may keep the remembrance of it.

7. At least, take this course till you see your way
clear to the table of the Lord, where you are to
renew the same covenant, and to seal it with more
affecting solemnities. And God grant that you may
be enabled to keep it, and, in the whole of your conversation, to walk according to it. May it be an
anchor to your soul in every temptation, and a cor
dial to it in every affliction. May the recollection
of it embolden your addresses to the throne of grace
now, and give additional strength to your departing
spirit, in a consciousness that it is ascending to your
covenant God and Father, and to that gracious Redeemer, whose power and faithfulness will securely
" keep what you commit to him against that day."
2 Tim. i. 12.

AN EXAMPLE OF SELF-DEDICATION; OR, A SOLEMN FORM OF RENEWING OUR COVENANT WITH GOD.

" Eternal and unchangeable JEHOVAH, thou great
Creator of heaven, and earth, and adorable Lord of
angels and men! I desire with the deepest humiliation and abasement of soul, to fall down at this time
in thine awful presence; and earnestly pray, that
thou wilt penetrate my very heart with a suitable
sense of thine unutterable and inconceivable glories?

" Trembling may justly take hold upon me," Job
xxi. 6, when I, a sinful worm, presume to lift up my
head to thee, presume to appear in thy majestic presence on such an occasion as this. " Who am I, O
Lord God, or what is my house?" 2 Sam. vii. 18.
what is my nature or descent, my character and desert, that I should speak of this, and desire that I may
be one party in a COVENANT, where thou, " the King
of kings, and Lord of lords," art the other? 1 blush
and am confounded, even to mention it before thee
But, O Lord, great as is thy Majesty, so also is thy
mercy. If thou wilt hold converse with any of thy
creatures, thy superlatively exalted nature must stoop,
must stoop infinitely low. And I know. that in and

through Jesus, the Son of thy love, thou condescend-
est to visit sinful mortals, and to allow their approach
to thee, and their covenant intercourse with thee;
nay, I know that the scheme and plan is thine own;
and that thou hast graciously sent to propose it to us;
as none untaught by thee would have been able to
form it, or inclined to embrace it even when actually
proposed.

" To thee, therefore, do I now come, invited by the
name of thy Son, and trusting in his righteousness
and grace. Laying myself at thy feet " with shame
and confusion of face, and smiting upon my breast,"
I say, with the humble publican, " God be merciful
to me a sinner," Luke xviii. 13. I acknowledge, O
Lord, that I have been a great transgressor. " My
sins have reached unto heaven, Rev. xviii. 5, and
mine iniquities are lifted up unto the skies," Jer. li.
9. The irregular propensities of my corrupted and
degenerate nature have, in ten thousand aggravated
instances, " wrought to bring forth fruit unto death,"
Rom. vii. 5. And if thou shouldst be strict to mark
mine offences, I must be silent under a load of guilt,
and immediately sink into destruction. But thou hast
graciously called me to return unto thee, though I
have been a wandering sheep, a prodigal son, a
" backsliding child," Jer. iii. 22. Behold, therefore, O
Lord, I come unto thee. I come, convinced not only
of my sin, but of my folly. I come from my very
heart ashamed of myself, and with an acknowledgment in the sincerity and humility of my soul, that
" I have played the fool, and have erred exceedingly," 1 Sam. xxvi. 21. I am confounded myself at
the remembrance of these things: but be thou " merciful to my unrighteousness, and do not remember
against me my sins and my transgressions," Heb.
viii. 12. Permit me, O Lord, to bring back unto thee
those powers and faculties which I have ungratefully
and sacrilegiously alienated from thy service; and receive, I beseech thee, thy poor revolted creature, who
is now convinced of thy right to him, and desires
nothing in the whole world so much as to be thine.

" Blessed God, it is with the utmost solemnity that I make this surrender of myself unto thee. " Hear, O heavens, and give ear, O earth; I avouch the Lord this day to be my God," Deut. xxvi. 17, and I avouch and declare myself this day to be one of his cove- nant-children and people.   Hear, O thou God of heaven, and record it in "the book of thy remem- brance," Mal. iii. 16, that henceforth I am thine, en- tirely thine.   I would not merely consecrate unto thee some of my powers, or some of my possessions; or give thee a certain proportion of my services, or all I am capable of for a limited time; but I would be wholly thine, and thine for ever. From this day do I solemnly renounce all the former lords, which have had dominion over me, Isa. xxvi. 13; every sin, and every lust; and bid, in thy name, an eternal defiance to the powers of hell, which have most un- justly usurped the empire over my soul, and to all the corruptions which their fatal temptations have in- troduced into it.   The whole frame of my nature, all the faculties of my mind, and all the members of my body, would I present before thee this day, " as a living sacrifice, holy and acceptable unto God, which I know to be my most reasonable service," Rom. xii. 1.   To thee I consecrate all my worldly possessions; in thy service I desire to spend all the remainder of my time upon earth, and beg thou wouldst instruct and influence me, so that, whether my abode here be longer or shorter, every year and month, every day and hour, may be used in such a manner, as shall most effectually promote thine honour and subserve the schemes of thy wise and gracious providence And I earnestly pray, that whatever influence thou givest me over others, in any of the superior relations of life in which I may stand, or in consequence of any peculiar regard which may be paid to me, thou wouldst give me strength and courage to exert my- self to the utmost for thy glory; resolving, not only that I will myself do it, but that all others, so far as I can rationally and properly influence them, " shall serve the Lord," Josh. xxiv. 15.   In this course, O

blessed God, would I steadily persevere to the very
end of my life; earnestly praying that every future
day of it may supply the deficiencies, and correct the
irregularities of the former; and that I may, by divine
grace, be enabled, not only to hold on in that happy
way, but daily to grow more active in it!

"Nor do I only consecrate all that I am, and have,
to thy service; but I also most humbly resign and
submit to thine holy and sovereign will, myself, and
all that I can call mine. I leave, O Lord, to thy management and direction, all I possess, and all I wish;
and set every enjoyment and every interest before
thee, to be disposed of as thou pleasest. Continue,
or remove, what thou hast given me; bestow or refuse what I imagine I want, as thou, Lord, shalt see
good! And though I dare not say I will never repine, yet I hope I may venture to say that I will
labour, not only to submit, but to acquiesce; not only
to bear what thou doest in thy most afflictive dispensations, but to consent to it, and to praise thee for it;
contentedly resolving, in all that thou appointest for
me, my will into thine, and looking on myself as nothing, and on thee, O God, as the great eternal ALL,
whose word ought to determine every thing, and
whose government ought to be the joy of the whole
rational creation.

"Use me, O Lord, I beseech thee, as the instrument of thy glory, and honour me so far as, either
by doing or suffering what thou shalt appoint, to
bring some revenue of praise to thee, and of benefit
to the world in which I dwell. And may it please
thee, from this day forward, to number me among
"thy peculiar people, that I may no more be a stranger and foreigner, but a fellow citizen with the saints,
and of the household of God!" Eph. ii. 19. Receive,
O heavenly Father, thy returning prodigal. Wash
me in the blood of thy dear Son; clothe me with his
perfect righteousness; and sanctify me throughout by
the power of thy Spirit. Destroy, I beseech thee,
more and more the power of sin in my heart; trans-

form me more into thine own image, and fashion me
to the resemblance of Jesus, whom henceforward I
would acknowledge as my teacher and sacrifice; my
intercessor and my Lord.   Communicate to me, I
beseech thee, all needful influences of thy purifying,
thy cheering, and thy comforting Spirit; and " lift up
that light of thy countenance upon me," which will
put the sublimest "joy and gladness into my soul!"
Psal. iv. 6, 7.

Dispose my affairs, O God, in a manner which may
be most subservient to thy glory, and my own truest
happiness; and when I have done and borne thy will
upon earth, call me from hence at what time, and in
what manner thou pleasest: only grant, that in my
dying moments, and in the near prospect of eternity, I
may remember these my engagements to thee, and
may employ my latest breath in thy service.   And do
thou, Lord, when thou seest the agonies of dissolving
nature upon me, remember this covenant too, even
though I should then be incapable of recollecting it.
Look down, O my heavenly Father, with a pitying
eye upon thy languishing, thy dying child; place
thine everlasting arms underneath me for my support; put strength and confidence into my departing
spirit; and receive it to the embraces of thine everlasting love.   Welcome it to the abodes "of them
that sleep in Jesus," 1 Thes. iv. 14, to wait with
them that glorious day, when the last of thy promises
to thy covenant-people shall be fulfilled in their
triumphant resurrection, and in that " abundant entrance," which shall be " administered to them into
that everlasting kingdom," 2 Pet. i. 11, of which thou
hast assured them by thy covenant, and in the hope
of which I now lay hold of it, desiring to live and
die as with my hand on that hope.

And when I am thus numbered among the dead,
and all the interests of mortality are over with me
for ever, if this solemn memorial should chance to
fall into the hands of any surviving friends, may it
be the means of making serious impressions on their
minds.   May they read it, not only as my language,

but as their own; and learn to "fear the Lord my God," and with me "to put their trust under the shadow of his wings" for time and for eternity! And may they also learn to adore with me that grace which inclines our hearts to enter into the covenant, and condescends to admit us into it when so inclined; ascribing with me, and with all the nations of the redeemed, to the Father, the Son, and the Holy Ghost, that glory, honour, and praise which is so justly due to each divine person for the part he bears in this illustrious work. Amen.

N. B. For the sake of those who may think the preceding form of self-dedication too long to be transcribed, (as it is probable many will,) I have, at the desire of a much esteemed friend, added the following abridgment of it, which should by all means be attentively weighed in every clause before it be executed; and any word or phrase which may seem liable to exception, changed, that the whole heart may consent to it.

Eternal and ever-blessed God! I desire to present myself before thee with the deepest humiliation and abasement of soul; sensible how unworthy such a sinful worm is to appear before the holy majesty of heaven, "the King of kings, and Lord of lords," and especially on such an occasion as this, even to enter into a covenant transaction with thee. But the scheme and plan is thine own. Thine infinite condescension has offered it by thy Son, and thy grace has inclined my heart to accept of it.

I come, therefore, acknowledging myself to have been a great offender; smiting on my breast, and saying, with the humble publican, "God be merciful to me a sinner!" I come invited by the name of thy Son, and wholly trusting in his perfect righteousness; entreating that, for his sake, thou wilt be merciful to my unrighteousness, and wilt no more remember my sins. Receive, I beseech thee, thy revolted creature who is now convinced of thy right to him, and desires nothing so much as that he may be thine.

This day do I, with the utmost solemnity, surrender myself to thee. I renounce all former lords that have had dominion over me; and I consecrate to

thee all that I am, and all that I have; the fa ulties
of my mind, the members of my body, my worldly
possessions, my time, and my influence over others;
to be all used entirely for thy glory, and resolutely
employed in obedience to thy commands, as long as
thou continuest me in life; with an ardent desire and
humble resolution to continue thine through all the
endless ages of eternity; ever holding myself in an
attentive posture to observe the first intimations of
thy will, and ready to spring forward, with zeal and
joy, to the immediate execution of it.

To thy direction also I resign myself, and all I am
and have, to be disposed of by thee in such a manner as thou shalt in thine infinite wisdom judge most
subservient to the purposes of thy glory.   To thee I
leave the management of all events, and say without
reserve, " Not my will, but thine be done;" rejoicing with a loyal heart in thine unlimited government,
as what ought to be the delight of the whole rational
creation.

Use me, O Lord, I beseech thee, as an instrument
of thy service.   Number me among thy peculiar
people.   Let me be washed in the blood of thy dear
Son; let me be clothed with his righteousness; let me
be sanctified by his Spirit.   Transform me more and
more into his image.   Impart to me, through him,
all needful influences of thy purifying, cheering, and
comforting Spirit.   And let my life be spent under
those influences, and in the light of thy gracious
countenance, as my Father and my God.   And
when the solemn hour of death comes, may I remember this thy covenant, well ordered in all things
and sure, as all my salvation and all my desire, 2
Sam. xxiii. 5, though every other hope and enjoyment is perishing.   And do thou, O Lord, remember it too.   Look down with pity, O my heavenly
Father, on thy languishing, dying child.   Embrace
me in thine everlasting arms.   Put strength and
confidence into my departing spirit, and receive it to
the abodes of them that sleep in Jesus, peacefully
and joyfully to wait the accomplishment of thy great

promise to all thy people, even that of ɩ glorious re
surrection, and of eternal happiness in thine heavenly
presence.   And if any surviving friend should, when
I am in the dust, meet with this memorial of my
solemn transactions with thee, may he make the engagement his own; and do thou graciously admit
him to partake in all the blessings of thy covenant,
through Jesus the great Mediator of it: to whom
with thee, O Father, and the Holy Spirit, be everlasting praises ascribed, by all the millions who are
thus saved by thee, and by all those other celestial
spirits, in whose work and blessedness thou shalt call
them to share. Amen.

CHAPTER XVIII.

OF ENTERING INTO CHURCH COMMUNION, BY AN ATTEND‧ANCE UPON THE LORD'S SUPPER.

The reader, being already supposed to have entered into covenant
with God, 1, is urged publicly to seal that engagement at the
table of the Lord, 2.   (1.) From a view of the ends for which that
ordinance was instituted, 3; whence its usefulness is strongly inferred, 4; and, (2.) from the authority of Christ's appointment,
which is solemnly pressed on the conscience, 5.   Objections from
apprehensions of unfitness, 6.   Weakness of grace, &c., briefly
answered, 7.   At least, serious thoughts on this subject are absolutely insisted upon, 8.   The chapter is closed with a prayer for
one who desires to attend, yet finds himself pressed with remaining doubts.

1. I HOPE this chapter will find you, by a most express consent, become one of God's covenant-people,
solemnly and cordially devoted to his service: and it
is my hearty prayer, that the covenant you have
made on earth may be ratified in heaven.   But for
your further instruction and edification, give me
leave to remind you, that our Lord Jesus Christ has
appointed a peculiar manner of expressing our regard
to him, and of solemnly renewing his covenant with
him, which, though it does not forbid any other pro

per way of doing it, must by no means be set aside
or neglected for any human methods, how prudent
and expedient soever they may appear to us.

2. Our Lord has wisely ordained, that the advantages of society should be brought into religion; and
as, by his command, professing Christians assemble
together for other acts of public worship, so he has
been pleased to institute a social ordinance, in which
a whole assembly of them is to come to his table,
and there to eat the same bread, and drink the same
cup. And this they are to do as a token of their
affectionate remembrance of his dying love, of their
solemn surrender of themselves to God, and of their
sincere love to one another, and to all their fellow
Christians.

3. That these are indeed the great ends of the
Lord's Supper, I shall not now stay to argue at large.
—You need only read what the apostle St. Paul has
written in the tenth and eleventh chapters of his first
Epistle to the Corinthians, to convince you fully of
this. He there expressly tells us, that our Lord commanded the bread to be eaten, and the wine to be
drunk in remembrance of him, 1 Cor. xi. 24, 25, or
as a commemoration or memorial of him: so that, as
often as we attend this institution, we show forth our
Lord's death, which we are to do even until he come
again, ver. 26. And it is particularly asserted, That
the cup is the new Testament in his blood, ver. 25;
that is, it is a seal of that covenant which was ratified by his blood. Now, it is evident that in consequence of this, we are to approach it with a view to
that covenant, desiring its blessings, and resolving by
divine grace to comply with its demands. On the
whole, therefore, as the apostle speaks, we have communion in the body and the blood of Christ, 1 Cor. x.
16; and partaking of his table, and of his cup, we
converse with Christ, and join ourselves to him as his
people: as the heathens had, in their idolatrous rites,
communion with their deities, and joined themselves
to them; and the Jews by eating their sacrifices, conversed with Jehovah, and joined themselves to him.

He fui ther reminds them, that though many, they were "one bread and one body, being all partakers of that one bread," 1 Cor. x. 17, and being "all made to drink into one spirit," 1 Cor. xii. 13; that is, meeting together as if they were but one family, and joining in the commemoration of that one blood which was their common ransom, and of the Lord Jesus their common head. Now, it is evident all these reasonings are equally applicable to Christians in succeeding ages. Permit me, therefore, by the authority of our divine Master, to press upon you the observation of this precept.

4. And let me also urge it, from the apparent tendency which it has to promote your truest advantage. You are setting out in the Christian life; and I have reminded you at large of the opposition you' must expect to meet with in it. It is the love of Christ which must animate you to break through all. What then can be more desirable than to bear about with you a lively sense of it? and what can awaken that sense more than the contemplation of his death as there represented? Who can behold the bread broken, and the wine poured out, and not reflect how the body of the blessed Jesus was even torn in pieces by his sufferings, and his sacred blood poured forth like water on the ground? Who can think of the heart-rending agonies of the Son of God, as the price of our redemption and salvation, and not feel his soul melted with tenderness, and inflamed with grateful affection? What an exalted view doth it give us of the blessings of the gospel-covenant, when we consider it as "established in the blood of God's only begotten Son?" And when we make our approach to God, as our heavenly Father, and give up ourselves to his service in this solemn manner, what an awful tendency has it to fix the conviction, that "we are not our own, being bought with such a price?" 1 Cor. vi. 19, 20. What a tendency has it to gnard us against every temptation to those sins which we have so solemnly renounced, and to engage **our** fidelity to him to whom we have "bound our

souls as with an oath?" Well may " our hearts be knit together in mutual love," Col. ii. 2, when " we consider ourselves as one in Christ," Gal. iii. 28: his blood becomes the cement of the society, joins us in spirit, not only to each other, but " to all that in every place call upon the name of Jesus Christ our Lord, both theirs and ours," 1 Cor. i. 2, and we anticipate in pleasing hope, that blessed day, when the assembly shall be complete, and we shall all " be for ever with the Lord," 1 Thess. iv. 17. Well may these views engage us to deny ourselves, and to " take up our cross and follow our crucified Master," Matt. xvi. 24: well may they engage us to do our utmost by prayer, and all other suitable endeavours, to serve his followers and his friends; to serve those whom he has purchased with his blood, and who are to be his associates and ours in the glories of a happy immortality.

5. It is also the express institution and command of our blessed Redeemer, that the members of such societies should be tenderly solicitous for the spiritual welfare of each other; and that, on the whole, his churches may be kept pure and holy, that they should " withdraw themselves from every brother that walketh disorderly;" 2 Thess. iii. 6; that they should " mark such as cause offences or scandals among them, contrary to the doctrine which they have learned, and avoid them," Rom. xvi. 17; that if any obey not the word of Christ by his apostles, they should have no fellowship or communion with such, that they may be ashamed, 2 Thess. iii. 14; that they should not eat with such as are notoriously irregular in their behaviour, but, on the contrary, should put away from among themselves such wicked persons, 1 Cor. v. 11, 13. It is evident, therefore, that the institution of such societies is greatly for the honour of Christianity, and for the advantage of its particular professors, and consequently, every consideration of obedience to our common Lord, and of prudent regard to our own benefit, and that of our brethren, will require, that those who love the Lord Jesus Christ in sincerity should enter into them, and assem

ole among them in these their most solemn and peculiar acts of communion at his table.

6. I entreat you, therefore, and, if I may presume
to say it, in his name, and by his authority, I charge
it on your conscience, that this precept of our dying
Lord go not, as it were, for nothing with you; but
that, if you indeed love him, you keep this as well as
the rest of his commandments.—I know you may be
ready to form objections. I have elsewhere debated
many of the chief of them at large, and I hope, not
without some good effect.* The great question is that
which relates to your being prepared for a worthy
attendance: and, in conjunction with what hath been
said before, I think that may be brought to a very
short issue. Have you, so far as you know your own
heart, been sincere in that deliberate surrender of
yourself to God through Christ, which I recommended in the former chapter? If you have, (whether it
were with or without the particular form or manner
of doing it there recommended,) you have certainly
taken hold of the covenant, and therefore have a right
to the seal of it. And there is not, and cannot be, any
other view of the ordinance in which you can have
any further objection to it. If you desire to remember
Christ's death, if you desire to renew the dedication
of yourself to God through him, if you would list
yourself among his people, if you would love them,
and do them good according to your ability; and, on
the whole, would not allow yourself in the practice
of any one known sin, or in the omission of any one
known duty, then I will venture confidently to say,
not only that you will be welcome to the ordinance,
but that it was instituted for such as you.

7. As for other objections, a few words may suffice,
by way of reply. The weakness of the religious
principle in your soul, if it be really implanted there,
is so far from being an argument against your seeking such a method to strengthen it, that it rather
strongly enforces the necessity of doing it.—The ne-

* See the fourth of my sermons to young persons; viz. "The Young
Christian invited to an early Attendance on the Lord's Table."

glect of this solemnity, by so many that call themselves Christians, should rather engage you so much
the more to distinguish your zeal for an institution
in this respect so much slighted and injured. And as
for the fears of aggravated guilt in case of apostasy,
do not indulge them. This may, by the divine blessing, be an effectual remedy against the evil you fear;
and, it is certain, that after what you must already
have known and felt before you could be brought
into your present situation, (on the supposition I
have now been making,) there can be no room to
think of a retreat; no room, even for the wretched
hope of being less miserable than the generality of
those that have˙ perished. Your scheme, therefore,
must be to make your salvation as sure, and to make
it as glorious as possible: and I know not any appointment of our blessed Redeemer which may have
a more comfortable aspect upon that blessed end,
than this which I am now recommending to you.

8. One thing I would at least insist upon, and I see
not with what face it can be denied, I mean, that you
should take this matter into serious consideration;
that you shall diligently inquire, whether you have
reason in your conscience to believe it is the will of
God, you should now approach to the ordinance, or
not; and that you should continue your reflections,
your inquiries, and your prayers, till you find further
encouragement to come, if that encouragement be
hitherto wanting. For of this be assured, that a state
in which you are on the whole unfit to approach this
ordinance is a state in which you are destitute of the
necessary preparations for death and heaven: in
which, therefore, if you would not allow yourself
to slumber on the brink of destruction, you ought not
to rest so much as-one single day.

⁂ PRAYER FOR ONE WHO EARNESTLY DESIRES TO APPROACH TO THE TABLE
OF THE LORD, YET HAS SOME REMAINING DOUBTS CONCERNING HIS RIGHT
TO THAT SOLEMN ORDINANCE.

Blessed Lord, I adore thy wise and gracious appointments for the edification of thy church in holi-

ness and in love. I thank thee that thou hast commanded thy servants to form themselves into societies; and I adore my gracious Saviour who has instituted, as with his dying breath, the holy solemnity of his supper, to be through all ages a memorial of his dying love, and a bond of that union which it is his sovereign pleasure that his people should preserve. I hope thou, Lord, art witness to the sincerity with which I desire to give myself up to thee; and that I may call thee to record on my soul, that if I now hesitate about this particular manner of doing it, it is not because I would allow myself to break any of thy commands, or to slight any of thy favours. I trust, thou knowest that my present delay arises only from an uncertainty as to my own duty, and a fear of profaning holy things by an unworthy approach to them. Yet surely, O Lord, if thou hast given me a reverence for thy command, a desire of communion with thee, and a willingness to devote myself wholly to thy service, I may regard it as a token for good that thou art disposed to receive me, and that I am not wholly unqualified for an ordinance which I so highly honour, and so earnestly desire; I therefore make it mine humble request unto thee, O Lord, this day, that thou wouldst graciously be pleased to instruct me in my duty, and to teach me the way which I should take! Examine me, O Lord, and prove me, try my reins and my heart, Psal. xxvi. 2. Is there any secret sin, in the love and practice of which I would indulge? Is there any of thy precepts, in the habitual breach of which I would allow myself? I trust I can appeal to thee as a witness that there is not. Let me not, then, wrong mine own soul by a causeless and sinful absence from thy sacred table. But grant, O Lord, I beseech thee, that thy word, thy providence and thy Spirit, may so concur, as to make my " way plain before me," Prov. xv. 19. Scatter my remaining doubts, if thou seest they have no just foundation. Fill me with a more assured faith, with a more ardent love; and plead thine own cause with my heart in such a manner as that I may not be able any longer to delay that approach, which, if I am thy servant indeed, is equally my duty and my privilege. In the mean time, grant that it may never be long out of my thoughts; but that I may give all diligence, if there be any remaining occasion of doubt, to remove it by a more affectionate concern to avoid whatever is displeasing to the eyes of thine holiness, and to practise the full extent of my duty. May the views of Christ crucified be so familiar to my mind, and may a sense of his dying love so powerfully constrain my soul, that my own growing experience may put it out of all question, that I am one of those for whom he intended this feast of love.

And even now, as joined to thy churches in spirit and in love, though not in so express and intimate a bond as I could wish, would I heartily pray that thy " blessing may be on all thy people;" that thou " wouldst feed thine heritage, and lift them up for ever," Psal. xxviii. 9. May every Christian society flourish in knowledge, in holiness, and in love! May all " thy priests be clothed with salvation," that by their means " thy chosen people may be made joyful," Psal. cxxxii. 16. And may there be a glorious accession to thy churches every where, of those who may fly " to them as a cloud, and as doves to their windows," Isa. lx. 8. May thy table, O Lord, be " furnished with guests," Matt. xxii. 10, and may all that " love thy salvation say, Let the Lord be magnified, who hath pleasure in the prosperity of his servants," Psal. xxxv. 27. And I earnestly pray, that all who profess to have received Christ Jesus the Lord may be duly careful to walk in him, Col. ii. 6, and that we may be all preparing for the general assembly of the first-born, and may join in that nobler and more immediate worship, where all these types and shadows shall be laid aside; where even these memorials shall be no longer necessary, but a living, present Redeemer shall be the everlasting joy of those who here in his absence have delighted to commemorate his death. Amen.

CHAPTER XIX.

1. I WOULD hope that upon serious consideration, self-examination and prayer, the reader may by this time be come to a resolution to attend the table of the Lord, and to seal his vows there. I will now suppose that solemn transaction to be over, or some other deliberate act to have passed, by which he has given himself up to the service of God; and that his concern now is to inquire how he may act according to the vows of God which are upon him. Now, for his further assistance here, besides the general view I have already given of the Christian temper and character, I will propose some more particular directions relating to maintaining that devout, spiritual and heavenly character, which may in the language of Scripture, be called " a daily walking with God; or, being in his fear all the day long," Prov. xxiii. 17. And I know not how I can express the idea and plan which I have formed of this in a more clear and distinct manner than I did in a letter, which I wrote many years ago* to a young person of eminent piety,

* N. B. It was in the year 1727.

with whom I had then an intimate friendship; and
who, to the great grief of all that knew him, died a
few months after he received it. Yet I hope he lived
long enough to reduce the directions into practice,
which I wish and pray that every reader may do, so
far as they may properly suit his capacities and circumstances in life, considering it as if addressed to
himself. I say (and desire it may be observed) that
I wish my reader may act on these directions, so far
as they may properly suit his capacities and circumstances in life; for I would be far from laying down
the following particulars as universal rules for all, or
for any one person in the world at all times. Let
them be practised by those that are able, and when
they have leisure; and when you cannot reach them
all, come as near the most important of them as you
conveniently can. With this precaution, I proceed
to the letter, which I would hope, after this previous
care to guard against the danger of mistaking it, will
not discourage any the weakest Christian. Let us
humbly and cheerfully do our best, and rejoice that
we have so gracious a Father who knows all our
infirmities, and so compassionate a High-priest to recommend to divine acceptance the feeblest efforts of
sincere duty and love.

MY DEAR FRIEND,

Since you desire my thoughts in writing, and at
large, on the subject of our late conversation, viz.
"By what particular methods, in our daily conduct,
a life of devotion and usefulness may be most happily maintained and secured?" I set myself with
cheerfulness to recollect and digest the hints which I
then gave you, hoping it may be of some service to
you in your most important interests, and may also
fix on my own mind a deeper sense of my obligations
to govern my own life by the rules I offer to others.
I esteem attempts of this kind among the pleasantest
fruits, and the surest cements of friendship; and, as
I hope ours will last for ever, I am persuaded a mu

tual care to cherish sentiments of this kind will add everlasting endearments to it.

2. The directions you will expect from me on this occasion naturally divide themselves into three heads. —How we are to regard God—in the beginning— the progress—and the close of the day. I will open my heart freely to you with regard to each, and will leave you to judge how far these hints may suit your circumstances; aiming at least to keep between the extremes of a superstitious strictness in trifles, and of an indolent remissness, which, if admitted in little things, may draw after it criminal neglects, and at length yet more criminal indulgences.

3. In the beginning of the day, it should certainly be our care—to lift up our hearts to God as soon as we awake, and while we are rising—and then, to set ourselves seriously and immediately to the secret devotions of the morning.

4. For the first of these, it seems exceedingly natural. There are so many things that may suggest a great variety of pious reflections and ejaculations, which are so obvious, that one would think a serious mind could hardly miss them. The ease and cheerfulness of our mind at our first awakening; the refreshment we find from sleep; the security we have enjoyed in that defenceless state; the provision of warm and decent apparel; the cheerful light of the returning sun; or (what is not unfit to mention to you,) the contrivances of art, taught and furnished by the great Author of all our conveniences, to supply us with many useful hours of life in the absence of the sun; the hope of returning to the dear society of our friends: the prospect of spending another day in the service of God, and the improvement of our own minds; and, above all, the lively hope of a joyful resurrection to an eternal day of happiness and glory; any of these particulars, and many more, which I do not mention, may furnish us with matter of pleasing reflection, and cheerful praise, while we are rising. And, for our further assistance, when we **are** alone at this time, it may not be improper to

speak sometimes to ourselves, and sometimes to **our** heavenly Father, in the natural expressions of joy and thankfulness.   Permit me, sir, to add, that if **we** find our hearts in such a frame at our first awaking, even that is just matter of praise, and the rather, as perhaps it is an answer to the prayer with which **we** lay down.

5. For the exercise of secret devotion in a morning, which I hope will generally be our first work, I cannot prescribe an exact method to another.   You must, my dear friend, consu.t your own taste in some measure.   The constituent parts of the service are, in the general, plain.   Were I to propose a particular model for those, who have half, or three quarters of an hour at command, (which, with prudent conduct, I suppose most may have) it should be thus:

6. To begin the stated devotions of the day with a solemn act of praise, offered to God on our knees, and generally with a low, yet distinct voice; acknowledging the mercies we had been reflecting on while rising; never forgetting to mention Christ, as the great foundation of all our enjoyments and our hopes, or to return thanks for the influences of the blessed Spirit, which have led our hearts to God, or are then engaging us to seek him.   This, as well as other offices of devotion afterwards mentioned, must be done attentively and sincerely; for, not to offer our praises heartily, is in the sight of God, not to praise him at all.   This address of praise may properly be concluded with an express renewal of our covenant with God, declaring our continued repeated resolution of being devoted to him, and particularly of living **to** his glory the ensuing day.

7. It may be proper, after this, to take a prospect of the day before us, so far, as we can probably foresee, in the general, where and how it may be spent; and seriously to reflect, How shall I employ myself for God this day?   What business is to be done, and in what order?   What opportunities may I expect, either of doing or of receiving good?   What temptations am I like.y to be assaulted with, in any place,

company, or circumstances, which may probably oc cur? In what instances have I lately failed? and how shall I be safest now?

8. After this review, it will be proper to offer up a short prayer, begging, that God would quicken us to each of these foreseen duties; that he would fortify us against each of these apprehended dangers; that he would grant us success in such or such a business, undertaken for his glory; and also that he would help us to discover and improve unforeseen opportunities, to resist unexpected temptations, and to bear patiently and religiously any afflictions which may surprise us in the day on which we are entering.

9. I would advise you after this to read some portion of Scripture; not a great deal, nor the whole Bible in its course; but some select lessons out of its most useful parts, perhaps ten or twelve verses; not troubling yourself much about the exact connexion, or other critical niceties which may occur, (though at other times I would recommend them to your inquiry, as you have ability and opportunity;) but considering them merely in a devotional and practical view. Here take such instructions as readily present themselves to your thoughts, repeat them over to your own conscience, and charge your heart religiously to observe them, and act upon them under a sense of the divine authority which attends them. And if you pray over the substance of this Scripture, with your Bible open before you, it may impress your memory and your heart yet more deeply, and may form you to a copiousness and variety both of thought and expression in prayer.

10. It might be proper to close these devotions with a psalm or hymn; and I rejoice with you, that through the pious care of many sacred poets, we are provided with so rich a variety for the assistance of the closet and family on these occasions, as well as for the service of the sanctuary.

11. The most material directions which have occurred to me, relating to the progress of the day, are these:—That we be serious in the devotion of the

day:—that we be diligent in the business of it, that is, in the prosecution of our worldly callings:—that we be temperate and prudent in the recreations of it:— that we carefully mark the providences of the day:— that we cautiously guard against the temptations of it:—that we keep up a lively and humble dependence upon the divine influence suitable to every emergen- cy of it:—that we govern our thoughts well in the solitude of the day,—and our discourses well in the conversations of it.   These, sir, were the heads of a sermon which you lately heard me preach on this occasion, and to which I know you referred in that request which I am now endeavouring to answer. I will, therefore, touch upon the most material hints which fell under each of these particulars.

12. (1.) For seriousness in devotion, whether pub- lic or domestic: Let us take a few moments, before we enter upon such solemnities, to pause, and reflect, on the perfections of the God we are addressing, on the importance of the business we are coming about, on the pleasure and advantage of a regular and de- vout attendance, and on the guilt and folly of an hypocritical formality.   When engaged, let us main- tain a strict watchfulness over our own spirits, and check the first wanderings of thought.   And when the duty is over, let us immediately reflect on the manner in which it has been performed, and ask our consciences whether we have reason to conclude that we are accepted of God in it?   For there is a certain manner of going through these offices, which our own hearts will immediately tell us it is impossible for God to approve: and if we have inadvertently fal- len into it, we ought to be deeply humbled before God for it, lest "our very prayer become sin," Psa. cix. 7.

13. (2.) As for the hours of worldly business; whe- ther it be, as with you, that of the hands; or whether it be the labour of a learned life, not immediately re- lating to religious matters: Let us set to the prosecu- tion of it with a sense of God's authority, and with a regard to his glory. Let us avoid a dreaming, slug- gish, indolent temper, which nods over its work, and

does only the business of one hour in two or three, In opposition to this, which runs through the life of some people, who yet think they are never idle; let us endeavour to dispatch as much as we well can in a little time; considering that it is but a little we have in all. And let us be habitually sensible of the need we have of the divine blessing to make our labour successful.

14. (3.) For seasons of diversion: Let us take care tha' our recreations be well chosen; that they be pursued with a good intention, to fit us for a renewed application to the labours of life; and thus that they be only used in subordination to the honour of God, the great end of all our actions. Let us take heed that our hearts be not estranged from God by them; and that they do not take up too much of our time; always remembering that the faculties of human nature, and the advantages of the Christian revelation, were not given us in vain; but that we are always to be in pursuit of some great and honourable end, and to indulge ourselves in amusements and diversions no further than as they make a part in a scheme of rational and manly, benevolent and pious conduct.

15. (4.) For the observation of providences: It will be useful to regard the divine interposition in our comforts and in our afflictions. In our comforts, whether more common or extraordinary: That we find ourselves in continued health; that we are furnished with food for our support and pleasure; that we have so many agreeable ways of employing our time; that we have so many agreeable friends, and those so good and so happy; that our business goes on so prosperously; that we go out and come in safely; and that we enjoy composure and cheerfulness of spirit, without which nothing else could be enjoyed. All these should be regarded as providential favours, and due acknowledgments should be made to God on these accounts, as we pass through such agreeable scenes. On the other hand, Providence is to be regarded in every disappointment, in every loss, in

every pain, in every instance of unkindness from those who have professed friendship: and we should endeavour to argue ourselves into a patient submission, from this consideration, that the hand of God is always mediately, if not immediately, in each of them; and that if they are not properly the work of Providence, they are at least under its direction. It is a reflection, which we should particularly make with relation to those little cross accidents, as we are ready to call them, and those infirmities and follies in the temper and conduct of our intimate friends, which may else be ready to discompose us. And it is the more necessary to guard our minds here, as wise and good men often lose the command of themselves on these comparatively little occasions, who calling up reason and religion to their assistance, stand the shock of great calamities with fortitude and resolution.

16. (5.) For watchfulness against temptations: It is necessary, when changing our place, or our employment, to reflect, " what snares attend me here?" And as this should be our habitual care, so we should especially guard against those snares which in the morning we foresaw. And when we are entering on those circumstances in which we expected the assault, we should reflect, especially if it be a matter of great importance, " Now the combat is going to begin: now God and the blessed angels are observing what constancy, what fortitude, there is in my soul; and how far the divine authority, and the remembrance of my own prayers and resolutions will weigh with me when it comes to the trial."

17. (6.) As for dependence on divine grace and influence: It must be universal; and since we always need it, we must never forget that necessity. A moment spent in humble fervent breathings after the communications of the divine assistance, may do more good than many minutes spent in mere reasonings; and though, indeed, this should not be neglected, since the light of reason is a kind of divine illumination, yet still it ought to be pursued in a due

sense of our dependence on the Father of lights, or where we "think ourselves wisest, we may become vain in our imaginations," Rom. i. 21, 22. Let us therefore always call upon God; and say for instance, when we are going to pray, " Lord, fix my attention, awaken my holy affections, and pour out upon me the spirit of grace and of supplication," Zech. xii. 10. When taking up the Bible, or any other good book, " Open thou mine eyes, that I may behold wondrous things out of thy law," Psal. cxix. 18. Enlighten mine understanding; warm my heart. May my good resolutions be confirmed, and all the course of my life in a proper manner regulated. When addressing ourselves to any worldly business, " Lord, prosper thou the work of mine hands upon me," Psal. xc. 17, and give thy blessing to my honest endeavours. When going to any kind of recreation. Lord, bless my refreshments; let me not forget thee in them, but still keep thy glory in view. When coming into company, Lord, may I do and get good! " Let no corrupt communication proceed out of my mouth, but that which is good to the use of edifying, that it may minister grace to the hearers," Eph. iv. 29. When entering upon difficulties, Lord, give me " that wisdom which is profitable to direct," Eccl. x. 10; teach me thy way, " and lead me in a plain path," Psal. xxvii. 11. When encountering with temptations, " Let thy strength, O gracious Redeemer, be made perfect in my weakness," 2 Cor. xii. 9. These instances may illustrate the design of this direction, though they be far from a complete enumeration of all the circumstances in which it is to be regarded.

18. (7.) For the government of our thoughts in solitude: Let us accustom ourselves, on all occasions, to exercise a due command over our thoughts. Let us take care of those entanglements of passion, and those attachments to any present interest in view, which would deprive us of our power over them. Let us set before us some profitable subject of thought; such as, the perfections of the blessed God,

17

the love of Christ, the value of time, the certainty
and importance of death and judgment, and of the
eternity of happiness or misery which is to follow.
Let us also at such intervals reflect on what we have
observed, as to the state of our own souls, with regard to the advance or decline of religion; or on the
last sermon we have heard, or the last portion of
Scripture we have read.   You may, perhaps, in this
connexion, sir, recollect what I have (if I remember
right) proposed to you in conversation; that it may
be very useful to select some one verse of Scripture,
which we had met with in the morning, and to treasure it up in our mind, resolving to think of that at
any time when we are at a loss for matter of pious
reflection in any intervals of leisure for entering upon
it. This will often be as a spring, from whence many
profitable and delightful thoughts may arise, which
perhaps we did not before see in that connexion and
force.   Or, if it should not be so, yet I am persuaded
it will be much better to repeat the same Scripture
in our mind an hundred times in a day, with some
pious ejaculations formed upon it, than to leave our
thoughts at the mercy of all those various trifles
which may otherwise intrude upon us, the variety
of which will be far from making amends for their
vanity.

19. (8.) Lastly, for the government of our discourse
in company: We should take care that nothing may
escape us which can expose us, or our Christian
profession, to censure and reproach: nothing injurious to those that are absent, or to those that are present; nothing malignant, nothing insincere, nothing
which may corrupt, nothing which may provoke,
nothing which may mislead those about us.   Nor
should we by any means be content that what we
say is innocent: it should be our desire that it may
be edifying to ourselves and others.   In this view
we should endeavour to have some subject of useful
discourse always ready, in which you may be assisted by the hints given about furniture for thought
under the former head. We should watch for decent

opportunities of introducing useful reflections, and if a pious friend attempt to do it, we should endeavour to second it immediately When the conversation does not turn directly on religious subjects, we snould endeavour to make it improving some other way; we should reflect on the character and capacities of our company, that we may lead them to talk of what they understand best; for their discourses on those subjects will probably be most pleasing to themselves, as well as most useful to us. And, in pauses of discourse, it may not be improper to lift up a holy ejaculation to God, that his grace may assist us and our friends in our endeavours to do good to each other; that all we say and do may be worthy the character of reasonable creatures, and of Christians.

20. The directions for a religious closing of the day, which I shall here mention, are only two.—Let us see to it, that the secret duties of the evening be well performed; and let us lie down on our beds in a pious frame.

21. (1.) For secret devotion in the evening I would propose a method something different from that in the morning; but still, as then, with due allowances for circumstances, which may make unthought of alterations proper. I should, sir, advise to read a portion of Scripture in the first place, with suitable reflections and prayer, as above; then to read a hymn or psalm: after this to enter on self-examination, to be followed by a longer prayer than that which followed reading, to be formed on this review of the day. In this address to the throne of grace it will be highly proper to entreat that God would pardon the omissions and offences of the day; to praise him for mercies temporal and spiritual; to recommend ourselves to his protection for the ensuing night: with proper petitions for others, whom we ought to bear on our hearts before him; and particularly for those friends with whom we have conversed or corresponded in the preceding day. Many other concerns will occur, both in morning and evening prayer, which

I have not here hinted at; but I did not apprehend that a full enumeration of these things belonged, by any means, to our present purpose.

22. Before I quit this head, I must take the liberty to remind you, that self-examination is so important a duty, that it will be worth our while to spend a few words upon it. And this branch of it is so easy, that when we have proper questions before us, any person of a common understanding may hope to go through it with advantage under a divine blessing. I offer you, therefore, the following queries, which I hope you will, with such alterations as you may judge requisite, keep near you for daily use. " Did I awake, as with God this morning, and rise with a grateful sense of his goodness? How were the secret devotions of the morning performed? Did I offer my solemn praises, and renew the dedication of myself to God, with becoming attention and suitable affections? Did I lay my scheme for the business of the day wisely and well? How did I read the Scripture, and any other devotional or practical piece, which I might afterwards conveniently review? Did it do my heart good, or was it a mere amusement? How have the other stated devotions of the day been attended, whether in the family or in public? Have I pursued the common business of the day with diligence and spirituality; doing every thing in season, and with all convenient dispatch, and " as unto the Lord?" Col. ii. 23. What time have I lost this day, in the morning or the forenoon, in the afternoon or the evening; (for these divisions will assist your recollection;) and what has occasioned the loss of it? With what temper, and under what regulations have the recreations of this day been pursued? Have I seen the hand of God in my mercies, health, cheerfulness, food, clothing, books, preservation in journeys, success of business, conversation and kindness of friends, &c.? Have I seen it in afflictions, and particularly in little things which had a tendency to vex and disquiet me? And with regard to this interposition, have I received my comforts thankfully, and my afflictions submis-

sively? How have I guarded against the temptations of the day, particularly against this or that temptation which I foresaw in the morning? Have I maintained an humble dependence on divine influences? Have I " lived by faith on the Son of God," Gal. ii. 20, and regarded Christ this day as my Teacher and Governor, my Atonement and Intercessor, my Example and Guardian, my Strength and Forerunner? Have I been looking forward to death and eternity this day, and considered myself as a probationer for heaven, and through grace an expectant of it? Have I governed my thoughts well, especially in such or such an interval of solitude? How was my subject of thought this day chosen, and how was it regarded? Have I governed my discourses well in such and such company? Did I say nothing passionate, mischievous, slanderous, imprudent, impertinent? Has my heart this day been full of love to God, and to all mankind? And have I sought, and found, and im proved opportunities of doing and of getting good? —With what attention and improvement have I read the Scripture this evening? How was self-examination performed the last night? and how have I profited this day by any remarks I then made on former negligences and mistakes? With what temper did I then lie down and compose myself to sleep?

23. You will easily see, sir, that these questions are so adjusted, as to be an abridgment of the most material advices I have given in this letter; and I believe I need not, to a person of your understanding, say any thing as to the usefulness of such inquiries. Conscience will answer them in a few minutes; but if you think them too large and particular, you may make a still shorter abstract for daily use, and reserve these, with such obvious alterations as will then be necessary, for seasons of more than ordinary exactness in review, which I hope will occur at least once a week. Secret devotion being then performed before drowsiness render us unfit for it, the interva' between that and our going to rest must be con

ducted by the rules mentioned under the next head And nothing will further remain to be considered here but,

24. (2.) The sentiments with which we should lie down and compose ourselves to sleep. Now, here it is obviously suitable to think of the divine goodness in adding another day, and the mercies of it, to the former days and mercies of our life: to take notice of the indulgence of Providence in giving us commodious habitations and easy beds, and continuing to us such health of body that we can lay ourselves down at ease upon them, and such serenity of mind as leaves us any room to hope for refreshing sleep: a refreshment to be sought not merely as an indulgence to animal nature, but as what our wise Creator, in order to keep us humble in the midst of so many infirmities, has been pleased to make necessary to our being able to pursue his service with renewed alacrity. Thus may our sleeping as well as our waking hours, be, in some sense, devoted to God. And when we are just going to resign ourselves to the image of death, (to what one of the ancients beautifully calls *its lesser mysteries;*) it is also evidently proper to think seriously of that end of all the living, and to renew those actings of repentance and faith which we should judge necessary, if we were to wake no more here. You have once, sir, seen a meditation of that kind in my hand: I will transcribe it for you in the postscript; and therefore shall add no more to this head, but here put a close to the directions you desired.

25. I am persuaded, the most important of them have, in one form or other, been long regarded by you and made governing maxims of your life. I shall greatly rejoice if the review of these, and the examination and trial of the rest, may be the means of leading you into more intimate communion with God, and so of rendering your life more pleasant and useful, and your eternity, whenever that is to commence, more glorious. There is not a human

creature upon earth whom I should not delight to serve in these important interests; but I can faithfully assure you, that I am with particular respect,

Dear Sir,

Your very affectionate friend and servant.

26. This, reader, with the alteration of a very few words, is the letter I wrote to a worthy friend, (now, I doubt not, with God,) about sixteen years ago: and I can assuredly say, that the experience of each of these years has confirmed me in these views, and established me in the persuasion, that one day thus spent is preferable to whole years of sensuality and the neglect of religion I chose to insert the letter as it is, because I thought the freedom and particularity of the advice I had given in it would appear most natural in its original form: and as I propose to enforce these advices in the next chapter, I shall conclude this with that meditation which I promised my friend as a postscript; and which I could wish you to make so familiar to yourself, as that you might be able to recollect the substance of it, whenever you compose yourself to sleep.

A SERIOUS VIEW OF DEATH, PROPER TO BE TAKEN AS WE LIE DOWN ON OUR BEDS.

O my soul, look forward a little with seriousness and attention, and " learn wisdom by the consideration of thy latter end," Deut. xxxii. 29. Another of thy mortal days is now numbered and finished: and as I have put off my clothes, and laid myself upon my bed for the repose of the night, so will the day of life quickly come to its period, so must the body itself be put off, and laid to its repose in a bed of dust. There let it rest; for it will be no more regarded by me than the clothes which I have now laid aside. I have another far more important concern to attend. Think, O my soul, when death comes, thou art to enter upon the eternal world, and to be fixed either in heaven or in hell. All the schemes

and cares, the hopes and fears, the pleasures and sorrows of life, will come to their period, and the world
of spirits will open upon thee. And, oh, how soon
may it open! perhaps before the returning sun brings
on the light of another day. To-morrow's sun may
not enlighten mine eyes, but only shine round a
senseless corpse, which may lie in the place of this
animated body: at least, the death of many in the
flower of their age, and many who were superior
to me in capacity, piety, and the prospects of usefulness, loudly warn me not to depend on a long life,
and engage me rather to wonder that I am continued
here so many years, than to be surprised if I am
speedily removed.

And now, O my soul, answer, as in the sight of
God, Art thou ready? art thou ready? Is there no
sin unforsaken, and so unrepented of, to fill me with
anguish in my departing moments, and to make me
tremble on the brink of eternity? Dread to remain
under the guilt of it, and this moment renew thy
most earnest applications to the mercy of God, and
the blood of a Redeemer, for deliverance from it.

But if the great account be already adjusted, if thou
hast cordially repented of thy numerous offences, if
thou hast sincerely committed thyself by faith into
the hands of the blessed Jesus, and hast not renounced thy covenant with him by returning to the allowed practice of sin, then start not at the thoughts of a
separation; it is not in the power of death to hurt a
soul devoted to God, and united to the great Re
deemer. It may take me from my worldly comforts,
it may disconcert and break my schemes for service
on earth; but, O my soul, diviner entertainments and
nobler services wait thee beyond the grave. For
ever blessed be the name of God, and the love of
Jesus, for these quieting, encouraging, joyful views'
I will now " lay me down in peace, and sleep," Psa..
iv. 8, free from the fears of what shall be the issue
of this night; whether life or death may be appointed
for me. " Father, into thine hands I commend my
spirit," Luke xxiii. 46; for " thou hast redeemed me,

O God of trut i," Psal. xxxi. 5; and therefore I can cheerfully refer it to thy choice whether I shall wake in this world or another.

CHAPTER XX.

A SERIOUS PERSUASIVE TO SUCH A METHOD OF SPENDING OUR DAYS, AS IS REPRESENTED IN THE FORMER CHAPTER.

Christians fix their views too low, and indulge too indolent a disposition, which makes it the more necessary to urge such a life as that under consideration, 1, 2. It is therefore enforced, (1.) From its being apparently reasonable, considering ourselves as the creatures of God, and as redeemed by the blood of Christ, 3. (2.) From its evident tendency to conduce to our comfort in life, 4. (3.) From the influence it will have to promote our usefulness to others, 5. (4.) From its efficacy to make afflictions lighter, 6. (5.) From its happy aspect on death, 7; and (6) On eternity, 8. Whereas not to desire improvement would argue a soul destitute of religion, 9. A prayer suited to the state of a soul who longs to attain the life recommended above.

1 I HAVE been assigning in the preceding chapter, what I fear will seem to some of my readers so hard a task, that they will want courage to attempt it; and it is indeed a life, in many respects, so far above that of the generality of Christians, that I am not without apprehensions that many who deserve the name, may think the directions, after all the precautions with which I have proposed them, are carried o an unnecessary degree of nicety and strictness. But I am persuaded much of the credit and comfort of Christianity is lost in consequence of its professors fixing their aims too low, and not conceiving of their high and holy calling in so elevated and sublime a view as the nature of religion would require, and the word of God would direct. I am fully convinced, that the expressions of " walking with God; of being in the fear of the Lord all the day long," Prov. xxiii. 17; and, above all, that of " loving the Lord our God

with all our heart and soul, and mind and strength,"
Mark xii. 30, must require, if not all these circumstances, yet the substance of all that I have been
recommending, so far as we have capacity, leisure
and opportunity; and I cannot but think, that many
might command more of the latter, and perhaps improve their capacities too, if they would take a due
care in the government of themselves, if they would
give up vain and unnecessary diversions, and certain
indulgences, which only suit and delight the lower
part of our nature, and (to say the best of them) deprive us of pleasures much better than themselves,
if they do not plunge us into guilt.   Many of these
rules would appear easily practicable, if men would
learn to know the value of time, and particularly to
redeem it from unnecessary sleep, which wastes so
many golden hours of the day: hours in which many
of God's servants are delighting themselves in him,
and drinking in full draughts of the water of life,
while these their brethren are slumbering upon their
beds, and lost in vain dreams, as far below the common entertainments of a rational creature, as the pleasures of the sublimest devotion are above them.

2. I know, likewise, that the mind is very fickle
and inconstant, and that it is a hard thing to preserve
such a government and authority over our thoughts
as would be very desirable, and as the plan I have
laid down will require.   But so much of the honour
of God, and so much of your own true happiness depends upon it, that I beg you will give me a patient
and attentive hearing while I am pleading with you;
and that you will seriously examine the arguments,
and then judge whether a care and conduct like that
which I have advised, be not in itself reasonable;
and whether it will not be highly conducive to your
comfort and usefulness in life, your peace in death,
and the advancement and increase of your eternal
glory.

3. Let conscience say whether such a life, as I
have described above, be not in itself highly reasonable.   Look over the substance of it again, and bring

It under a close examination; for I am very apprehensive that some weak objections may arise against the whole, which may, in their consequences, affect particulars, against which no reasonable man would presume to make any objection at all. Recollect, O Christian, and carry it with you in your memory and your heart, while you are pursuing this review, that you are the creature of God, that you are purchased with the blood of Jesus; and then say whether these relations in which you stand do not demand all that application and resolution which I would engage you to. Suppose all the counsels I have given reduced into practice: suppose every day begun and concluded with such devout breathings after God, and such holy retirements for morning and evening converse with him and your own heart: suppose a daily care in contriving how your time may be managed, and in reflecting how it has been employed: suppose this regard to God, this sense of his presence, and zeal for his glory to run through your acts of worship, your hours of business and recreation: suppose this attention to Providence, this guard against temptations, this dependence upon divine influence, this government of the thoughts in solitude and of the discourse in company: nay, I will add further, suppose every particular direction given to be pursued, excepting when particular cases occur, with respect to which you shall be able in conscience to say, " I wave it not from indolence and carelessness, but because I think it will just now be more pleasing to God to be doing something else;" which may often happen in human life where general rules are best concerted: suppose, I say, all this to be done, not for a day, or a week, but through the remainder of life, whether longer or shorter; and suppose this to be reviewed at the close of life, in the full exercise of your rational faculties, will there be reason to say, in the reflection, " I have taken too much pains in religion; the Author of my being did not deserve all this from me; less diligence, less fidelity, less zeal, than this might have been equivalent for the blood which was shed for my

redemption.   A part of my heart, a part of my time,
a part of my labours, might have sufficed for him
who has given me all my powers; for him, who
has delivered me from that destruction, which would
have made them my everlasting torment; for him
who is raising me to the regions of a blissful immortality?"   Can you with any face say this?   If you
cannot, then surely your conscience bears witness,
that all I have recommended under the limitations
above is reasonable; that duty and gratitude require
it ; and consequently that, by every allowed failure
'n it, you bring guilt upon your own soul, you offend
God, and act unworthily of your Christian profession.

4. I entreat you further to consider whether such
a conduct as I have been now recommending would
not conduce much to your comfort and usefulness in
life.   Reflect seriously what is true happiness.   Does
it consist in distance from God, or in nearness to him?
Surely you cannot be a Christian, surely you cannot
be a rational man, if you doubt whether communion
with the great Father of our spirits be a pleasure and
felicity; and if it be, then surely they enjoy most of
it who keep him most constantly in view.   You cannot but know in your own conscience, that it is this
which makes the happiness of heaven; and therefore
the more of it any man enjoys upon earth, the more of
heaven comes down into his soul.   If you have made
any trial of religion, though it be but a few weeks or
months since you first became acquainted with it,
you must be some judge of it upon your own experience, which have been the most pleasant days of
your life.   Have they not been those in which you
have acted most upon these principles; those in which
you have most steadily and resolutely carried them
through every hour of time, and every circumstance
of life?   The check which you must, in many instances, give to your own inclinations might seem
disagreeable: but it would surely be overbalanced in
a most happy manner by the satisfaction you would
find in a consciousness of self-government; in having
such a command of your thoughts, affections and

actions, as is much more glorious than any authority over others can be.

5. I would also entreat you to consider the influence which such a conduct as this might have upon the happiness of others. And it is easy to be seen it must be very great, as you would find your heart always disposed to watch every opportunity of doing good, and to seize it with eagerness and delight. It would engage you to make it the study and business of your life to order things in such a manner that the end of one kind and useful action might be the beginning of another; in which you would go on as naturally as the inferior animals do in those productions and actions by which mankind are relieved or enriched; or as the earth bears her successive crops of different vegetable supplies. And though mankind be, in this corrupt state, so unhappily inclined to imitate evil examples rather than good; yet it may be expected that while your light shines before men, some seeing your good works, will endeavour to transcribe them in their own lives, and so to " glorify your Father which is in heaven," Matt. v. 16. The charms of such beautiful models would surely impress some, and incline them at least to attempt an imitation; and every attempt would dispose to another. And thus, through the divine goodness, you might be entitled to a share in the praise, and the reward, not only of the good you had immediately done yourself, but likewise of that which you had engaged others to do. And no eye but that of an all-searching God can see into what distant times or places the blessed consequences may reach. In every instance in which these consequences appear, it will put a generous and sublime joy into your heart, which no worldly prosperity could afford, and which would be the liveliest emblem of that high delight which the blessed God feels, in seeing and making his creatures happy.

6. It is true indeed, that amidst all these pious and benevolent cares, afflictions may come, and in some measure interrupt you in the midst of your projected schemes. But surely these afflictions will sit much

lighter when your heart is gladdened with the peaceful and joyful reflections of your own mind, and with
so honourable a testimony of conscience before God
and man.   Delightful will it be to go back to past
scenes in your pleasing review, and to think that you
have not only been sincerely humbling yourself for
those past offences, which afflictions may bring to
your remembrance; but that you have given substantial proofs of the sincerity of that humiliation, by
real reformation of what has been amiss, and by acting with strenuous and vigorous resolution on the
contrary principle.   And while converse with God,
and doing good to men, are made the great business
and pleasure of. life, you will find a thousand opportunities of enjoyment, even in the midst of those afflictions, which would render you so incapable of
relishing the pleasures of sense, that the mention of
them might, in those circumstances, seem an insult
and a reproach.

7. At length death will come; that solemn and important hour, which hath been passed through by so
many thousands who have in the main lived such a
life, and by so many millions who have neglected it.
And let conscience say, if there was ever one of all
these millions who had then any reason to rejoice in
that neglect; or any one, among the most strict and
exemplary Christians, who then lamented that his
heart and life had been too zealously devoted to God?
Let conscience say, whether they have wished to
have a part of that time, which they have thus employed, given back to them again, that they might be
more conformed to this world, that they might plunge
themselves deeper into its amusements, or pursue its
honours, its possessions or its pleasures with greater
eagerness than they had done?   If you were yourself
dying, and a dear friend or child stood near you,
and this book, and the preceding chapter of it should
chance to come into your thoughts, would you caution
that friend or child against conducting himself by such
rules as I have advanced?   The question may perhaps seem unnecessary where the answer is so plain

and so certain. Well then, let me beseech you to learn how you should live, by reflecting how you would die, and what course you would wish to look back upon, when you are just quitting this world, and entering upon another. Think seriously; what if death should surprise you on a sudden, and you should be called into eternity at an hour's or a minute's warning, would you not wish that your last day should have thus been begun, and the course of it, if it were a day of health and activity, should have been thus managed? Would you not wish that your Lord should find you engaged in such thoughts, and in such pursuits? Would not the passage, the flight from earth to heaven, be most easy, most pleasant, in this view and connexion? And, on the other hand, if death should make more gradual approaches, would not the remembrance of such a pious, holy, humble, diligent, and useful life, make a dying bed much softer and easier than it would otherwise be? You would not die depending upon these things: God forbid that you should! Sensible of your many imperfections, you would, no doubt, desire to throw yourself at the feet of Christ, that you might appear before God adorned with his righteousness, and washed from your sins in his blood. You would also, with your dying breath, ascribe to the riches of his grace every good disposition you had found in your heart, and every worthy action you had been enabled to perform: but would it not give you a delight worthy of being purchased with ten thousand worlds, to reflect, that, " his grace bestowed on you had not been in vain," 1 Cor. xv. 10, but that you had, from an humble principle of grateful love, glorified your heavenly Father on earth, and, in some degree, though not with the perfection you could desire, " finished the work which he had given you to do:" John xvii. 4; that you had been living for many years past as on the borders of heaven, and endeavouring to form your heart and life to the temper and manners of its inhabitants?

8. And, once more, let me entreat you to reflect on

the view you will have of this matter when you come
into a world of glory, if (which I hope will be the hap
py case,) divine mercy conduct you thither. Will not
your reception there be affected by your care, or negligence, in this holy course? Will it appear an indifferent thing in the eye of the blessed Jesus, who
distributes the crowns, and allots the thrones there,
whether you have been among the most zealous, or
the most indolent of his servants? Surely you must
wish to have " an entrance administered unto you
abundantly into the kingdom of your Lord and Saviour:" 2 Pet. i. 11: and what can more certainly
conduce to it than to be always abounding in his
work? 1 Cor. xv. 58. You cannot think so meanly of
that glorious state as to imagine that you shall there
look round about with a secret disappointment, and
say in your heart, that you overvalued the inheritance
you have received, and pursued it with too much
earnestness. You will not surely complain that it
had too many of your thoughts and cares: but, on
the contrary, you have the highest reason to believe,
that if any thing were capable of exciting your indignation and your grief there, it would be that, amidst
so many motives, and so many advantages, you exerted yourself no more in the prosecution of such a
prize.

9. But I will not enlarge on so clear a case, and
therefore conclude the chapter with reminding you,
that to allow yourself deliberately to sit down satisfied with any imperfect attainments in religion, and
to look upon a more confirmed and improved state
of it as what you do not desire, nay, as what you
secretly resolve that you will not pursue, is one of
the most fatal designs we can well imagine, that you
are an entire stranger to the first principles of it.

A PRAYER SUITED TO THE STATE OF A SOUL WHO DESIRES
TO ATTAIN THE LIFE RECOMMENDED ABOVE.

Blessed God, I cannot contradict the force of these
reasonings; O that I might feel more than ever the

lasting effects of them! Thou art the great fountain
of being and of happiness; and as from thee my being was derived, so from thee my happiness directly
flows; and the nearer I am to thee, the purer and the
more delicious is the stream. " With thee is the
fountain of life: in thy light" may I " see light,"
Psal. xxxvi. 9. The great object of my final hope
is to dwell for ever with thee; give me now some
foretaste of that delight. Give me, I beseech thee,
to experience the blessedness of " that man who fear-
eth the Lord, and who delighteth greatly in his commandments," Psal. cxii. 1; and so form my heart by
thy grace, that I may " be in the fear of the Lord all
the day long," Prov. xxiii. 17.

To thee may my awaking thoughts be directed,
and with the first ray of light that visits mine opening eyes, " lift up, O Lord, the light of thy countenance upon me," Psal. iv. 6. When my faculties
are roused from that broken state in which they lay,
while buried, and as it were annihilated, in sleep,
may my first actions be consecrated to thee, O God,
who givest me light; who givest me, as it were,
every morning a new life and a new reason. Enable
my heart to pour itself out before thee with a filial
reverence, freedom and endearment! And may I
hearken to God, as I desire that he should hearken
unto me. May thy word be read with attention
and pleasure. May my soul be delivered into the
mould of it; and may I " hide it in mine heart, that
I sin not against thee," Psal. cxix. 11. Animated
by the great motives there suggested, may I every
morning be renewing the dedication of myself to
thee, through Jesus Christ 'hy beloved Son; and be
deriving from him new supplies of that blessed Spirit
of thine, whose influences are the life of my soul.

And being thus prepared, do thou, Lord, lead me
forth by the hand to all the duties and events of the
day. In that calling, wherein thou hast been pleased
to call me, " may I abide with thee," 1 Cor. vii. 20;
not being " slothful in business, but fervent in spirit,
serving the Lord," Rom. xii. 11. May I know the

value of time, and always improve it to the best advantage, in such duties as thou hast assigned me, how low soever they may seem, or how painful soever they may be. To thy glory, O Lord, may the labours of life be pursued; and to thy glory may the refreshments of it be sought. "Whether I eat, or drink, or whatsoever I do," 1 Cor. x. 31, may that end still be kept in view, and may it be attained; and may every refreshment and release from business prepare me to serve thee with greater vigour and resolution.

May mine eye be watchful to observe the descent of mercies from thee; and may a grateful sense of thine hand in them add a favour and relish to all. And when afflictions come, which, in a world like this, I would accustom myself to expect, may I remember that they come from thee; and may that fully reconcile me to them, while I firmly believe that the same love which gives us our daily bread, appoints us our daily crosses: which I would learn to take up, that I may "follow my dear Lord," Mark viii. 34, with a temper like that which he manifested when ascending Calvary for my sake; saying like him, "The cup which my Father hath given me, shall I not drink it?" John xviii. 11. And when I enter into temptation, do thou, Lord, "deliver me from evil," Matt. vi. 13. Make me sensible, I entreat thee, of my own weakness, that my heart may be raised to thee for present communications of proportionable strength. When I am engaged in the society of others, may it be my desire and my care that I may do and receive as much good as possible, and may I continually answer the great purposes of life, by honouring thee, and diffusing useful knowledge and happiness in the world. And when I am alone, may I remember my heavenly Father is with me; and may I enjoy the pleasure of thy presence, and feel the animating power of it, awakening my soul to an earnest desire to think, and act, as in thy sight.

Thus let my days be spent: and let them always

be closed in thy fear, and under a sense of thy gracious presence. Meet me, O Lord, in mine evening
retirements. May I choose the most proper time for
them; may I diligently attend to reading and prayer;
and when I review my conduct, may I do it with an
impartial eye. Let not self-love spread a false co-
louring over it; but may I judge myself, as one that
expects to be judged of the Lord, and is very solicitous he may be approved by thee, " who searchest
all hearts, and canst not forget any of my works,"
Amos viii. 7. Let " my prayer come daily before
thee as incense," and let " the lifting up of my hands
be as the morning and the evening sacrifice," Psal.
cxli. 2. May I resign my powers to sleep in sweet
calmness and serenity; conscious that I have lived to
God in the day, and cheerfully persuaded that I am
accepted of thee in Christ Jesus my Lord, and humbly hoping in thy mercy through him, whether my
days on earth be prolonged, or " the residue of them
be cut off in the midst," Isa. xxxviii. 10. If death
comes by a leisurely advance, may it find me thus
employed; and if I am called on a sudden to exchange worlds, may my last days and hours be found
to have been conducted by such maxims as these;
that I may have a sweet and easy passage from the
services of time to the infinitely nobler services of an
immortal state. I ask it through him, who while on
earth was the fairest pattern and example of every
virtue and grace, and who now lives and reigns with
thee, " able to save unto the uttermost," Heb. vii. 25;
to him, having done all, I would fly, with humble
acknowledgment that I am " an unprofitable servant," Luke xvii. 10; to him be glory for ever and
ever. Amen

CHAPTER XXI.

A CAUTION AGAINST VARIOUS TEMPTATIONS, BY WHICH THE YOUNG CONVERT MAY BE DRAWN ASIDE FROM THE COURSE RECOMMENDED ABOVE.

Dangers continue after the first difficulties (considered, chap. xvi.) are broken through, 1. Particular cautions, (1.) Against a slug-gish and indolent temper, 2. (2.) Against the excessive love of sensual pleasure, 3. Leading to a neglect of business, and need less expense, 4. (3.) Against the snares of vain company, 5. (4.) Against excessive hurry of worldly business, 6; which is enforced by the fatal consequences these have had in many cases, 7. The chapter concludes with an exhortation to die to this world, and live to another, 8; and the young convert's prayer for divine protection against the dangers arising from these snares.

1. THE representation I have been making of the pleasure and advantage of a life spent in devotedness to God, and communion with him, as I have described it above, will, I hope, engage you, my dear reader, to form some purposes, and make some attempt to obtain it. But, from considering the nature, and ob-serving the course of things, it appears exceedingly evident, that, besides the general opposition, which I formerly mentioned, as likely to attend you in your first entrance on a religious life, you will find, even after you have resolutely broken through this, that a variety of hinderances in any attempts of exemplary piety, and in the prosecution of a remarkably strict and edifying course, will present themselves daily in your path. And whereas you may, by a few reso-lute efforts, baffle some of the former sort of enemies, these will be perpetually renewing their onsets, and a vigorous struggle must be continually maintained with them. Give me leave now, therefore, to be particular in my cautions against some of the chief of them. And here I would insist upon the difficul-ties which will arise from indolence and the love of pleasure, from vain company, and from worldly cares. Each of these may prove ensnaring to any, and

especially to young persons, to whom I would **now** have particular regard.

2. I entreat you, therefore, in the first place, that you would guard against a sluggish and indolent temper. The love of ease insinuates itself into the heart, under a variety of plausible pretences, which are often allowed to pass, when temptations of a grosser nature would not be admitted. The misspending a little time seems to wise and good men but a small matter; yet this sometimes runs them into great inconveniences. It often leads them to break in upon the seasons regularly allotted to devotion, and to defer business, which might immediately be done, but being put off from day to day, is not done at all; and thereby the services of life are at least diminished, and the rewards of eternity diminished proportionably; not to insist upon it, that very frequently this lays the soul open to further temptations, by which it falls, in consequence of being found unemployed. Be, therefore, suspicious of the first approaches of this kind. Remember that the soul of man is an active being, and that it must find its pleasure in activity. Gird up, therefore, the "loins of your mind," 1 Pet. i. 13. Endeavour to keep yourself always well employed. Be exact, if I may with humble reverence use the expression, in your appointments with God. Meet him early in the morning; and say not with the sluggard, when the proper hour of rising is come, " A little more sleep, a little more slumber," Prov. vi. 10. That time which prudence shall advise you, give to conversation, and to other recreations; but when that is elapsed, and no unforeseen and important engagement prevents, rise and be gone. Quit the company of your dearest friends, and retire to your proper business, whether it be in the field, the shop, or the closet; for by acting contrary to the secret dictates of your mind, as to what it is just at the present moment best to do, though it be but in the manner of spending half an hour, some degree of guilt is contracted, and a habit is cherished, which may draw after it much worse

consequences. Consider, therefore, what duties are to be dispatched, and in what seasons. Form your plan as prudently as you can, and pursue it resolutely: unless any unexpected incident arises, which leads you to conclude that duty calls you another way. Allowances for such unthought of interruptions must be made; but if in consequence of this, you are obliged to omit any thing of importance which you purposed to have done to-day, do it if possible to-morrow; and do not cut yourself out new work till the former plan be dispatched; unless you really judge it, not merely more amusing, but more important. And always remember, that a servant of Christ should see to it that he determine on these occasions as in his Master's presence.

3. Guard also against an excessive love of sensitive and animal pleasure, as that which will be a great hinderance to you in that religious course which I have now been urging. You cannot but know that Christ has told us, that "a man must deny himself, and take up his cross daily, if he desire to become his disciple," Luke ix. 23. Christ the Son of God, "the Former and the Heir of all things, pleased not himself;" Rom. xv. 3, but submitted to want, to difficulties and hardships, in the way of duty, and some of them in the extremest kind and degree, for the glory of God, and the salvation of men. In this way we are to follow him; and as we know not how soon we may be called even to "resist unto blood, striving against sin," Heb. xii. 4, it is certainly best to accustom ourselves to that discipline which we may possibly be called out to exercise, even in such rigorous heights. A soft and delicate life will give force to temptations, which might easily be subdued by one who has habituated himself to "endure hardship, as a good soldier of Jesus Christ," 2 Tim. ii. 3. It also produces an attachment to this world, and an unwillingness to leave it; which ill becomes those who are strangers and pilgrims on earth, and who expect so soon to be called away to that better country which they profess to seek, Heb. xi. 13—16. Add to this, that what the

world calls a life of pleasure, is necessarily a life of expense too, and may, perhaps, lead you, as it has done may others, and especially many who have been setting out in the world, beyond the limits which providence has assigned; and so, after a short course of indulgence, may produce proportionable want. And while in other cases it is true, that pity should be shown to the poor, it is a poverty that is justly contemptible, because it is the effect of a man's own folly; and when your want thus "comes upon you as an armed man," Prov. vi. 11, you will not only find yourself stripped of the capacity you might otherwise have secured for performing those works of charity, which are so ornamental to a Christian profession, but, probably, will be under strong temptations to some low artifice, or mean compliance. quite beneath the Christian character, and that of an upright man. Many who once made a high profession, after a series of such sorry and scandalous shifts, have fallen into the infamy of bankrupts, and of the worst kinds of bankrupts; I mean such as have lavished away on themselves what was indeed the property of others, and so have injured, and perhaps ruined, the industrious, to feed a foolish, luxurious, or ostentatious humour, which, while indulged, was the shame of their own families, and when it can be indulged no longer, is their torment. This will be a terrible reproach to religion: such a reproach to it, that a good man would rather choose to live on bread and water, or indeed to die for want of them, than to occasion it.

4. Guard, therefore, I beseech you, against any thing which might tend that way, especially by diligence in business, and by prudence and frugality in expense; which, by the divine blessing, may have a very happy influence to make .your affairs prosperous, your health vigorous, and your mind easy. But this cannot be attained without keeping a resolute watch over yourself, and strenuously refusing to comply with many proposals which indolence or sensuality will offer in very plausible forms, and for

which it will plead that it asks but very little. Take
heed, lest, in this respect, you imitate those fond parents, who, by indulging their children in every little
thing they have a mind to, encourage them, by insensible degrees, to grow still more encroaching and im-
perious in their demands; as if they chose to be ruined with them, rather than to check them in what
seems a trifle. Remember and consider that excellent remark, sealed by the ruin of so many thousands;
" He that despiseth small things, shall fall by little
and little."

5. In this view, give me leave also seriously and
tenderly to caution you, my dear reader, against
the snares of vain company. I speak not, as before,
of that company, which is openly licentious and profane. I hope there is something now in your temper
and views which would engage you to turn away
from such with detestation and horror. But I beseech you to consider, that those companions may be
very dangerous who might at first give you but very
little alarm; I mean those, who, though not the declared enemies of religion, and professed followers of
vice and disorder, yet nevertheless have no practical
sense of divine things on their hearts, so far as can
be judged by their conversation and behaviour. You
must often of necessity be with such persons, and
Christianity not only allows, but requires, that you
should, on all expedient occasions of intercourse with
them, treat them with civility and respect; but choose
not such for your most intimate friends, and do not
contrive to spend most of your leisure moments
among them. For such converse has a sensible tendency to alienate the soul from God, and to render
it unfit for all spiritual communion with him. To
convince you of this, do but reflect on your own experience, when you have been for many hours together among persons of such a character. Do you not
find yourself more indisposed for devotional exercises? Do you not find your heart, by insensible degrees, more and more inclined to a conformity to this
world, and to look with a secret disrelish on those

objects and employments to which reason directs as
the noblest and the best? Observe the first symptoms and guard against the snare in time: and, for
this purpose endeavour to form friendships founded
in piety, and supported by it. " Be a companion of
them that fear God, and of them that keep his precepts." Psal cxix. 63. You well know, that in the
sight of God " they are the excellent of the earth;"
let them therefore " be all your delight," Psal. xvi. 3.
And that the peculiar benefit of their friendship may
not be lost, endeavour to make the best of the hours
you spend with them. The wisest of men has observed, that when " counsel in the heart of a man is
like deep waters," that is, when it lies low and con-
cealed, " a man of understanding will draw it out."
Prov. xx. 5. Endeavour, therefore, on such occasions, so far as you can do it with decency and con-
venience, to give the conversation a religious turn.
And when serious and useful subjects are started in
your presence, lay hold of them, and cultivate them;
and, for that purpose, " let the word of Christ dwell
richly in you," Col. iii. 16, and be continually made
" the man of your counsel." Psal. cxix. 24.

6. If it be so, it will secure you, not only from the
snares of idleness and luxury, but from the contagion
of every bad example. And it will also engage you
to guard against those excessive hurries of worldly
business, which would fill up all your time and
thoughts, and thereby choke the good word of God,
and render it in a great measure, if not quite unfruit-
ful, Matt. xiii. 22. Young people are generally of
an enterprising disposition, having experienced comparatively little of the fatigue of business, and of the
disappointments and incumbrances of life, they easily
swallow them upon, and annihilate them in their
imagination, and fancy that their spirit, their application and address, will be able to encounter and sur-
mount every obstacle or hinderance. But the event
proves it otherwise. Let me entreat you, therefore,
to be cautious how you plunge yourself into a greater
variety of business than you are capable of managing

as you ought, that is, in consistency with the care of your souls, and the service of God; which certainly ought not on any pretence to be neglected. It is true, indeed, that a prudent regard to your worldly interest would require such a caution; as it is ob- vious to every careful observer, that multitudes are undone by grasping at more than they can conve- niently manage. Hence it has frequently been seen, that while they have seemed " resolved to be rich," they have " pierced themselves through with many sorrows," 1 Tim. vi. 10; have ruined their own fami- lies, and drawn down many others into desolation with them; whereas, could they have been contented with moderate .employments, and moderate gains, they might have prospered in their business, and might, by sure degrees, under a divine blessing, have advanced to great and honourable increase. But if there were no danger at all to be apprehended on this head; if you were as certain of becoming rich and great, as you are of perplexing and fatiguing yourself in the attempt; consider, I beseech you, how precarious these enjoyments are. Consider how often a " plentiful table becomes a snare, and that which should have been for a man's welfare becomes a trap," Psal. lxix. 22. Forget not that short lesson, which is so comprehensive of the highest wisdom, " One thing is needful," Luke x. 42. Be daily think- ing, while the gay and great things of life are glitter- ing before your eyes, how soon death will come, and impoverish you at once; how soon it will strip you of all possessions but those which a naked soul can carry along with it into eternity, when it drops the body into the grave. ETERNITY! ETERNITY! ETER- NITY! Carry the view of it about with you, if it be possible, through every hour of waking life; and be fully persuaded that you have no business, no inter- est in life, that is inconsistent with it: for whatsoever would be injurious in this view, is not your business, is not your interest. You see, indeed, that the gene- rality of men act as if they thought the great thing which God requires of them, in order to secure his

favour, was to get as much of the world as possible;
at least, as much as they can without any gross
immorality, and without risking the loss of all, for
making a little addition. And, as if it were to abet
this design, they tell others, and perhaps tell themselves, they only seek opportunities of greater usefulness, but, in effect, if they mean any thing more by
this than a capacity of usefulness, which, when they
have it, they will not exert, they generally deceive
themselves; and one way or another, it is a vain pretence. In most instances men seek the world, either
that they may hoard up riches for the mean and
scandalous satisfaction of looking upon them while
they are living, and of thinking, that when they are
dead, it will be said of them, that they have left so
many hundreds or thousands of pounds behind them:
very probably to ensnare their children, or other
heirs, for the vanity is not peculiar to those who
have children of their own; or else that they may
lavish away their riches on their lusts. and drown
themselves in a gulf of sensuality, in which, if reason
be not lost, religion is soon swallowed up, and with
it all the noblest pleasures which can enter into the
heart of man. In this view, the generality of rich
people appear to me objects of much greater compassion than the poor; especially as when both live
(which is frequently the case) without any fear of
God before their eyes, the rich abuse the greater
variety and abundance of his favours, and therefore
will probably feel in that world of future ruin which
awaits impenitent sinners, a more exquisite sense of
their misery.

7. And let me observe to you, my dear reader, lest
you should think yourself secure from any such danger, that we have great reason to apprehend there
are many now in a very wretched state, who once
thought seriously of religion when they were first
setting out, in lower circumstances of life, but they
have since forsaken God for Mammon, and are now
priding themselves in those golden chains, which, in
all probability, before it be long, will leave them to

remain in those of darkness. When, therefore, an attachment to the world may be followed with such fatal consequences, " let not thine heart envy sin. ners," Prov. xxiii. 17; and do not, out of a desire of gaining what they have, be guilty of such folly, as to expose yourself to this double danger of failing in the attempt, or of being undone by the success of it. Contract your desire: endeavour to be easy and content with a little; and if Providence call you out to act in a larger sphere, submit to it in obedience to Providence; but number it among the trials of life, which it will require a larger proportion of grace to bear well. For be assured, that as affairs and interests multiply, cares and duties will certainly increase, and probably disappointments and sorrows will increase in an equal proportion.

8. On the whole, learn by divine grace, to die to the present world; to look upon it as a low state of being, which God never intended for the final and complete happiness, or the supreme care, of any one of his children; a world where something is indeed to be enjoyed, but chiefly from himself; where a great deal is to be borne with patience and resignation; and where some important duties are to be performed, and a course of discipline to be passed through, by which you are to be formed for a better state; to which, as a Christian, you are near, and t which God will call you, perhaps on a sudden, but undoubtedly, if you hold on your way, in the fittest time, and the most convenient manner. Refer, therefore, all this to him. Let your hopes and fears, your expectations and desires, with regard to this world, oe kept as low as possible; and all your thoughts be united, as much as may be, in this one centre, What it is that God would, in present circumstances, have you to be; and what is that method of conduct by which you may most effectually please and glorify aim.

Blessed God! in the midst of ten thousand snares
and dangers which surround me from without and
from within, permit me to look up unto thee with
my humble entreaty, that thou wouldst "deliver me
from them that rise up against me," Psal. lix. 1, and
that "thine eyes may be upon me for good," Jer.
xxiv. 6.   When sloth and indolence are ready to
seize me, awaken me from that idle dream, with lively and affectionate views of that invisible and eternal
world to which I am tending.   Remind me of what
infinite importance it is that I diligently improve
those transient moments which thou hast allotted me
as the time of my preparation for it.

When sinners entice me, may I not consent, Prov.
i. 10.   May holy converse with God give me a disrelish for the converse of those who are strangers to
thee, and who would separate my soul from thee!
May "I honour them that fear the Lord," Psal. xv.
4; and walking with such wise and holy men, may I
find I am daily advancing in wisdom and holiness,
Prov. xiii.   Quicken me, O Lord, by their means,
that by me thou mayest also quicken others!   Make
me the happy instrument of enkindling and animating the flame of divine love in their breasts; and
may it catch from heart to heart, and grow every
moment in its progress.

Guard me, O Lord, from the love of sensual pleasure.   May I seriously remember, that "to be carnally minded is death," Rom. viii. 6.   May it please
thee, therefore, to purify and refine my soul by the
influences of thy Holy Spirit, that I may always shun
unlawful gratifications more solicitously than others
pursue them; and that those indulgences of animal
nature, which thou hast allowed, and which the constitution of things renders necessary, may be soberly
and moderately used.   May I still remember the superior dignity of my spiritual and intelligent nature,

and may the pleasures of the man and the Christian be sought as my noblest happiness.   May my soul rise on the wings of holy contemplation to the regions of invisible glory, and may I be endeavouring to form myself, under the influences of divine grace, for the entertainments of those angelic spirits, that live in thy presence in a happy incapacity of those gross delights by which spirits dwelling in flesh are so often ensnared, and in which they so often lose the memory of their high original, and of those noble hopes which alone are proportionable to it.

Give me, O Lord, to know the station in which thou hast fixed me, and steadily to pursue the duties of it.   But deliver me from those excessive cares of this world, which would so engross my time and my thoughts, that the one thing needful should be forgotten.   May my desires after worldly possessions be moderated, by considering their uncertain and unsatisfying nature, and while others are laying up treasures on earth, may I be " rich towards God," Luke xii. 21.   May I never be too busy to attend to those great affairs which lie between thee and my soul ; never be so engrossed with the concerns of time, as to neglect the interests of eternity.   May I pass through earth with my heart and hopes set upon heaven, and feel the attractive influence stronger and stronger, as I approach still nearer and nearer to that desirable centre ; till the happy moment come, when every earthly object shall disappear from my view, and the shining glories of the heavenly world shall fill my improved and strengthened sight, which shall then be cheered with that which would now over-whelm me.   Amen.

CHAPTER XXII.

THE CASE OF A SPIRITUAL DECAY AND LANGUOR IN RELIGION.

Declensions in religion and relapses into sin, with their sorrowful consequences, are, in the general, too probable, 1. The cause of declension and languor in religion described, negatively, 2; and positively, 3; as discovering itself, (1.) By a failure in the duties of the closet, 4. (2.) By a neglect of social worship, 5. (3.) By want of love to our fellow-Christians, 6. (4.) By an undue attachment to sensual pleasures or secular cares, 7. (5.) By prejudices against some important principles in religion, 8; a symptom peculiarly sad and dangerous, 9, 10. Directions for recovery, 11, immediately to be pursued, 12. A prayer for one under spiritual decays.

1. IF I am so happy as to prevail upon you in the exhortations and cautions I have given, you will probably go on with pleasure and comfort in religion; and your path will generally be " like the morning light, which shineth more and more unto the perfect day," Prov. iv. 18. Yet I dare not flatter myself with an expectation of such success as shall carry you above those varieties in temper, conduct and state, which have been more or less the complaint of the best of men. Much do I fear that, how warmly soever your heart may be now impressed with the representation I have been making, though the great objects of your faith and hope continue unchangeable, your temper towards them will be changed. Much do I fear that you will feel your mind languish and tire in the good ways of God; nay, that you may be prevailed upon to take some step out of them, and may thus fall a prey to some of those temptations which you now look upon with a holy scorn. The probable consequence of this will be, that God will hide his face from you; that he will stretch forth his afflicting hand against you; and that you will still see your sorrowful moments, how cheerfully soever you may now be " rejoicing in the Lord, and joy'ng in the God of your salvation," Hab. iii.

18. I hope, therefore, it may be of some service, if this too probable event should happen, to consider these cases a little more particularly; and I heartily pray that God would make what I shall say concerning them the means of restoring, comforting, and strengthening your soul, if he ever suffers you in any degree to deviate from him.

2. We will first consider the case of spiritual declensions and languor in religion. And here I desire that before I proceed any further, you would observe, that I do not comprehend under this head, every abatement of that fervour which a young convert may find, when he first becomes experimentally acquainted with divine things. Our natures are so framed, that the novelty of objects strikes them in something of a peculiar manner; not to urge how much more easily our passions are impressed in the earlier years of life, than when we are more advanced in the journey of it. This, perhaps, is not sufficiently considered. Too great a stress is commonly laid on the flow of affections; and for want of this, a Christian who is ripened in grace, and greatly advanced in his preparations for glory, may sometimes be ready to lament imaginary rather than real decays, and to say, without any just foundation, " O that it were with me as in months past," Job xxix. 2. Therefore you can hardly be too frequently told, that religion consists chiefly " in the resolution of the will for God, and in a constant care to avoid whatever we are persuaded he would disapprove, to despatch the work he has assigned us in life, and to promote his glory in the happiness of mankind." To this we are chiefly to attend, looking in all to the simplicity and purity of those motives from which we act, which we know are chiefly regarded by that God who searches the heart; humbling ourselves before him at the same time under a sense of our many imperfections, and flying to the blood of Christ and the grace of the gospel.

3. Having given this precaution, I will now a little more particularly describe the case which I call the

state of a Christian who is declining in religion, so far as it does not fall in with those which I shall consider in the following chapters. And I must observe, that it chiefly consists " in a forgetfulness of divine objects, and a remissness in those various duties to which we stand engaged by that solemn surrender which we have made of ourselves to the service of God." There will be a variety of symptoms, according to the different circumstances and relations in which the Christian is placed; but some will be of a more universal kind. It will be peculiarly proper to touch on these; and so much the rather, as these declensions are often unobserved, like the gray hairs which were upon Ephraim, when he knew it not, Hos. vii. 9.

4. Should you, my good reader, fall into this state, it will probably first discover itself by a failure in the duties of the closet. Not that I suppose they will at first, or certainly conclude that they will at all, be wholly omitted, but they will be run over in a cold and formal manner. Sloth, or some of those other snares which I cautioned you against in the former chapter, will so far prevail upon you, that though perhaps you know and recollect that the proper season for retirement is come, you will sometimes indulge yourself upon your bed in the morning, sometimes in conversation or business in the evening, so as not to have convenient time for it; or, perhaps, when you come into your closet at that season, some favourite book you are desirous to read, some correspondence that you choose to carry on, or some other amusement will present itself, and plead to be dispatched first. This will probably take up more time than you imagine; and then secret prayer will be hurried over, and perhaps reading the Scripture quite neglected. You will plead, perhaps, that it is but for once; but the same allowance will be made a second and a third time; and it will grow more easy and familiar to you each time, than it was the last. And thus God will be mocked, and your own soul will be defrauded of its spiritual meals, if I may be

allowed the expression; the word of God will be slighted, and self-examination quite disused; and secret prayer itself will grow a burden rather than a delight, and a trifling ceremony rather than a devout homage fit for the acceptance of our Father who is in heaven.

5. If immediate and resolute measures be not taken for our recovery from these declensions, they will spread further, and reach the acts of social worship. You will fee the effects in your family, and in public ordinances. And if you do not feel them, the symptoms will be so much the worse. Wandering thoughts will, as it were, eat out the very heart of these duties. It is not, I believe, the privilege of the most eminent Christians to be entirely free from them: but, probably, in these circumstances, you will find but few intervals of strict attention, or of any thing which wears the appearance of inward devotion. And when these heartless duties are concluded, there will scarce be a reflection made how little God has been enjoyed in them, how little he has been honoured by them. Perhaps the sacrament of the Lord's Supper, being so admirably adapted to fix the attention of the soul, and to excite its warmest exercise of holy affections, may be the last ordinance in which these declensions will be felt. And yet who can say that the sacred table is a privileged place? Having been unnecessarily straitened in your preparations, you will attend with less fixedness and enlargement of heart than usual. And perhaps a dissatisfaction in the review, when there has been a remarkable alienation or insensibility of mind, may occasion a disposition to forsake your place and your duty there. And when your spiritual enemies have once gained this point over you, it is probable you will fall by swifter degrees than ever, and your resistance to their attempts will grow weaker and weaker.

6. When your love to God our Father, and to the Lord Jesus Christ fails, your fervor of Christian affection to your brethren in Christ will proportionably

decline, and your concern for usefulness in life abate; especially where any thing is to be done for spiritual edification. You will find one excuse or another for the neglect of religious discourse, perhaps not only among neighbours and Christian friends, when very convenient opportunities offer, but even with regard to those who are members of your own families, and to those who, if you are fixed in the superior relations of life, are committed to your care.

7. With this remissness an attachment either to sensual pleasure or to worldly business will increase. For the soul must have something to employ it, and something to delight itself in; and as it turns to one or the other of these, temptations of one sort or another will present themselves. In some instances, perhaps the strictest bounds of temperance, and the regular appointments of life, may be broken in upon through a fondness for company, and the entertainments which often attend it. In other instances, the interests of life appearing greater than they did before, and taking up more of the mind, contrary interests of other persons may throw you into disquietude, or plunge you in debate and contention; in which it is extremely difficult to preserve either the serenity or the innocence of the soul. And perhaps, if ministers and other Christian friends observe this, and endeavour, in a plain and faithful way, to reduce you from your wandering, a false delicacy of mind, often contracted in such a state as this, will render these attempts extremely disagreeable. The ulcer of the soul (if I may be allowed the expression) will not bear being touched when it most needs it; and one of the most generous and self-denying instances of Christian friendship shall be turned into an occasion of coldness and distaste, yea perhaps of enmity.

8. And possibly, to sum up all, this disordered state of mind may lead you into some prejudices against those very principles which might be most effectual for your recovery: and your great enemy may succeed so far in his attempts against you as to persuade you that you have lost nothing in religion, when you

have almost lost all.   He may, very probably, lead
you to conclude, that your former devotional frames
were mere fits of enthusiasm; and that the holy re-
gularity of your walk before God was an unnecessary strictness and scrupulosity.   Nay, you may think
it a great improvement in understanding that you
have learnt from some new matters, that if a man
treat his fellow-creatures with humanity and good
nature, judging and reviling only those who would
disturb others by the narrowness of their notions (for
these are generally exempted from other objects of
the most universal and disinterested benevolence so
often boasted of) he must necessarily be in a very
good state, though he pretend not to converse much
with God, provided that he think respectfully of
him, and do not provoke him by any gross immoralities.

9. I mention this in the last stage of religious declensions, because I apprehend that to be its proper
place; and I fear it will be found by experience to
stand upon the very confines of that gross apostasy
into deliberate and presumptuous sin, which will
claim our consideration under the next head; and because, too, it is that symptom which most effectually
tends to prevent the success, and even the use, of any
proper remedies, in consequence of a fond and fatal
apprehension that they are needless.   It is, if I may
borrow the simile, like those fits of lethargic drowsiness which often precede apoplexies and death.

10. It is by no means my design at this time to
reckon up, much less to consider at large, those dan
gerous principles which are now ready to possess the
mind, and to lay the foundation of a false and treacherous peace.   Indeed they are in different instances
various, and sometimes run into opposite extremes;
but if God awaken you to read your Bible with attention, and give you to feel the Spirit with which it is
written, almost every page will flash conviction upon
the mind, and spread a light to scatter and disperse
these shades of darkness.

11. What I chiefly intend in this address, is to en-

gage you, if possible, as soon as you perceive the first symptoms of these declensions, to be upon your guard, and to endeavour as speedily as possible to recover yourself from them. And I would remind you, that the remedy must begin where the first cause of complaint prevailed, I mean, in the closet. Take some time for recollection, and ask your own conscience seriously, How matters stand between the blessed God and your soul? Whether they are as they once were, and as you could wish them to be, if you saw your life just drawing to a period, and were to pass immediately into the eternal state? One serious thought of eternity shames a thousand vain excuses, with which, in the forgetfulness of it, we are ready to delude our own souls. And when you feel that secret misgiving of heart, which will naturally arise on this occasion, do not endeavour to palliate the matter, and to find out slight and artful coverings for what you cannot forbear secretly condemning; but honestly fall under the conviction, and be humbled for it. Pour out your heart before God, and seek the renewed influences of his Spirit and grace. Return with exactness to secret devotion, and to self-examination. Read the Scripture with yet greater diligence, and especially the more devotional and spiritual parts of it. Labour to ground it in your heart, and to feel what you have reason to believe the sacred penmen felt when they wrote, so far as circumstances may agree. Open your soul with all simplicity to every lesson which the word of God would teach you; and guard against those things which you perceive to alienate your mind from inward religion, though there be nothing criminal in the things themselves. They may perhaps in the general be lawful; to some, possibly, they may be expedient; but if they produce such an effect, as was mentioned above, it is certain, they are not convenient for you. In these circumstances, above all, seek the converse of those Christians whose progress in religion seems most remarkable, and who adorn their profession in the most amiable manner. Labour to obtain their temper and sentiments, and lay open your case and your heart to them with all the freedom which prudence will permit. Employ yourself at seasons of leisure in reading practical and devotional books, in which the mind and the heart of the pious author is transfused into the work, and in which you can (as it were,) taste the genuine spirit of Christianity. And, to conclude, take the first opportunity that presents itself of making an approach to the table of the Lord, and spare neither time nor pains in the most serious preparation for it. There renew your covenant with God; put your soul anew into the hand of Christ, and endeavour to view the wonders of his dying love in such a manner as may rekindle the languishing flame, and quicken you to more vigorous resolutions than ever, " to live unto him who died for you," 2 Cor. v. 15. And watch over your own heart, that the good impressions you then felt may continue. Rest not till you have made greater progress than before: for it is certain more is yet behind; and it is only by a certain zeal to go forward that you can be secure from the danger of going backward, and of revolting more and more.

12. I only add, that it is necessary to take these precautions as soon as posssible; or you will probably find a much swifter progress than you are aware in the down-hill road, and you may possibly be left of God to fall into some gross and aggravated sins, so as to fill your conscience with an agony and horror, which the pain of broken bones, Psal. li. 8, can but imperfectly express.

A PRAYER FOR ONE UNDER SPIRITUAL DECAYS.

Eternal and unchangeable Jehovah! thy perfections and glories are, like thy being, immutable; Jesus, thy Son, is " the same yesterday, to-day, and for ever," Heb. xiii. 8. The eternal world to which I am hastening is always equally important, and presses upon the attentive mind for a more fixed and solemn regard, in proportion to the degree in which it comes nearer and nearer. But, alas! my views, and my affections, and my best resolutions, are continually varying, like this poor body, which goes through daily and hourly alterations in its state and circumstances. Whence, O Lord, whence this sad change, which I now experience, in the frame and temper of my mind towards thee? Whence this alienation of my soul from thee? Why can I not come to thee with all the endearments of filial love as I once could? Why is thy service so remissly attended, if attended at all? and why are the exercises of it, which were once my greatest pleasure, become a burden to me? "Where, O God, is the blessedness I once spake of," Gal. iv. 15, when my joy in thee as my heavenly Father was so conspicuous that strangers might have observed it; and when my heart did so overflow with love to thee, and with zeal for thy service, that it was matter of self-denial to me to limit and restrain the genuine expressions of those strong emotions of my soul, even where prudence and duty required it?

Alas, Lord, whither am I fallen! Thine eye sees me still; but O, how unlike what it once saw me! Cold and insensible as I am, I must blush on the reflection. Thou "seest me in secret," Matt. vi. 6, and seest me, perhaps, often amusing myself with trifles in those seasons which I used solemnly to devote to thine immediate service. Thou seest me coming into thy presence as by constraint; and when I am before thee, so straitened in my spirit, that I hardly know what to say to thee, though thou art the God with whom I have to do, and though the keeping up an humble and dutiful correspondence with thee is beyond all comparison the most important business of my life. And even when I am speaking to thee, with how much coldness and formality is it! It is, perhaps, the work of the imagination, the labour of the lips; but where are those ardent desires, those intense breathings after God, which I once felt? Where is that pleasing repose in thee which I was once conscious of, as being near my divine rest, as being happy in that nearness, and resolving that, if possible, I would no more be removed from it? But, O, how far am I now removed! When these short devotions, if they may be called devotions, are over in what long intervals do I forget thee, and appear so little animated with thy love, so little devoted to thy service, that a stranger might converse with me a considerable time without knowing that I had ever formed any acquaintance with thee, without discovering that I had so much as known or heard any thing of God. Thou callest me to thine house, O Lord, on thine own day; but how heartless are my services there! I offer thee no more than a carcase. My thoughts and affections are engrossed with other objects, while I " draw near thee with my mouth, and honour thee with my lips," Isa. xxix. 13. Thou callest me to thy table; but my heart is so frozen, that it hardly melts even at the foot of the cross; hardly feels any efficacy in the blood of Jesus. O wretched creature that I am! Unworthy of being called thine! unworthy of a place among thy children, or of the meanest situation in thy family; rather worthy to be cast out, to be forsaken, yea, to be utterly destroyed!

Is this, Lord, the service which I once promised, and which thou hast so many thousand reasons to expect? Are these the returns I am making for thy daily providential care, for the sacrifice of thy Son, for the communications of thy Spirit, for the pardon of my numberless aggravated sins, for the hopes, the undeserved and so often-forfeited hopes of eternal glory? Lord, I am ashamed to stand or to kneel before thee. But pity me, I beseech thee, and help me; for I am a pitiable object indeed! " My soul cleaveth unto the dust," and lays itself as in the dust before thee; but O, " quicken me according to thy word," Psal. cxix. 25. Let me trifle no longer, for I am upon the brink of a precipice. I am thinking of my ways; O give me grace to turn my feet unto thy testimonies; to make haste without any further delay, that I may keep thy commandments, Psal.

cxix. 59, 60. "Search me, O Lord, and try me," Psal. cxxxix. 23. Go to the first root of this distemper which spreads itself over my soul, and recover me from it. Represent sin unto me, O Lord, I beseech thee, that I may see it with abhorrence; and represent the Lord Jesus Christ to me in such a light, that I may "look upon him and mourn," Zech. xii. 10, that I may look upon him and love. May I awake from this stupid lethargy into which I am sinking; and may Christ give me more abundant degrees of spiritual life and activity than I have ever yet received. And may I be so quickened and animated by him, that I may more than recover the ground I have lost, and may make a more speedy and exemplary progress than in my best days I have ever yet done. Send down upon me, O Lord, in a more rich and abundant effusion, thy good Spirit. May he dwell in me, as in a temple which he has consecrated to himself, 1 Cor. iii. 16; and while all the service is directed and governed by him, may holy and acceptable sacrifices be continually offered, Rom. xii. 1. May the incense be constant, and may it be fragrant. May the sacred fire burn and blaze perpetually, Lev. v. 13; and may none of its vessels ever be profaned, by being employed to an unholy or forbidden use. Amen.

CHAPTER XXIII.

1. THE declensions which I have described in the
foregoing chapter, must be acknowledged worthy of
deep lamentation: but happy will you be, my dear
reader, if you never know, by experience, a circumstance yet more melancholy than this. Perhaps,
when you consider the view of things which you
now have, you imagine that no considerations can
ever bribe you, in any single instance, to act contrary
to the present dictates or suggestions of your conscience, and of the Spirit of God as setting it on work.
No: you think it would be better for you to die; and
you think rightly. But Peter thought and said so
too: "Though I should die with thee, yet will I not
deny thee," Matt. xxvi. 35; and yet after all, he fell;
and therefore " be not high-minded, but fear," Rom.
ix. 20. It is not impossible but you may fall into
that very sin of which you imagine you are least in
danger, or into that against which you have most
solemnly resolved, and of which you have already
most bitterly repented. You may relapse into it
again and again; but O, if you do, nay, if you should
deliberately and presumptuously fall but once, how
deep will it pierce your heart! how dear will you
pay for all the pleasure with which the temptation
has been baited! how will this separate between God
and you   What a desolation, what a dreadful deso

,ation will it spread over your soul! it is grievous to think of it. Perhaps in such a state you may feel more agony and distress in your own conscience, when you come seriously to reflect, than you ever felt when you were first awakened and reclaimed; because the sin will be attended with some very high aggravations beyond those of your unregenerate state. I well knew the person that said, " The agonies of a sinner in the first pangs of his repentance were not to be mentioned on the same day with those of the backslider in heart, when he comes to be filled with his own way," Prov. xiv. 14.

2. Indeed it is enough to wound one's heart to think how yours will be wounded; how all your comforts, all your evidences, all your hopes, will be clouded; what thick darkness will spread itself on every side, so that neither sun, nor moon, nor stars will appear in your heaven. Your spiritual consolations will be gone; and your temporal enjoyments will also be rendered tasteless and insipid. And if afflictions be sent, as they probably may, in order to reclaim you, a consciousness of guilt will sharpen and envenom the dart. Then will the enemy of your soul, with all his art and power, rise up against you, encouraged by your fall, and labouring to trample you down in utter hopeless ruin. He will persuade you that you are already undone beyond recovery: he will suggest that it signifies nothing to attempt it any more; for that every effort, every amendment, every act of repentance, will but make your case so much the worse, and plunge you lower and lower into hell.

3. Thus will he endeavour by terrors to keep you from that sure remedy which yet remains. But yield not to him. Your case will indeed be sad; and if it be now your case, it is deplorably so; and to rest in it would be still much worse. Your heart would be hardened yet more and more: and nothing could be expected but sudden and aggravated destruction. Yet, blessed be God, it is not quite hopeless. " Your wounds are corrupted because of your foolishness,"

Psal. xxxviii. 5; but the gangrene is not incurable. " There is balm in Gilead, there is a Physician there,' Jer. viii. 22. Do not, therefore, render your condition hopeless, by now saying, " There is no hope," Jer. ii. 25, and drawing a fatal argument from that false supposition for going after the idols you have loved. Let me address you in the language of God to his backsliding people, when they were ready to apprehend that to be their case, and to draw such a conclusion from it: " Only return unto me, saith the Lord," Jer. iii. 1, 13. Cry for renewed grace; and, in the strength of it labour to return. Cry with David under the like guilt. ' " I have gone astray like a lost sheep, seek thy servant; for I do not forget thy commandments," Psal. cxix. 176; and that remembrance of them is, I hope, a token for good. But if thou wilt return at all, do it immediately. Take not one step more in that fatal path to which thou hast turned aside. Think not to add one sin more to the account, and then to repent; as if it would be but the same thing on the whole. The second error may be worse than the first; it may make way for another and another, and draw on a terrible train of consequences beyond all you can now imagine. Make haste, therefore, and do not delay. Escape and fly as for thy life, Gen. ix. 17, " before the dart strike through thy liver," Prov. vii. 23. " Give not sleep to thine eyes, nor slumber to thine eye-lids," Prov. vi. 4: lie not down upon thy bed under unpardoned guilt, lest evil overtake thee, lest the sword of divine justice should smite thee; and, whilst thou proposest to return to-morrow, thou shouldst this night go and take possession of hell.

4. Return immediately; and permit me to add, return solemnly. Some very pious and excellent divines have expressed themselves upon this head in a manner which seems liable to dangerous abuse; when they urge men after a fall " not to stay to survey the ground, nor consider how they came to be thrown down, but immediately to get up and renew the race." In slighter cases the advice is good · but when con-

science has suffered such violent outrage, by the commission of known, wilful, and deliberate sin, (a case which one would hope should but seldom happen to those who have once sincerely entered on a religious course,) I can by no means think that either reason or Scripture encourages such a method. Especially would it be improper, if the action itself has been of so heinous a nature, that even to have fallen into it on the most sudden surprise of temptation, must greatly have ashamed, and terrified, and distressed the soul. Such an affair is dreadfully solemn, and should be treated accordingly. If this has been the sad case with you, my then unhappy reader, I would pity you, and mourn over you; and would beseech you, as you tender your peace, your recovery, the health and the very life of your soul, that you would not loiter away an hour. Retire immediately for serious reflection. Break through other engagements and employments, unless they be such as you cannot in conscience delay for a few hours, which can seldom happen in the circumstances I now suppose. This is the one thing needful. Set yourself to it, therefore, as in the presence of God, and hear at large, patiently and humbly, what conscience has to say, though it chide and reproach severely. Yea, earnestly pray that God would speak to you by conscience, and make you more thoroughly to know and feel " what an evil and bitter thing it is, that you have " thus forsaken him," Jer. ii. 19. Think of all the aggravating circumstances attending your offence, and especially those which arise from abused mercy and goodness; which arise not only from your solemn vows and engagements to God, but from the views you have had of a Redeemer's love, sealed even in blood. And are these the returns? Was it not enough that Christ should have been thus injured by his enemies? must he be " wounded in the house of his friends too?" Zech. xiii. 6. Were " you delivered to work such abominations as these," Jer. vii. 10. Did the blessed Jesus groan and die **for** you, that you might sin with boldness and freedom that you might extract, as it were, the very spirit and essence of sir. and offend God to a height of ingratitude and base ness which would otherwise have been in the nature of things impossible! Oh, think how justly God might cast you out from his presence! how justly he might number you among the most signal instances of his vengeance! And think how "your heart would endure, or your hands be strong, if he would deal thus with you!" Ezek. xxii. 14. Alas! all your former experiences would enhance your sense of the ruin and misery that must be felt in an eternal banishment from the divine presence and favour.

5. Indulge such reflections as these. Stand the humbling sight of your sins in such a view as this The more odious and more painful it appears, the greater prospect there will be of your benefit by attending to it. But the matter is not to rest here. All these reflections are intended, not to grieve, but to cure; and to grieve no more than may promote the cure. You are indeed to look upon sin; but you are also, in such circumstances, if ever, "to look upon Christ: to look upon him whom you have now pierced" deeper than before, and to mourn for him with sincerity and tenderness, Zech. xii. 10.—The God whom you have injured and affronted, whose laws you have broken, and whose justice you have, as it were, challenged by this foolish wretched apostasy, is nevertheless "a most merciful God," Deut. iv. 31. You cannot be so ready to return to him, as he is ready to receive you. Even now does he, as it were, solicit a reconciliation by those tender impressions which he is making upon your heart. But remember how he will be reconciled. It is in the very same way in which you made your first approaches to him in the name, and for the sake of his dear Son. Come, therefore, in an humble dependence upon him. Renew your application to Jesus, that his blood may, as it were, be sprinkled upon your soul, that your soul may thereby be purified, and your guilt removed. This very sin of yours which the blessed God fore saw, increased the weight of your Redeemer's suffer

ings: it was concerned in shedding his blood. Humbly go, and place your wounds, as it were, under the droppings of that precious balm by which alone they can be healed. That compassionate Saviour will delight to restore you, when you lie as an humble suppliant at his feet, and will graciously take part with you in that peace and pleasure which he gives. Through him renew your covenant with God, that broken covenant, the breach of which divine justice might teach you to know " by terrible things in righteousness," Psal. lxv. 5; but mercy allows of an accommodation. Let the consciousness and remembrance of the breach engage you to enter into a covenant anew, under a deeper sense than ever of your own weakness, and a more cordial dependence on divine grace for your security, than you have ever yet entertained. I know you will be ashamed to present yourself among the children of God in his sanctuary, and especially at his table, under a consciousness of so much guilt; but break through that shame, if Providence open you the way. You would be humbled before your offended Father; but surely there is no place where you are more likely to be humbled, than when you see yourself in his house; and no ordinance administered there can lay you lower than that in which " Christ is evidently set forth as crucified before your eyes," Gal. iii. 1. Sinners are the only persons who have business there; the best of men come to that sacred table as sinners; as such make your approach to it; yea, as the greatest of sinners, as one who needs the blood of Jesus as much as any creature upon earth.

6. And let me remind you of one thing more. If your fall has been of such a nature as to give any scandal to others, be not at all concerned to save appearances, and to moderate those mortifications which deep humiliation before them would occasion. The depth and pain of that mortification is indeed an excellent medicine, which God has in his wise goodness appointed for you in such circumstances as these. In such a case, confess your fault with the greatest

frankness; aggravate it to the utmost; entreat pardon
and prayer from those whom you have offended.
Then, and never till then, will you be in the way to
peace: not by palliating a fault, not by making vain
excuses, not by objecting to the manner in which
others may have treated you; as if the least excess
of rigour in a faithful admonition were a crime equal
to some great immorality that occasioned it. This
can only proceed from the madness of pride and self-
love: it is the sensibility of a wound which is hardened, swelled and inflamed; and it must be reduced
and cooled, and suppled, before it can possibly be
cured. To be censured and condemned by men,
will be but a little grievance to a soul thoroughly
humbled and broken under a sense of having incurred the condemning sentence of God. Such a one
will rather desire to glorify God, by submitting to deserved blame; and will fear deceiving others into a
more favourable opinion of himself than he inwardly
knows himself to deserve. These are the sentiments
which God gives to the sincere penitent in such a
case; and by this means he restores him to that credit
and regard among others, which he does not know
how to seek; but which, nevertheless, for the sake
both of his comfort and usefulness, God wills that he
should have; and which it is, humanly speaking,
impossible for him to recover any other way. But
there is something so honourable in the frank acknowledgment of a fault, and in deep humiliation for
it, that all who see it must needs approve it. They
pity an offender who is brought to such a disposition,
and endeavour to comfort him with returning expressions, not only of their love, but of their esteem
too.

7. Excuse this digression, which may suit some
cases; and which would suit many more, if a regular
discipline were to be exercised in churches; for on
such a supposition, the Lord's Supper could not be
approached after visible and scandalous falls, without
solemn confession of the offence, and declarations of
repentance. On the other hand, there may be in-

stances of sad apostasy, where the crime, though highly aggravated before God, may not fall under human notice.   In this case, remember, that your business is with him to whose piercing eye every thing appears in its just light; before him, therefore, prostrate your souls and seek a solemn reconciliation with him, confirmed by the memorials of his dying Son.   And when this is done, imagine not, that because you have received the tokens of pardon, the guilt of your apostasy is to be forgot at once.   Bear it still in your memory for future caution: lament it before God in the frequent returns of secret devotion especially; and view with humiliation the scars of those wounds which your own folly occasioned, even when by divine grace they are thoroughly healed. For God establishes his covenant, not to remove the sense of every past abomination, but " that thou mayest remember thy ways, and be confounded, and never open thy mouth any more because of thy shame, even when I am pacified towards thee for all that thou hast done, saith the Lord," Ezek. xvi. 63.

8. And now, upon the whole, if you desire to attain such a temper, and to return by such steps as these, then immediately fall down before God, and pour out your heart in his presence, in language like this:

A PRAYER FOR ONE WHO HAS FALLEN INTO GROSS SIN, AFTER RELIGIOUS RESOLUTIONS AND ENGAGEMENTS.

O MOST holy, holy, holy, Lord God! when I seriously reflect on thy spotless purity, and on the strict and impartial methods of thy steady administration, together with that almighty power of thine, which is able to carry every thought of thine heart into immediate and full execution, I may justly appear before thee this day with shame and terror, in confusion and consternation of spirit.   This day, O my God, this dark mournful day, would I take occasion to look back to that sad source of our guilt and our misery, the apostasy of our common parents, and

say, with thine offending servant David, " Behold
I was shapen in iniquity, and in sin did my mother
conceive me," Psal. li. 5.   This day would I lament
all the fatal consequences of such a descent with regard to myself.   And, O, how many have they been!
The remembrance of the sins of my unconverted
state, and the failings and infirmities of my after life,
may justly confound me.   How much more such a
scene as now lies before my conscience, and before
thine all-seeing eye!   For " thou, O Lord, knowest
my foolishness, and my sins are not hid from thee,"
Psal. lxix. 5.   " Thou tellest all my wanderings from
thy statutes," Psal. lvi. 8; thou seest, and thou re-
cordest, every instance of my disobedience to thee,
and of my rebellion against thee; thou seest it in
every aggravated circumstance which I can discern,
and in many more which I have never observed or
reflected upon.   How then shall I " appear in thy
presence, or lift up my face to thee," Ezra ix. 6.
" I am full of confusion," Job x. 15, and feel a secret
regret in the thought of applying to thee; but, " O
Lord, to whom should I go but unto thee?" John
vi. 68; unto thee, on whom depends my life or my
death: unto thee, who alone canst take away that
burden of guilt which now presses me down to the
dust: who alone canst restore to my soul that rest
and peace which I have lost, and which I deserve
for ever to lose.

Behold me, O Lord God, falling down at thy feet.
Behold me, pleading guilty in thy presence, and
surrendering myself to that justice which I cannot
escape.   I have not one word to offer in my own
vindication, in my own excuse.   Words, far from
being able to clear up my innocence, can never sufficiently describe the enormity and demerit of my sin.
Thou, O Lord, and thou only, knowest to the full,
how heinous and how aggravated it is.   Thine
infinite understanding alone can fathom the infinite
depth of its malignity.   I am, on many accounts,
most unable to do it.   I cannot conceive the glory of
thy sacred majesty, whose authority I have despised.

nor the number and variety of those mercies which I have sinned against. I cannot conceive the value of the blood of thy dear Son, which I have ungratefully trampled under my feet; nor the dignity of that blessed Spirit of thine, whose agency I have, as far as I could, been endeavouring to oppose, and whose work I have been, as with all my might, labouring to undo, and to tear up, as it were, that plantation of his grace, which I should rather have been willing to have guarded with my life, and watered with my blood. O the baseness and madness of my conduct! that I should thus, as it were, rend open the wounds of my soul, of which I had died long ere this, had not thine own hand applied a remedy, had not thine only Son bled to prepare it!—that I should violate the covenant that I have " made with thee by sacrifice," Psal. l. 5, by the memorials of such a sacrifice too, even of Jesus Christ my Lord, whereby I am become "guilty of his body and blood," 1 Cor. xi. 27;—that I should bring such dishonour upon religion too, by so unsuitable a walk, and perhaps open the mouths of its greatest enemies, to insult it upon my account, and prejudice some against it to their everlasting destruction!

I wonder, O Lord God, that I am here to own all this. I wonder that thou hast not long ago appeared "as a swift witness against me:" Mal. iii. 5: that thou hast not discharged the thunderbolts of thy flaming wrath against me, and crushed me into hell: making me there a terror to all about me as well as to myself, by a vengeance and ruin, to be distinguished even there, where all are miserable, and all hopeless.

O God, thy patience is marvellous, but how much more marvellous is thy grace, which, after all this, invites me to thee! While I am here giving judgment against myself that I deserve to die, to die for ever, thou art sending me the words of everlasting life, and "calling me, as a backsliding child, to return · unto thee," Jer. iii. 22. Behold, therefore, O Lord, invited by thy word, and encouraged by thy grace,

I come; and, great as my transgressions are, I humbly beseech thee freely to pardon them; because I know, that though my "sins have reached unto heaven," Rev. xviii. 5, and "are lifted up even to the skies," Jer. li. 9, "thy mercy, O Lord, is above the heavens," Psal. cviii. 4. Extend thy mercy to me, O heavenly Father; and display, in this illustrious instance, the riches of thy grace, and the prevalency of thy Son's blood. For surely, if such crimson sins as mine may be made "white as snow, and as wool," Isa. i. 18, and if such a revolter as I am, be brought to eternal glory, earth must, so far as it is known, be filled with wonder, and heaven with praise: and the greatest sinner may cheerfully apply for pardon, if I, the chief of sinners, find it. And, O, that when I have lain mourning, and, as it were, bleeding at thy feet, as long as thou thinkest proper, thou wouldst at length heal this soul of mine which hath sinned against thee, Psal. xli. 4, and "give me beauty for ashes, the oil of joy for mourning, and the garment of praise for the spirit of heaviness." Isa. lxi. 3. O that thou wouldst at length "restore unto me the joy of thy salvation, and make me to hear songs of gladness, that the bones which thou hast broken may yet rejoice," Psal. li. 8, 12. Then, when a sense of thy forgiving love is shed abroad upon my heart, and it is cheered with the voice of pardon, I will proclaim thy grace to others; " I will teach transgressors thy ways, and sinners shall be converted unto thee:" Psal. li. 13; those that have been backsliding from thee shall be encouraged to seek thee by my happy experience, which I shall gladly proclaim for thy glory, though it be to my own shame and confusion of face. And may this "joy of the Lord be my strength," Neh. viii. 10. So that in it I may serve thee henceforward with vigour and zeal far beyond what I have hitherto known!

This I would ask, with all humble submission to thy will; for I presume not to insist upon it. If thou shouldst see fit to make me a warning to others, by appointing that I should walk all my days in dark

ness, and at last die under a cloud, " thy will be oone."
But, O God, extend mercy for thy Son's sake, to this
sinful soul at last; and give me some place, though it
were at the feet of all thine other servants in the regions of glory! O bring me at length, though it
should be through the gloomiest valley that any have
ever passed, into that blessed world where I shall depart from God no more; where I shall wound my
own conscience and dishonour thy holy name no
more. Then shall my tongue be loosed, how long
soever it might here be bound under the confusion of
guilt; and immortal praises shall be paid to that victorious blood, which has redeemed such an infamous
slave of sin, as I must acknowledge myself to be,
and brought me, from returns into bondage and repeated pollution, to share the dignity and holiness of
those who are kings and priests unto God, Rev. i. 6
Amen.

CHAPTER XXIV.

THE CASE OF THE CHRISTIAN UNDER THE HIDINGS OF GOD'S FACE.

The phrase scriptural, 1. It signifies the withdrawing the tokens
of the divine favour, 2; chiefly as to spiritual considerations, 3.
This may become the case of any Christian, 4; and will be found
a very sorrowful one, 5. The following directions, therefore, are
given to those who suppose it to be their own:—I. To inquire
whether it be indeed a case of spiritual distress, or whether a disconsolate frame may not proceed from indisposition of body, 6; or
difficulties as to worldly circumstances, 7. If it be found to be
indeed such as the title of the chapter proposes, be advised. II
To consider it as a merciful dispensation of God, to awaken and
bestir the soul, and excite to a strict examination of conscience
and reformation of what has been amiss, 8, 9. III. To be humble
and patient while the trial continues, 10. IV. To go on steadily
in the way of duty, 11. V. To renew a believing application to
the blood of Jesus, 12. An humble supplication for one under
these mournful exercises of mind, when they are found to proceed
from the spiritual cause supposed.

1. THERE is a case which often occurs in the Christ
'an life, which they who accustom themselves much

to the exercise of devotion, have been used to cal!
hidings of God's face. It is a phrase borrowed from
the word of God, which I hope may shelter it from
contempt at the first hearing. It will be my business
in this chapter to state it as plainly as I can, and then
to give some advice as to your own conduct when
you fall into it, as it is very probable you may, before
you have finished your journey through this wilderness.

2. The meaning of it may partly be understood by
the opposite phrase of *God's causing his face to
shine* upon a person, or *lifting upon him the light
of his countenance.* This seems to carry in it an
allusion to the pleasant and delightful appearance
which the face of a friend has, and especially if in a
superior relation of life, when he converses with those
whom he loves and delights in. Thus Job, when
speaking of the regard paid him by his attendants,
says, "If I smiled upon them, they believed it not,
and the light of my countenance they cast not down;"
Job xxix. 24, that is, they were careful, in such an
agreeable circumstance, to do nothing to displease
me, or (as we speak) to cloud my brow. And
David, when expressing his desire of the manifes-
tation of God's favour to him, says, "Lord, lift thou
up the light of thy countenance upon me;" and, as
the effect of it, declares, "thou hast put gladness into
my heart more than if corn and wine increased,"
Psal. iv. 6, 7. Nor is it impossible that, in this phrase,
as used by David, there may be some allusion to the
bright shining forth of the Shechinah, that is, the
lustre which dwelt in the cloud as the visible sign of
the divine presence with Israel, which God was
pleased peculiarly to manifest upon some public occasions, as a token of his favour and acceptance.—On
the other hand, therefore, for God to hide his face,
must imply his withholding the tokens of his favour,
and must be esteemed a mark of his displeasure.
Thus *Isaiah* uses it; "Your iniquities have separated
between you and your God, and your sins have hid
his face from you, that he will not hear," Isa. lix. 4

And again, " Thou hast hid thy face from us," as not regarding the calamities we suffer, "and hast consumed us, because of our iniquities," Isa. lxiv. 7. So likewise for God " to hide his face from our sins," Psal. li. 9, signifies to overlook them, and to take no further notice of them. The same idea is, at other times, expressed by " God's hiding his eyes," Isa. i. 15, from persons of a character disagreeable to him when they come to address him with their petitions, not vouchsafing, as it were, to look towards them. This is plainly the scriptural sense of the word; and agreeably to this, it is generally used by Christians in our day, and every thing which seems a token of divine displeasure towards them is expressed by it.

3. It is further to be observed here, that the things which they judge to be manifestations of divine favour towards them, or complacency in them, are not only, nor chiefly, of a temporal nature, or such as merely relate to the blessings of this animal and perishing life. David, though the promises of the law had a continual reference to such, yet was taught to look further, and describes them as preferable to, and therefore plainly distinct from " the blessings of the corn-floor, or the wine-press." Psal. iv. 7. And if you, whom I am now addressing, do not know them to be so, it is plain you are quite ignorant of the subject we are inquiring into, and indeed have yet to learn the first lessons of true religion. All that David says of " beholding the beauty of the Lord," Psal. xxvii. 4, or being " satisfied as with marrow and fatness, when he remembered him upon his bed," Psal. lxiii. 5, 6, as well as " with the goodness of his house, even of his holy temple," ·Psal. lxv. 4, is to be taken in the same sense, and can need very little explication to the truly experienced soul. But those that have known the light of God's countenance, and the shinings of his face, will, in proportion to the degree of that knowledge, be able to form some notion of the hiding of his face, or the withdrawing of the tokens he has given his people of his presence and

favour, which sometimes greatly embitters prosperity, as where the contrary is found, it sweetens afflictions, and often swallows up the sense of it.

4. And give me leave to remind you, my Chris tian friend (for under that character I now address my reader) that to be thus deprived of the sense of God's love, and of the tokens of his favour, may soon be the case with you, though you may now have the pleasure to see " the candle of the Lord shining upon you," or though it may even seem to be sunshine and high noon in your soul. You may lose your lively views of the divine perfections, and glories, in the contemplation of which you now find that inward satisfaction. You may think of the divine wisdom and power, of the divine mercy and fidelity, as well as of his righteousness and holiness, and feel little inward complacency of soul in the view; it may be with respect to any lively impression, as if it were the contemplation merely of a common object. It may seem to you as if you had lost all idea of those important words, though the view has sometimes swallowed up your whole soul in transports of admi- ration, astonishment and love. You may lose your delightful sense of the divine favour. It may be matter of great and sad doubt with you, whether you do indeed belong to God; and all the work of his blessed Spirit may be so veiled and shaded in the soul, that the peculiar characters by which the hand of that sacred Agent might be distinguished, shall be in a great measure lost; and you may be ready to ima- gine you have only deluded yourself in all the former hopes you have entertained. In consequence of this, those ordinances, in which you now rejoice, may grow very uncomfortable to you, even when you do indeed desire communion with God in them. You may hear the most delightful evangelical truths open- ed, you may hear the privileges of God's children most affectionately represented, and not be aware that you have any part or lot in the matter; and from that very coldness and insensibility, may be drawing a further argument, that you have nothing to do with

them. And then your heart may meditate terror, Isa. xxxiii. 18; and under the distress that over- whelms you, your dearest enjoyments may be reflect- ed upon as adding to the weight of it, and making it more sensible, while you consider that you had once such a taste for these things, and have now lost it all. So that perhaps it may seem to you, that they who never felt any thing at all of religious impressions, are happier than you, or at least are less miserable. You may perhaps, in these melancholy hours, even doubt whether you have ever prayed at all; and whether all that you called your enjoyment of God were not some false delight, excited by the great enemy of souls, to make you apprehend that your state was good, that so you might continue his more secure prey.

5. Such as this may be your case for a consider- able time; and ordinances may be attended in vain, and the presence of God may be in vain sought in them. You may pour out your soul in private, and then come to public worship, and find little satisfac- tion in either; but be forced to take up the Psalmist's complaint; "My God, I cry in the day-time, but thou hearest not; and in the night-season, and am not silent;" Psal. xxii. 2, or that of Job, " Behold, I go forward, but he is not there, and backward, but I cannot perceive him; on the left hand where he doth work, but I cannot behold him; he hideth himself on the right hand that I cannot see him:' Job xxiii. 9. So that all which looked like religion in your mind shall seem, as it were, to be melted into grief, or chilled into fear, or crushed into a deep sense of your own unworthiness; in consequence of which you shall not dare so much as to lift up your eyes before God, and be almost ashamed to take your place in a worshipping assembly among any that you think his servants. I have known this to be the case of some excellent Christians, whose improvements in religion have been distinguished, and whom God has honoured above many of their brethren in what he has done for them, and by them. Give me leave,

therefore, having thus described it, to offer you some plain advices with regard to it; and let not that be imputed to enthusiastic fancy which proceeds from an intimate and frequent view of facts on the one hand, and from a sincere affectionate desire on the other, to relieve the tender pious heart in so desolate a state. At least, I am persuaded the attempt will not be overlooked or disapproved by "the great Shepherd of the sheep," Heb. xiii. 20, who hath charged us to "comfort the feeble minded," 1 Thess. v. 14.

6. And here I would first advise you most carefully to inquire whether your present distress does indeed arise from causes which are truly spiritual; or whether it may not rather have its foundation in some disorder of body, or in the circumstances of life, in which you are providentially placed, which may break your spirits, and deject your mind? The influence of the inferior part of our nature on the nobler, the immortal spirit, while we continue in this embodied state, is so evident, that no attentive person can, in the general, fail to have observed it; and yet there are cases in which it seems not to be sufficiently considered; and perhaps your own may be one of them. The state of the nerves is often such as necessarily to suggest gloomy ideas even in dreams, and to indispose the soul for taking pleasure in any thing: and when it is so, why should it be imagined to proceed from any peculiar divine displeasure, if it does not find its usual delight in religion? or why should God be thought to have departed from us, because he suffers natural causes to produce natural effects, without interposing by miracle to break the connexion? When this is the case, the help of the physician is to be sought rather than that of the divine, or, at least, by all means, together with it; and medicine, diet, exercise, and air, may, in a few weeks, effect that which the strongest reasonings, the most pathetic exhortations or consolations, might for many months have attempted in vain.

7. In other instances, the dejection and feebleness of the mind may arise from something uncomfortable

in our worldly circumstances; these may cloud as well as distract the thoughts, and embitter the temper, and thus render us in a great degree unfit for religious services or pleasures; and when it is so, the remedy is to be sought in submission to divine Providence; in abstracting our affections, as far as possible, from the present world; in a prudent care to ease ourselves of the burden, so far as we can, by moderating un-necessary expenses, and by diligent application to business in humble dependence on the divine bless-ing; in the mean time, endeavouring by faith to look up to him, who sometimes suffers his children to be brought into such difficulties, that he may endear himself more sensibly to them by the method he shall take for their relief.

8. On the principles here laid down, it may per-haps appear, on inquiry, that the distress complained of may have a foundation very different from what was at first supposed. But where the health is sound, and the circumstances easy; when the animal spirits are disposed for gaiety and entertainment, while all taste for religious pleasure is in a manner gone; when the soul is seized with a kind of lethargic insensibi-lity, or, what I had almost called a paralytic weak-ness, with respect to every religious exercise, even though there should not be that deep terrifying dis-tress, or pungent amazement, which I before repre-sented as the effect of melancholy; nor that anxiety about the accommodations of life, which strait cir-cumstances naturally produce: I would in that case vary my advice, and urge you, with all possible at-tention and impartiality, to search into the cause which has brought upon you that great evil, under which you justly mourn. And probably, in the ge-neral, the cause is sin; some secret sin, which has not been discovered or observed by the eye of the world; for enormities that draw on them the obser-vation and censure of others, will probably fall under the case mentioned in the former chapter, as they must be instances of known and deliberate guilt. Now, the eye of God has seen these evils which have

escaped the notice of your fellow creatures; and, in consequence of this care to conceal them from others, while you could not but know they were open to him, God has seen himself in a peculiar manner affronted and injured, I had almost said, insulted, by them; and hence his righteous displeasure. O! let that never be forgotten, which is so plainly said, so commonly known, so familiar to almost every religious ear, yet too little felt by any of our hearts. "Your iniquities have separated between you and your God, and your sins have hid his face from you that he will not hear," Isa. lix. 1, 2. And this is, on the whole, a merciful dispensation of God, though it may seem severe; regard it not, therefore, merely as your calamity, but as intended to awaken you, tha you may not content yourself even with lying in tears of humiliation before the Lord, but, like Joshua, rise and exert yourself vigorously to put away from you that accursed thing, whatever it be. Let this be your immediate and earnest care that your pride may be humbled, that your watchfulness may be maintained, that your affections to the world may be deadened, and that, on the whole, your fitness for heaven may in every respect be increased. These are the designs of your heavenly Father, and let it be your great concern to co-operate with them.

9. Receive it therefore, on the whole, as the most important advice that can be given you, "immediately to enter on a strict examination of your conscience."—Attend to its gentlest whispers. If a suspicion arises in your mind that any thing has not been right, trace that suspicion, search into every secret folding of your heart, improve to the purposes of a fuller discovery, the advice of your friends, the reproaches of your enemies: recollect for what your heart has smitten you at the table of the Lord; for what it would smite you if you were upon a dying bed, and within this hour to enter on eternity. When you have made any discovery, note it down, and go on in your search till you can say, "These are the remaining corruptions of my heart; these are the sins

and follies of my life; this have I neglected; this have I done amiss." And when the account is as complete as you can make it, set yourself, in the strength of God, to a strenuous reformation of every thing that seems amiss as soon as ever you discover it; " Return to the Almighty, and thou shalt be built up, and put iniquity far from thy tabernacle; then shalt thou have thy de-light in the Almighty, and shalt lift up thy face unto God. Thou shalt make thy prayer unto him, and he shall hear thee; thou shalt pay thy vows unto him, and his light shall shine upon thy ways," Job xxii. 23, 26, 27.

10. In the mean time, be waiting for God with the deepest humility, and submit yourself to the discipline of your heavenly Father, acknowledging his justice, and hoping in his mercy; even when your conscience is least severe in its remonstrances, and discovers nothing more than the common infirmities of God's people; yet still bow yourself down before him, and own, that so many are the evils of your best days, so many the imperfections of your best services, that by them you have deserved all, and more than all, that you suffer: deserved, not only that your sun should be clouded, but that it should go down, and arise no more, but leave your soul in a state of everlasting darkness. And while the shade continues, be not impatient. Fret not yourself in any wise, but rather with a holy calmness and gentleness of soul, " wait on the Lord," Psal. xxxvii. 8, 34. Be willing to stay his time, willing to bear his frown, in humble hope that he will at length " return and have compassion on you," Jer. xii. 15. He " has not utterly forgotten to be gracious, nor resolved that he will be favour-able no more," Psal. lxxvii. 7, 9. " For the Lord will not cast off for ever; but though he cause grief, yet will he have compassion according to the multi-tude of his mercies," Lam. iii. 31, 32. It is compa-ratively but for a small moment that he hides his face from you; but you may humbly hope, that with great mercies he will gather you, and that with ever-lasting kindness he will have mercy on you, Isa. liv.

7, 8. These suitable words are not mine, but nis, and they wear this as in the very front of them, " That a soul under the hidings of God's face may at ,east be one whom he will gather, and to whom he will extend everlasting favour."

11. But while the darkness continues, " go on in the way of your duty." Continue the use of means and ordinances: read, and meditate: pray, yea, and sing the praises of God too, though it may be with a heavy heart. Follow " the footsteps of his flock," Cant. i. 8; you may perhaps meet " the Shepherd of souls" in doing it. Place yourself at least in his way. It is possible you may by this means get a kind look from him; and one look, one turn of thought, which may happen in a moment, may, as it were, create a heaven in your soul at once. Go to the table of the Lord. If you cannot rejoice, go and mourn there. " Go and mourn that Saviour, whom by your sins you have pierced," Zech. xii. 10; go and lament the breaches of that covenant, which you have there so often confirmed. Christ may, perhaps, " make himself known unto you in the breaking of bread," Luke xxiv. 35; and you may find, to your surprise, that he has been near you, when you imagined he was at the greatest distance from you; near you, when you thought you were cast out from his presence. Seek your comfort in such enjoyments as these, and not in the vain amusements of this world, and in the pleasures of sense. I shall never forget that affectionate expression, which I am well assured broke out from an eminently pious heart, then almost ready to break under its sorrows of this kind: " Lord, if I may not enjoy thee, let me enjoy nothing else; but go down mourning after thee to the grave!" I wondered not to hear, that almost as soon as this sentiment had been breathed out before God in prayer, the burden was taken off, and the joy of God's salvation restored.

12. I shall add but one advice more, and that is, ' That you renew your application to the blood of fesus, through whom the reconciliation between God

and your soul has been accomplished." It is he that
is our peace, and by his blood it is that we are made
nigh, Eph. ii. 13, 14; it is in him, as the Beloved of
his soul, that God declares he is well pleased, Matt.
iii. 17; and it is in him that we are made accepted,
to the glory of his grace, Eph. i. 6.   Go, therefore, O
Christian, and apply by faith to a crucified Saviour:
go, and apply to him as to a merciful High Priest,
"and pour out thy complaint before him, and show
before him thy trouble," Psal. cxlii. 2.   Lay open
the distress and anguish of thy soul to him, who once
knew what it was to say, (O astonishing! that he of
all others should ever have said it,) "My God, my
God, why hast thou forsaken me?" Matt. xxvii. 46.
Look up for pity and relief to him, who himself suffered, being not only tempted, but with regard to
sensible manifestations, deserted, that he might thus
know how to pity those that are in such a melancholy case, and be ready, as well as "able, to suc-
cour them," Heb. ii. 18.   He is "Emmanuel, God
with us," Matt. i. 23; and it is only in and through
him, that his Father shines forth upon us with the
mildest beams of mercy and of love.   Let it be, therefore, your immediate care to renew your acquaintance with him.   Review the records of his life and
death: hear his words: behold his actions: and when
you do so, surely you will find a secret sweetness
diffusing itself over your soul.   You will be brought
into a calm, gentle, silent frame, in which faith and
love will operate powerfully, and God may probably
cause the still small voice of his comforting Spirit to
be heard, 1 Kings xix. 12, till your soul bursts out
into a song of praise, and you may be "made glad,
according to the days in which you have been afflicted," Psal. xc. 15.   In the mean time, such language as the following supplication speaks, may be
suitable.

A HUMBLE SUPPLICATION FOR ONE UNDER THE HIDINGS
OF GOD'S FACE.

Blesssed God! " with thee is the fountain of life,"
Psal. xxxvi. 9, and of happiness. I adore thy name,
that I have ever tasted of thy streams; that I have
ever felt the peculiar pleasure arising from the light
of thy countenance, and the shedding abroad of thy
love in my soul. But, alas! these delightful seasons
are now to me no more; and the " remembrance of
them engages me to pour out my soul within me,"
Psal. xlii. 4. I would come, as I have formerly
done, and call thee, with the same endearment, my
Father and my God: but, alas! I know not how to
do it. Guilt and fears arise, and forbid the delightful
language. I seek thee, O Lord, but I seek thee in
vain. I would pray, but my lips are sealed up. I
would read thy word, but all the promises of it are
veiled from mine eyes. I frequent those ordinances,
which have been formerly most nourishing and comfortable to my soul; but, alas! they are only the shadows of ordinances: the substance is gone: the animating spirit is fled, and leaves them now at best but
the image of what I once knew them.

But, Lord, " hast thou cast off for ever, and wilt
thou be favourable no more?" Psal. lxxvii. 7. Hast
thou in awful judgment determined that my soul
must be left to a perpetual winter, the sad emblem
of eternal darkness? Indeed, I deserve it should be
so. I acknowledge, O Lord, I deserve to be cast
away from thy presence with disdain; to be sunk
lower than I am, much lower: I deserve to have the
" shadow of death upon mine eyelids," Job xvi. 16,
and even to be surrounded with the thick gloom of
the infernal prison. But hast thou not raised multitudes, who have deserved, like me, " to be delivered
into chains of darkness," 2 Pet. ii. 4, to the visions
of thy glory above, where no cloud can ever inter
pose between thee and their rejoicing spirits? " Have
mercy upon me, O Lord, have mercy upon me,"
Psal. cxxiii. 3; and though mine iniquities have now

justly " caused thee to hide thy face from me," Isa.
lix. 2, yet be thou rather pleased, agreeably to the
gracious language of thy word, to " hide thy face
from my sins, and to blot out all mine iniquities,"
Psal. li. 9. Cheer my heart with the tokens of thy
returning favour, and " say unto my soul, I am thy
salvation," Psal. xxxv. 3.

Remember, O Lord God, remember that dreadful
day in which Jesus thy dear Son endured what my
sins have deserved! Remember that agony, in which
he poured out his soul before thee, and said, " My
God, my God, why hast thou forsaken me?" Matt.
xxvii. 46. Did he not, O Lord, endure all this, that
humble penitents might through him be brought near
unto thee, and might behold thee with pleasure, as
their Father and their God? Thus do I desire to
come unto thee, blessed Saviour; art thou not appointed " to give unto them that mourn in Zion beauty for ashes, the oil of joy for mourning, and the garment of praise for the spirit of heaviness," Isa. lxi.
3.—O wash away my tears, anoint my head with
the oil of gladness, and clothe me with the garments
of salvation, Isa. lxi. 10.

" O that I knew where I might find thee," Job
xxiii. 3.—O that I knew what it is that has engaged
thee to depart from me! I am " searching and try-
ing my ways," Lam. iii. 40. O that thou wouldst
" search me, and know my heart: try me, and know
my thoughts; and if there be any wicked way in me,
discover it, and lead me in the way everlasting,"
Psal. cxxxix. 23, 24, in that way in which I may find
rest and peace for my soul, Jer. vi. 16, and feel the
discoveries of thy love in Christ!

O God, " who didst command the light to shine
out of darkness," 2 Cor. iv. 6, speak but the word,
and light shall dart into my soul at once! " Open thou
my lips, and my mouth shall show forth thy praise,"
Psal. li. 15, shall burst out into a cheerful song, which
shall display before those whom my present dejections
may have discouraged, the pleasures and supports of
religion!

Yet, Lord, on the whole, I submit to thy will.   If it is thus that my faith must be exercised, by walking in darkness for days, and months, and years to come, how long soever they may seem, how long soever they may be, I will submit.   Still will I adore thee as "the God of Israel, and the Saviour, though thou art a God that hidest thyself," Isa. xiv. 15; still will "I trust in the name of the Lord, and stay myself upon my God," Isa. l. 10, "trusting in thee, though thou slay me," Job xiii. 15, and "waiting for thee more than they that watch for the morning, yea, more than they that watch for the morning," Psal. cxxx. 6.   Peradventure "in the evening time it may be light," Zech. xiv. 7.   I know that thou hast some-times manifested thy compassions to thy dying ser-vants, and given them, in the lowest ebb of their na-tural spirits, a full tide of divine glory, thus turning "darkness into light before them," Isa. xlii. 16.   So may it please thee to gild the valley of the shadow of death with the light of thy presence, when I am passing through it, and to stretch forth "thy rod and thy staff to comfort me," Psal. xxiii. 4, that my trem-blings may cease, and the gloom may echo with songs of praise!   But if it be thy sovereign pleasure that distress and darkness should still continue to the last motion of my pulse, and the last gasp of my breath, O let it cease with the parting struggle and bring me to that "light which is sown for the righteous, and to that gladness which is reserved for the upright in heart," Psal. xcvii. 11, to the unclouded regions of everlasting splendour and joy, where the full anoint-ings of the Spirit shall be poured out on all thy peo-ple, and thou wilt no more "hide thy face from any of them!" Ezek. xxxix. 29.

This, "Lord, is thy salvation, for which I am wait-ing," Gen. xlix. 18, and whilst I feel the desires of my soul drawn out after it, I will never despair of obtaining it.   Continue and increase those desires, and at length satisfy and exceed them all, "through the riches of thy grace in Christ Jesus!"   Amen.

CHAPTER XXV.

THE CHRISTIAN STRUGGLING UNDER GREAT AND HEAVY AFFLICTIONS.

Here it is advised, (1.) That afflictions should be expected, 1. (2.) That the righteous hand of God should be acknowledged in them when they come, 2. (3.) That they should be borne with patience, 3. (4.) That the divine conduct in them should be cordially approved, 4. (5.) That thankfulness should be maintained in the midst of trials, 5. (6.) That the design of afflictions should be diligently inquired into, and all proper assistance taken in discovering it, 6, (7.) That when it is discovered, it should humbly be complied with and answered, 7. A prayer suited to such a case.

1. SINCE "man is born unto trouble as the sparks fly upward," Job v. 7, and Adam has entailed on all his race the sad inheritance of calamity in their way to death, it will certainly be prudent and necessary that we should all expect to meet with trials and afflictions; and that you, reader, whoever you are, should be endeavouring to gird on your armour, and put yourself into a posture to encounter those trials which will fall to your lot as a man, and a Christian. Prepare yourself to receive your afflictions, and to endure them, in a manner agreeable to both those characters.   In this view, when you see others under the burden, consider how possible it is that you may be called out to the very same difficulties, or to others equal to them. Put your soul as in the place of theirs. Think how you could endure the load under which they lie; and endeavour at once to comfort them, and to strengthen your own heart; or rather, pray that God would do it.   And observing how liable mortal life is to such sorrows, moderate your expectations from it; raise your thoughts above it; and form your schemes of happiness only for that world where they cannot be disappointed: in the mean time, blessing God, that your prosperity is lengthened out thus far and ascribing it to his special providence that you continue so long unwounded, when so many showers

of arrows are flying around you, and so many are
falling by them on the right hand and on the left.

2. When at length your turn comes, as it certainly
will, from the first hour in which an affliction seizes
you, realize to yourself the hand of God in it, and
lose not the view of him in any second cause, which
may have proved the immediate occasion. Let it be
your first care " to humble yourself under the mighty
hand of God, that he may exalt you in due time," 1
Pet. v. 6. Own, that " he is just in all that is brought
upon you," Neh. ix. 33, and " that in all these things
he punishes you less than your iniquities deserve,"
Ezra ix. 13. Compose yourself to bear his hand with
patience, to glorify his name by a submission to his
will, and to fall in with the gracious design of this
visitation, as well as to wait the issue of it quietly,
whatever the event may be.

3. Now that " patience may have its perfect work,"
James i. 4, reflect frequently and deeply upon your
own meanness and sinfulness. Consider how often
every mercy has been forfeited, and every judgment
deserved. And consider too, how long the patience
of God has borne with you, and how wonderfully it
is still exerted towards you; and, indeed, not only his
patience, but his bounty too. Afflicted as you are,
(for I speak to you now as actually under the pres-
sure,) look round and survey your remaining mercies,
and be gratefully sensible of them. Make the supposition of their being removed: what if God should
stretch out his hand against you, and add poverty to
pain, or pain to poverty, or the loss of friends to both;
or the death of surviving friends to that of those whom
you are now mourning over; would not the wound
be more grievous? Adore his goodness that this is
not the case: and take heed, lest your unthankfulness
should provoke him to multiply your sorrows. Consider also the need you have of discipline; how
wholesome it may prove to your soul, and what merciful designs our heavenly Father has in all the cor-
rections he sends upon his children.

4. Nay, I will add that, in consequence of all these

considerations, it may well be expected, not only that you should submit to your afflictions, as what you cannot avoid, but that you should sweetly acquiesce in them, approve them; that you should not only justify, but glorify God, in sending them; that you should glorify him with your heart, and with your lips too. Think not praise unsuitable on such an occasion; nor think that praise alone to be suitable which takes its rise from remaining comforts: but know that it is your duty, not only to be thankful in your afflictions, but to be thankful on account of them.

5. God himself has said, " In every thing give thanks;" 1 Thess. v. 18, and he has taught his servants to say, " Yea also we glory in tribulation," Rom. v. 3. And most certain it is, that to true believers they are instances of divine mercy; for " whom the Lord loveth he chasteneth, and scourgeth every son whom he receiveth" with peculiar and distinguishing endearment, Heb. xii. 6. View your present afflictions in this light as chastisements of love; and then let your own heart say, whether love does not demand praise. Think with yourself, it is thus that God is making me conformable to his own Son; it is thus that he is training me up for complete glory. Thus he kills my corruptions; thus he strengthens my graces; thus he is wisely contriving to bring me nearer to himself, and to ripen me for the honours of his heavenly kingdom. It is "if need be," that I am in heaviness; 1 Pet. i. 6, and he surely knows what that need is better than I can pretend to teach him; and knows what peculiar propriety there is in this affliction to answer my present necessity, and do me that peculiar good which he is graciously intending me by it. " This tribulation shall work patience, and patience experience, and experience a more assured hope; even a hope which shall not make ashamed, while the love of God is shed abroad in my heart," Rom. v. 3, 4, 5, and shines through my affliction like the sun through a gently descending

cloud, darting in light upon the shade, and mingling fruitfulness with weeping.

6. Let it be then your earnest care, while you thus look on your affliction, whatever it may be, as coming from the hand of God, to improve it to the purposes for which it was sent. And that you may so improve it, let it be your first concern to know what those purposes are. Summon up all the attention of your soul to "hear the rod, and him who hath appointed it;" Mic. vi. 9, and pray earnestly that you may understand its voice. Examine your life, your words, and your heart; and pray, that God would so guide your inquiries, that you may return unto the Lord that smiteth you, Isa. ix. 13. To assist you in this, call in the help of pious friends, and particularly of your minister: entreat not only their prayers but their advices too, as to the probable design of Providence; and encourage them freely to tell you any thing which occurs to their minds upon this head. And if such an occasion should lead them to touch upon some of the imperfections of your character and conduct, look upon it as a great token of their friendship, and take it not only patiently but thankfully. It does but ill become a Christian at any time to resent reproofs and admonitions, and least of all does it become him when the rebukes of his heavenly Father are upon him: he ought rather to seek admonitions at such a time as this, and voluntarily to offer his wounds to be searched by a faithful and skilful hand.

7. And when, by one means or another, you have got a ray of light to direct you in the meaning and language of such dispensations, take heed that you do not in any degree, "harden yourself against God, and walk contrary to him," Lev. xxvi. 27. Obstinate reluctance to the apprehended design of any provi dential stroke is inexpressibly provoking to him. Se yourself therefore to an immediate reformation of whatever you discover amiss; and labour to learr 'he general lessons of greater submission to God's

will, of a more calm indifference to the world, and of a closer attachment to divine converse, and to the views of an approaching invisible state. And what-ever particular proportion or correspondence you may observe between this or that circumstance in your affliction and your former transgressions, be especial-ly careful to act according to that more peculiar and express voice of the rod. Then you may perhaps have speedy and remarkable reason to say, that " it hath been good for you, that you have been afflict-ed;" Psal. cxix. 71, and, with a multitude of others, may learn to number the times of your sharpest trials, among the sweetest and the most exalted mo-ments of your life. For this purpose, let prayer be your frequent employment; and let such sentiments as these, if not in the very same terms, be often and affectionately poured out before God.

AN HUMBLE ADDRESS TO GOD UNDER THE PRESSURE OF HEAVY AFFLICTION.

O thou supreme, yet all-righteous and gracious Governor of the whole universe! Mean and incon-siderable as this little province of thy spacious em-pire may appear, thou dost not disregard the earth and its inhabitants: but attendest to its concerns with the most condescending and gracious regard. " Thou reignest, and I rejoice in it," as it is indeed matter of universal joy, Psal. xcvii. 1. I believe thy uni versal providence and care; and I firmly believe thy wise, holy, and kind interposition in every thing which relates to me, and to the circumstances of my abode in this thy world. I would look through all inferior causes unto thee, whose eyes are upon all thy creatures; to thee " who formest the light, and createst darkness, who makest peace, and createst evil;" Isa. xlv. 7, to thee, Lord, who, at thy plea-sure, canst exchange the one for the other, canst turn the brightest noon into midnight, and the darkest midnight into noon.

O thou wise and merciful Governor of the world!
I have often said " Thy will be done:" and now thy
will is painful to me. But shall I, upon that account,
unsay what I have so often said? God forbid. I come
rather to lay myself down at thy feet, and to declare
my full and free submission to all thy sacred pleasure. O Lord, thou art just and righteous in all! I
acknowledge, in thy venerable and awful presence,
that I have deserved this, and ten thousand times
more; Ezra ix. 13. I acknowledge, that " it is of thy
mercy that I am not utterly consumed," Lam. iii. 22,
and that any the least degree of comfort yet remains.
O Lord, I most readily confess, that the sins of one
day of my life have merited all these chastisements;
and that every day of my life hath been more or
less sinful. Smite therefore, O thou righteous Judge!
and I will still adore thee, that instead of the scourge,
thou hast not given a commission to the sword, to do
all the dreadful work of justice, and to pour out my
blood in thy presence.

But shall I speak unto thee only as my Judge? O
Lord, thou hast taught me a tender name: thou con-
descendest to call thyself my Father, and to speak
of correction as the effect of thy love. O welcome,
welcome, those afflictions which are the tokens of
thy paternal affection, the marks of my adoption into
thy family! Thou knowest what discipline I need;
thou seest, O Lord, that bundle of folly which there
is in the heart of thy poor, froward and thoughtless
child; and knowest what rods, and what strokes are
needful to drive it away. I would therefore " be in
humble subjection to the Father of spirits," who
" chasteneth me for my profit;" would be in subjection to him, and live, Heb. xii. 9, 10. I would
bear thy strokes, not merely because I cannot resist
them, but because I love and trust in thee. I would
sweetly acquiesce and rest in thy will, as well as
stoop to it; and would say, " Good is the word of the
Lord," 2 Kings xx. 19. And I desire, that not only my
lips but my soul may acquiesce. Yea, Lord, I would
praise thee, that thou wilt show so much regard to

me as to apply such remedies as these to the diseases of my mind, and art thus kindly careful to train me up for glory. I have no objection against being afflicted, against being afflicted in this particular way; " The cup which my Father puts into my mine hand, shall I not drink it?" John xviii. 11. By thine assistance and support I will. Only be pleased, O Lord, to stand by me, and sometimes to grant me a favourable look in the midst of my sufferings. Support my soul, I beseech thee, by thy consolations mingled with my tribulations; and I shall glory in those tribulations that are thus allayed. It has been the experience of many who have reflected on afflicted days with pleasure, and have acknowledged that their comforts have swallowed up their sorrows. And after all that thou hast done, " are thy mercies restrained?" Isa. lxiii. 15. " Is thy hand waxed short?" Numb. xi. 23, or canst thou not still do the same for me?

If my heart be less tender, less sensible, thou canst cure that disorder, and canst make this affliction the means of curing it. Thus let it be; and at length, in thine own due time, and in the way which thou shalt choose, work out deliverance for me; and " show me thy marvellous loving kindness, O thou that savest by thy right hand them that put their trust in thee," Psal. xvii. 7. For I well know, that how dark soever this night of affliction seems, if thou sayest, " Let there be light, there shall be light." But I would urge nothing before the time thy wisdom and goodness shall appoint. I am much more concerned that my afflictions may be sanctified than that they may be removed. Number me, O God, among the " happy persons, whom" whilst " thou chastenest," thou " teachest out of thy law!" Psal. xciv. 12. Show me, I beseech thee, " wherefore thou contendest with me;" Job x. 2, and purify me by the fire, which is so painful to me while I am passing through it! Dost thou not " chasten thy children" for this very end, " that they may be partakers of thy holiness!" Heb. xii. 10. Thou knowest, O God, it is this my

23

soul is breathing after. I am partaker of thy bounty every day and moment of my life; I am partaker of thy gospel, and, I hope, in some measure too, a partaker of the grace of it operating on my heart. O may it operate more and more, that I may largely partake of thine holiness too; that I may come nearer and nearer in the temper of my mind to thee, O blessed God, the supreme model of perfection. Let my soul be, as it were, melted, though with the intensest heat of the furnace, if I may but thereby be made fit for being delivered into the mould of the gospel, and bearing thy bright and amiable image!

O Lord " my soul longeth for thee; it crieth out for the living God!" Psal. lxxxiv. 2. In thy presence, and under the support of thy love, I can bear any thing; and am willing to bear it, if I may grow more lovely in thine eyes, and more meet for thy kingdom. The days of my affliction will have an end; the hour will at length come, when " thou wilt wipe away all my tears," Rev. xxi. 4. Though it tarry, I would " wait for it," Heb. ii. 3. My foolish heart, in the midst of all its trials, is ready to grow fond of this earth, disappointing and grievous as it is: and graciously, O God, dost thou deal with me in breaking those bonds that would tie me faster to it. O let my soul be girding itself up, and, as it were, stretching its wings, in expectation of that blessed hour, when it shall drop all its sorrows and incumbrances at once, and soar away to expatiate with infinite delight in the regions of liberty, peace, and joy! Amen.

CHAPTER XXVI

THE CHRISTIAN ASSISTED IN EXAMINING INTO HIS GROWTH IN GRACE.

The examination important, 1.	False marks of growth to be avoid
ed, 2.	True marks proposed: such as, (1.) Increasing love to
God, 3.	(2.) Benevolence to men, 4.	(3.) Candour of disposi-
tion, 5.	(4) Meekness under injuries, 6.	(5.) Serenity amidst
the uncertainties of life, 7.	(6.) Humility, 8, especially as ex-
pressed in evangelical exercises of mind towards Christ and the
Spirit, 9.	(7.) Zeal for the divine honour, 10.	(8.) Habitual and
cheerful willingness to exchange worlds, whenever God shall appoint, 11. Conclusion, 12. The Christian breathing after growth
in grace.

1. If by divine grace you have been " born again,
not of corruptible seed, but of incorruptible," 1 Pet.
i. 2, 3, even " by that word of God, which liveth and
abideth for ever," not only in the world, and in the
church, but in particular souls in which it is sown;
you will, " as new-born babes, desire the sincere milk
of the word, that you may grow thereby," 1 Pet. ii.
2.	And though, in the most advanced state of reli-
gion on earth, we are but infants in comparison of
what we hope to be, when in the heavenly world we
arrive " unto a perfect man, unto the measure of the
stature of the fulness of Christ;" Eph. iv. 13, yet, as
we have some exercise of a sanctified reason, we
shall be solicitous that we may be growing and
thriving.	And you, my reader, if " so be that you
have tasted that the Lord is gracious," 1 Pet. ii. 3,
will, I doubt not, feel this solicitude.	I would
therefore endeavour to assist you in making the inquiry, whether religion be on the advance in your
soul.	And here I shall warn you against some false
marks of growth; and then shall endeavour to lay
down others on which you may depend as more
solid.—In this view, I would observe, that you are
not to measure your growth in grace only, or chiefly,
by your advances in knowledge, or in zeal, or any

other passionate impression of the mind; no, nor b,
the fervour of devotion alone; but by the habitual de
termination of the will for God, and by your prevail
mg disposition to obey his commands, to submit to
his disposal, and to promote his cause in the world.

2. It must be allowed, that knowledge and affec
tion in religion are indeed desirable.   Without some
degree of the former, religion cannot be rational; and
it is very reasonable to believe, that without some de
gree of the latter it cannot be sincere, in creatures
whose natures are constituted like ours.   Yet there
may be a great deal of speculative knowledge, and
a great deal of rapturous affection, where there
is no true religion at all; and therefore much more,
where there is no advanced state of it.—The ex-
crcise of our rational faculties upon the evidences
of divine revelation, and upon the declaration of it
as contained in Scripture, may furnish a very wicked
man with a well-digested body of orthodox divinity
in his head, when not one single doctrine of it has
ever reached his heart.   An eloquent description of
the sufferings of Christ, of the solemnities of judgment, of the joys of the blessed, and the miseries of
the damned, might move the breast even of a man
who did not firmly believe them; as we often find
ourselves strongly moved by well-wrought narrations,
or discourses, which at the same time, we know to
have their foundation in fiction.   Natural constitution, or such accidental causes as are, some of them,
too low to be here mentioned, may supply the eyes
with a flood of tears, which may discharge itself
plenteously upon almost any occasion that shall first
arise.   And a proud impatience of contradiction, directly opposite as it is to the gentle spirit of Christianity, may make a man's blood boil when he hears
the notions he has entertained, and especially those
which he has openly and vigorously espoused, disputed and opposed.   This may possibly lead him, in
terms of strong indignation, to pour out his zeal and
his rage before God in a fond conceit, that, as the
God of truth, he is the patron of those favourite doc

t/ines, by whose fair appearances perhaps he himself
is misled.—And if these speculative refinements, or
these affectionate sallies of the mind, be consistent
with a total absence of true religion, they are much
more evidently consistent with a very low state of
it. I would desire to lead you, my friend, into sub-
limer notions and juster marks: and refer you to other
practical writers, and, above all, to the book of God
to prove how material they are. I would therefore
entreat you to bring your own heart to answer, as in
the presence of God, to such inquiries as these:

3. Do you find "divine love, on the whole, advancing in your soul?"—Do you feel yourself more
and more sensible of the presence of God? and does
that sense grow more delightful to you than it formerly was? Can you, even when your natural spirits are weak and low, and you are not in any frame
for the ardours and ecstasies of devotion, nevertheless find a pleasing rest, a calm repose of heart, in the
thought that God is near you, and that he sees the
secret sentiments of your soul, while you are, as it
were, labouring up the hill, and casting a longing eye
towards him, though you cannot say you enjoy any
sensible communications from him? Is it agreeable
to you to open your heart to his inspection and regard? to present it to him laid bare of every disguise,
and to say with David, "Thou, Lord, knowest thy
servant?" 2 Sam. vii. 20. Do you find a growing
esteem and approbation of that sacred law of God,
which is the transcript of his moral perfections? Do
you inwardly "esteem all his precepts concerning all
things to be right?" Ps. cxix. 128. Do you discern,
not only the necessity, but the reasonableness, the
beauty, the pleasure, of obedience; and feel a growing scorn and contempt for those things which may
be offered as the price of your innocence, and would
tempt you to sacrifice or to hazard your interest in the
divine favour and friendship? Do you find an ingen
uous desire to please God, not only because he is so
powerful, and has so many good, and so many evil
things entirely at his command, but from a veneration

23*

of his most amiable nature and character; and do you find your heart habitually reconciled to a most humble subjection, both to his commanding and to his disposing will? Do you perceive that your own will is now more ready and disposed in every circumstance, to bear the yoke, and to submit to the divine determination, whatever he appoints to be borne or forborne? Can you "in patience possess your soul?" Luke xxi. 19. Can you maintain a more steady calmness and serenity when God is striking at your dearest enjoyments in this world, and acting most directly contrary to your present interests, to your natural passions and desires? If you can, it is a most certain and noble sign that grace is growing up in you to a very vigorous state.

4. Examine also, "what affections you find in your heart towards those who are round about you, and towards the rest of mankind in general."—Do you find your heart overflow with undissembled and un-restrained benevolence? Are you more sensible than you once were of those many endearing bonds which unite all men, and especially all Christians, into one community; which make them brethren and fellow-citizens? Do all the unfriendly passions die and wither in your soul, while the kind social affections grow and strengthen? And though self-love was never the reigning passion since you became a true Christian, yet as some remainders of it are still too ready to work inwardly, and to show themselves, especially as sudden occasions arise, do you perceive that you get ground of them? Do you think of yourself only as one of a great number, whose particular interests and concerns are of little importance when compared with those of the community, and ought by all means, on all occasions to be sacrificed to them?

5. Reflect especially "on the temper of your mind towards those whom an unsanctified heart might be ready to imagine it had some just excuse for excepting out of the list of those it loves, and towards whom you are ready to feel a secret aversion, or at least an

alienation from them."—How does your mind stand affected towards those who differ from you in their religious sentiments and practices? I do not say that Christian charity will require you to think every error harmless. It argues no want of love to a friend in some cases to fear lest his disorder should prove more fatal than he seems to imagine; nay, sometimes the very tenderness of friendship may increase that apprehension. But to hate persons because we think they are mistaken, and to aggravate every difference in judgment or practice, into a fatal and damnable error, that destroys all Christian communion and love, is a symptom generally much worse than the evil it condemns. Do you love the image of Christ in a person who thinks himself obliged in conscience to profess and worship in a manner different from yourself? Nay further, can you love and honour that which is truly amiable and excellent in those in whom much is defective; in those in whom there is a mixture of bigotry and narrowness of spirit, which may lead them perhaps to slight, or even to censure you? Can you love them as the disciples and servants of Christ, who, through a mistaken zeal, may be ready to " cast out your name as evil," Luke vi. 22, and to warn others against you as a dangerous person? This is none of the least triumphs of charity, nor any despicable evidence of an advance in religion.

6. And, on this head, reflect further, " how can you bear injuries?"—There is a certain hardness of soul in this respect, which argues a confirmed state in piety and virtue. Does every thing of this kind hurry and ruffle you, so as to put you on contrivances how you may recompense, or, at least, how you may disgrace and expose him who has done you the wrong? Or can you stand the shock calmly, and easily divert your mind to other objects, only (when you recollect these things) pitying and praying for those who, with the worst tempers and views, are assaulting you? This is a Christ-like temper indeed, and he will own it as such; will own you as one of his soldiers, as one of his heroes especially if it rises

so far, as instead of " being overcome of evil, to over come evil with good," Rom. xii. 21.   Watch over your spirit, and over your tongue, when injuries are offered; and see whether you be ready to meditate upon them, to aggravate them to yourself, to complain of them to others, and to lay on all the load of blame that you in justice can: or whether you be ready to put the kindest construction upon the offence, to excuse it as far as reason will allow, and, where, after all, it will wear a black and odious aspect, to forgive it, heartily to forgive it, and that even before any submission is made or pardon asked; and in token of the sincerity of that forgiveness, to be contriving what can be done, by some benefit or other toward the injurious person to teach him better temper.

7. Examine further " with regard to the other evils and calamities of life, and even with regard to its uncertainties, how can you bear them?—Do you find your soul in this respect gathering strength?   Have you fewer foreboding fears and disquieting alarms than you once had as to what may happen in life? Can you trust the wisdom and goodness of God to order your affairs for you, with more complacency and cheerfulness than formerly?   Do you find you are able to unite your thoughts more in surveying present circumstances. that you may collect immediate duty from them, though you know not what God will next appoint or call you to?   And when you feel the smart of affliction, do you make a less matter of it?   Can you transfer your heart more easily to heavenly and divine objects, without an anxious solicitude, whether this or that burden be removed, so it may be but sanctified to promote your communion with God, and your ripeness for glory?

8. Examine also, " whether you advance in humility."—This is a silent, but most excellent grace; and they who are most eminent in it, are dearest to God, and most fit for the communications of his presence to them.   Do you then feel your mind more emptied of proud and haughty imaginations; not

prone so much to look back upon past services which it has performed, as forward to those which are yet before you, and inward upon the remaining imperfections of your heart? Do you more tenderly observe your daily slips and miscarriages, and find yourself disposed to mourn over those things before the Lord, that once passed with you as slight matters; though when you come to survey them as in the presence of God, you find they were not wholly involuntary, or free from guilt? Do you feel in your breast a deeper apprehension of the infinite majesty of the blessed God, and of the glory of his natural and moral perfections; so as, in consequence of those views, to perceive yourself as it were annihilated in his presence, and to shrink into "less than nothing and vanity?" Isa. xl. 17. If this be your temper, God will look upon you with peculiar favour, and will visit you more and more with the distinguished blessings of his grace.

9. But there is another great branch and effect of Christian humility, which it would be an unpardonable negligence to omit. Let me, therefore, further inquire, Are you more frequently renewing your application, your sincere, steady, determined application, to the righteousness and blood of Christ, as being sensible how unworthy you are to appear before God otherwise than in him? And do the remaining corruptions of your heart humble you before him, though the disorders of your life are in a great measure cured? Are you more earnest to obtain the quickening influences of the Holy Spirit? and have you such a sense of your own weakness, as to engage you to depend, in all the duties you perform, upon the communications of his grace to "help your infirmities?" Rom. viii. 26. Can you, at the close of your most religious, exemplary, and useful days, blush before God for the deficiencies of them, while others perhaps may be ready to admire and extol your conduct? And while you give the glory of all that has been right to Him from whom the strength and grace has been derived, are you coming to the

blood of sprinkling to free you from the guilt which
mingles itself even with the best of your services?
Do you learn to receive the bounties of Providence,
not only with thankfulness as coming from God, but
with a mixture of shame and confusion too, under a
consciousness that you do not deserve them, and are
continually forfeiting them? And do you justify
Providence in your afflictions and disappointments,
even while many are flourishing around you in the
full bloom of prosperity, whose offences have been
more visible at least, and more notorious than yours?

10. Do you also advance in " zeal and activity for
the service of God, and the happiness of mankind?"
Does your love show itself solid and sincere, by a continual flow of good works from it? Can you view the
sorrows of others with tender compassion, and with
projects and contrivances what you may do to relieve
them? Do you feel in your breast that you are more
frequently "devising liberal things," Isa. xxxii. 8, and
ready to wave your own advantage or pleasure that
you may accomplish them? Do you find your imagination teeming, as it were, with conceptions and schemes
for the advancement of the cause and interest of
Christ in the world, for the propagation of his gospel,
and for the happiness of your fellow-creatures? And
do you not only pray, but act for it; act in such a
manner as to show that you pray in earnest; and feel
a readiness to do what little you can in this cause,
even though others who might, if they pleased, very
conveniently do a vast deal more, will do nothing?

11. And not to enlarge on this copious head, reflect once more, " how your affections stand with regard to this world and another"—Are you more
deeply and practically convinced of the vanity of
these " things which are seen and are temporal?" 2
Cor. iv. 18. Do you perceive your expectations from
them, and your attachments to them, to diminish? You
are willing to stay in this world as long as your Father pleases, and it is right and well: but do you find
your bonds so loosened to it, that you are willing,
heartily willing, to leave it at the shortest warning:

so that if God should see fit to summon you away on a sudden, though it should be in the midst of your enjoyments, pursuits, expectations, and hopes, you would cordially consent to that remove; without say· ing, Lord, let me stay a little while longer to enjoy this or that agreeable entertainment, to finish this or that scheme? Can you think with an habitual calmness, and hearty approbation, if such be the divine pleasure, of waking no more when you lie down on your bed, of returning home no more when you go out of your house? And yet, on the other hand, how great soever the burdens of life are, do you find a willingness to bear them, in submission to the will of your heavenly Father, though it should be to many future years; and though they should be years of far greater affliction than you have ever yet seen? Can you say calmly and steadily, if not with such overflowings of tender affection as you could desire, " Behold thy servant, thy child, is in thine hand, do with me as seemeth good in thy sight!" 2 Sam. xv. 26. My will is melted into thine, to be lifted up, or laid down, to be carried out, or brought in, to be here or there, in this or that circumstance, just as thou pleas· est, and as shall best suit with thy great extensive plan, which it is impossible that I, or all the angels in heaven, should mend.

12. These, if I understand matters right, are some of the most substantial evidences of growth and esta- blishment in religion. Search after them: bless God for them, so far as you discover them in yourself; and study to advance in them daily, under the influ- ences of divine grace, to which I heartily recommend you, and to which I entreat you frequently to recom- mend yourself.

THE CHRISTIAN BREATHING EARNESTLY AFTER GROWTH IN GRACE.

O thou ever blessed Fountain of natural and spi- ritual life! I thank thee that I live, and know the exercises and pleasures of a religious life. I bless thee that thou hast infused into me thine own vital breath, though I was once " dead in trespasses and sins," Eph. ii. 1, so that I am become in a sense peculiar to thine own children, " a living soul," Gen. ii. 7. But it is my earnest desire, that I may not only live, but grow; " grow in grace, and in the knowledge of my Lord and Saviour Jesus Christ," 2 Pet iii. 18, upon an acquaintance with whom my progress in it so evidently depends! In this view, I humbly entreat thee, that thou wilt form my mind to right notions in religion, that I may not judge of grace by any wrong conceptions of it, nor measure my advances in it by those things which are merely the effects of nature, and possibly its corrupt effects!

May I be seeking after an increase of divine love to thee, my God and Father in Christ: of unreserved resignation to thy wise and holy will, and of extensive benevolence to my fellow-creatures! May I grow in patience and fortitude of soul, in humility and zeal, in spirituality and a heavenly disposition of mind, and in a concern " that whether present or absent, I may be accepted of the Lord," 2 Cor. v. 9, that whether I live or die, it may be for his glory! In a word, as thou knowest I hunger and thirst after righteousness, make me whatever thou wouldst delight to see me. Draw on my soul, by the gentle influences of thy gracious Spirit, every trace and every feature, which thine eye, O heavenly Father, may survey with pleasure, and which thou mayest acknowledge as thine own image.

I am sensible, O Lord, I have not as yet attained; yea, my soul is utterly confounded to think " how far I am from being already perfect:" but this one thing (after the great example of thine apostle,) I would endeavour to do; forgetting the things which are behind, " I would press forward to those which are before," Phil. iii. 12, 13. O that thou wouldst feed my soul by thy word and Spirit! Having been, as I humbly hope and trust, regenerated by it, " being born again, not of corruptible seed, but of incorruptible, even by the word which liveth and abideth for ever," 1 Pet.

23, as "a new-born babe, I desire the sincere milk of the word, that I may grow thereby," 1 Pet. ii. 2. " And may my profiting appear unto all men," 1 Tim. iv. 15, till at length " I come unto a perfect man, unto the measure of the stature of the fulness of Christ;" Eph. iv. 13, and after having enjoyed the pleasure of those that flourish eminently in the courts below, be fixed in the paradise above! I ask and hope it through Him of " whose fulness we have all received, even grace for grace:" John i. 16. " To Him be glory, both now and for ever!" 2 Pet. iii. 18. Amen.

CHAPTER XXVII.

THE ADVANCED CHRISTIAN REMINDED OF THE MERCIES OF GOD, AND EXHORTED TO THE EXERCISE OF HABITUAL LOVE TO HIM, AND JOY IN HIM.

A holy joy in God our privilege as well as our duty, 1. The Christian invited to the exercise of it, 2. (1.) By the representation of temporal mercies, 3. (2.) By the consideration of spiritual favours, 4. (3.) By the views of eternal happiness, 5. And (4.) Of the mercies of God to others, the living and the dead, 6. The chapter closes with an exhortation to this heavenly exercise, 7. And with an example of the genuine workings of this grateful joy in God.

1. I WOULD now suppose my reader to find, on an examination of his spiritual state, that he is growing in grace. And if you desire that this growth may at once be acknowledged and promoted, let me call your soul to that more affectionate exercise of love to God, and joy in him, which suits, and strengthens, and exalts, the character of the advanced Christian; and which I beseech you to regard, not only as your privilege, but as your duty too. Love is the most sublime generous principle of all true and acceptable

24

obedience; and with love, when so wiseiy and hap
pily fixed, when so certainly returned, joy, proportionable joy, must naturally be connected. It may
justly grieve a man that enters into the spirit of Christianity to see how low a life the generality even ot
sincere Christians commonly live in this respect.
" Rejoice then in the Lord, ye righteous, and give
 hanks at the remembrance of his holiness," Psal.
xcvii. 12, and of all those other perfections and glories which are included in that majestic, that wonderful, that delightful name, THE LORD THY GOD!
Spend not your sacred moments merely in confession,
or petition, though each must have their daily share :
but give a part, a considerable part, to the celestial
and angelic work of praise. Yea, labour to carry
about with you continually a heart overflowing with
such sentiments, warmed and inflamed with such affections.

2. Are there not continually rays enough diffused
from the great Father of light and love to enkindle it
in our bosom? Come, my Christian friend and brother, come and survey with me the goodness of our
heavenly Father. And O! that he would give me
such a sense of it, that I might represent it in a suitable manner; that " while I am musing the fire may
burn" in my own heart, Psal. xxxix. 3, and be communicated to yours! and O! that it might pass with
the lines I write, from soul to soul; awakening in the
breast of every Christian that reads them, sentiments
more worthy of the children of God, and the heirs of
glory; who are to spend an eternity in those sacred
exercises to which I am now endeavouring to excite
you!

3. Have you not reason to adopt the words of David, and say, " How many are thy gracicus thoughts
unto me, O Lord! how great is the sum of them!
When I would count them, they are more in number
than the sand," Psal. cxxxix. 17. 18. You indeed
know where to begin the survey; for the favours of
God to you began with your being. Commemorate
it therefore with a grateful heart, that the " eyes

which saw your substance, being yet imperfect," beheld you with a friendly care, " when you were made in secret," and have watched over you ever since; and that the hand, which drew the plan of your members, when as yet there was none of them, Psal. cxxxix. 15, 16, not only fashioned them at first, but from that time has been concerned in keeping all your bones, so that not " one of them is broken," Psal. xxxiv. 20, and that indeed it is to this you owe it that you live. Look back upon the path you have trod, from the day that God brought you out of the womb, and say, whether you do not, as it were, see all the road thick set with the marks and memorials of the divine goodness. Recollect the places where you have lived, and the persons with whom you have most intimately conversed; and call to mind the mercies you have received in those places, and from those persons, as the instruments of the divine care and goodness. Recollect the difficulties and dangers with which you have been surrounded; and reflect attentively on what God has done to defend you from them, or to carry you through them. Think how often there has been " but a step between you and death;" and how suddenly God has sometimes interposed to set you in safety, even before you apprehended your danger. Think of those chambers of illness in which you have been confined, and from whence perhaps you once thought you should go forth no more; but said, with Hezekiah, " In the cutting off of my days I shall go to the gates of the grave; I am deprived of the residue of my years," Isa. xxxviii. 10. God has, it may be, since that time, added many years to your life; and you know not how many may be in reserve, or how much usefulness and happiness may attend each. Survey your circumstances in relative life; how many kind friends are surrounding you daily, and studying how they may contribute to your comfort. Reflect on those remarkable circumstances in providence, which occasioned the knitting of some bonds of this kind, which, next to those which join your soul to God, you num·

ber among the happiest. And forget not, in how many instances, when these dear lives have been threatened, lives perhaps, more sensibly dear than your own, God has given them back from the borders of the grave, and so added new endearments arising from that tender circumstance to all your after converse with them. Nor forget, in how gracious a manner he has supported some others in their last moments, and enabled them to leave behind a sweet odour of piety, which has embalmed their memories, revived you when ready to faint under the sorrows of the last separation, and, on the whole, made even the recollection of their death delightful.

4. But it is more than time that I lead on your thoughts to the many spiritual mercies which God has bestowed upon you. Look back, as it were, to the "rock from whence you were hewn, and to the hole of the pit from whence you were digged," Isa. li. 1. Reflect seriously on the state wherein divine grace found you: under how much guilt, under how much pollution! in what danger, in what ruin! Think what was, and, O! think with yet deeper reflection, what would have been the case! The eye of God. which penetrates into eternity, saw that your mind, amused with the trifles of present time, and sensual gratification, was utterly ignorant and regardless of it; it saw you on the borders of eternity, and pitied you; saw that you would in a little time have been such a helpless wretched creature, as the sinner that is just now dead, and has, to his infinite surprise and everlasting terror, met his unexpected doom, and would, like him, stand thunderstruck in astonishment and despair. This God saw, and he pitied you; and being merciful to you, he provided in the counsels of his eternal love and grace, a Redeemer for you, and purchased you to himself with the blood of his Son; a price which, if you will pause upon it, and think seriously what it was, must surely affect you to such a degree as to make you fall down before God in wonder and shame, to think it should ever have been given for you. To accomplish these blessed purposes, he sent his grace

into your heart; so that, though "you were once
darkness, you are now light in the Lord," Eph. v. 8.
He made that happy change which you now feel in
your soul, and by his Holy Spirit which is given to
you, he shed abroad that principle of love, Rom. v.
5, which is enkindled by this review, and now flames
with greater ardour than before.   Thus far he has
supported you in your Christian course; and, "hav
ing obtained help from him, it is, that you continue
even to this day," Acts xxvi. 22.   He has not only
blessed you, but made you a blessing, Gen. xii. 2: and
though you have not been so useful as that holy generosity of heart, which he has excited, would have
engaged you to desire, yet some good you have done
in the station in which he has fixed you.   Some of
your brethren of mankind have been relieved, perhaps too some thoughtless creature reclaimed to virtue and happiness, by his blessing on your endeavours.
Some in the way to heaven are praising God for you;
and some, perhaps, already there are longing for your
arrival, that they may thank you in nobler and more
expressive forms for benefits, the importance of which
they now sufficiently understand, though while here
they could never conceive it.

5. Christian, look round on the numberless bless
ings of one kind and of another with which you are
already encompassed; and advance your prospect
still further to what faith yet discovers within the
veil.   Think of those now unknown transports with
which thou shalt drop every burden in the grave,
and thine immortal spirit shall mount, light and joyful, holy and happy, to God, its original, its support,
and its hope; to God, the source of being, of holiness,
and of pleasure; to Jesus, through whom all these
mercies are derived to thee, and who will appoint
thee a throne near his own, to be for ever the specta-
tor and partaker of his glory.   Think of the rapture
with which thou shalt attend his triumph in the resurrection day, and receive this poor mouldering corruptible body, transformed into his glorious image,
and then think. " these hopes are not mine alone, but

24*

the hopes of thousands and millions. Multitudes, whom I number among the dearest of my friends upon earth, are rejoicing with me in these apprehen-sions and views; and God gives me sometimes to see the smiles on their cheeks, the sweet humble hope that sparkles in their eyes, and shines through the tears of tender gratitude; and to hear that little of their inward complacency and joy which language can express. Yes, and multitudes more, who were once equally dear to me with these, though I have laid them in the grave, and wept over their dust, are .iving to God, living in the possession of inconceivable delights, and drinking large draughts of the water of life, which flows in perpetual streams at his right haud."

6. O Christian, thou art still intimately united and allied to them. Death cannot break a friendship thus cemented; and it ought not to render thee insensible of the happiness of those friends for whose memory thou retainest so just an honour. They live to God, as his servants; they "serve him, and see his face;" Rev. xxii. 3, 4, and they make but a small part of that glorious assembly. Millions equally worthy of thine esteem and affections with themselves inhabit those blissful regions: and wilt thou not rejoice in their joy? and wilt thou not adore that everlasting spring of holiness and happiness from whence each of these streams is derived? Yea, I will add, while the blessed angels are so kindly regarding us, while they are administering to thee, O Christian, and bear-ing thee in their arms, "as an heir of salvation," Heb. i. 14, wilt thou not rejoice in their felicity too? and wilt thou not adore that God, who gives them all the superior glory of their more exalted nature, and gives them a heaven, which fills them with bless-edness, even while they seem to withdraw from it that they may attend on thee?

7. This, and infinitely more than this, the blessed God is, and was, and shall ever be. The felicities of the blessed spirits that surround his throne, and thy felicities, O Christian, are immortal. These heavenly

luminaries shall glow with an undecaying flame; and thou shalt shine and glitter among them, when the sun and stars are gone out. Still shall the unchanging Father of lights pour forth his beams upon them; and the lustre they reflect from him, and their happiness in him, shall be everlasting, shall be ever growing. Bow down, O thou child of God, thou heir of glory, bow down, and let all that is around thee, and all that is before thee, in the prospects of an unbounded eternity, concur to elevate and transport thy soul. that thou mayest, as far as possible, begin the work and blessedness of heaven, in falling down before the God of it, in opening thine heart to his gracious influences, and in breathing out before him that incense of praise which these warm beams of his presence and love have so great a tendency to produce, and to ennoble with a fragrancy resembling that of his paradise above.

THE GRATEFUL SOUL REJOICING IN THE BLESSINGS OF PROVIDENCE AND GRACE, AND POURING OUT ITSELF BEFORE GOD IN VIGOROUS AND AFFECTIONATE EXERCISES OF LOVE AND PRAISE.

O my God, it is enough! I have mused, and "the fire burneth!" Psal. xxxix. 3. But, O! in what language shall the flame break forth! What can I say but this, that my heart admires thee, and adores thee, and loves thee! My little vessel is as full as it can hold; and I would pour out all that fulness before thee, that it may grow capable of receiving more and more. Thou art "my hope, and my help; my glory and the lifter up of my head," Psal. iii. 3. " My heart rejoiceth in thy salvation;" Psal. xiii. and when I set myself under the influences of thy good Spirit to converse with thee, a thousand delightful thoughts spring up at once; a thousand sources of pleasure are unsealed, and flow in upon my soul with such refreshment and joy, that they seem to crowd into every moment the happiness of days, and weeks, and months.

I bless thee, O God, for this soul of mine, which

thou hast created; which thou hast taught to say and I hope to the happiest purpose, "Where is God my maker?" Job xxxv. 10.   I bless thee for the knowledge with which thou hast adorned it.   I bless thee for that grace with which, I trust, I may (not without humble wonder) say, Thou hast sanctified it; though, alas! the celestial plant is fixed in too barren a soil, and does not flourish to the degree I could wish.

I bless thee also for that body which thou hast given me, and which thou preservest as yet in its strength and vigour; not only capable of relishing the entertainments which thou providest for its various senses, but (which I esteem far more valuable than any of them for its own sake,) capable of acting with some vivacity in thy service.   I bless thee for that ease and freedom with which these limbs of mine move themselves, and obey the dictates of my spirit, I hope, as guided by thine.   I bless thee that "the keepers of the house do not yet tremble, nor the strong men bow themselves; that they that look out of the windows are not yet darkened, nor the daughters of music brought low."—I bless thee, O God of my life, that "the silver cord is not yet loosed, nor the golden bowl broken," Eccl. xii. 3, 4, 6.   For it is thine hand that braces all my nerves, and thine infinite skill that prepares those spirits which flow in so freely, and, when exhausted, recruit so soon and so plentifully.

I praise thee for that royal bounty which thou providest for the daily support of mankind in general, and for mine in particular; for the various tables which thou spreadest before me, and for the overflowing cup which thou puttest into mine hands, Psal. xxiii. 5.   I bless thee, that these bounties of thy providence do not serve, as it were, to upbraid a disabled appetite, and are not like messes of meat set before the dead.   I bless thee too, that "I eat not my morsel alone; Job xxxi. 17, but share it with so many agreeable friends, who add the relish of a social life to that of the animal, at our seasons of common repast. I thank thee for so many dear relatives at home, for so many kind friends abroad, who are capable of serving me in various instances, and disposed to make an obliging use of that capacity.

Nor would I forget to acknowledge thy favour, in rendering me capable of serving others, and giving me in any instances to know how much more " blessed it is to give than to receive," Acts xx. 35. I thank thee for a heart which feels the sorrows of the necessitous, and a mind which can make it my early care and refreshment to contrive, according to my little ability, for their relief: for " this also cometh forth from thee, O Lord," Isa. xxviii. 9, the great author of every benevolent inclination, of every prudent scheme, of every successful attempt to spread happiness around us, or in any instance to lessen distress.

And, surely, O Lord, if I thus acknowledge the pleasures of sympathy with the afflicted, much more must I bless thee for those of sympathy with the happy, with those that are completely blessed. I adore thee for the streams that water paradise, and maintain it in ever-flourishing, ever-growing delight. I praise thee for the rest, the joy, the transport, thou art giving to many that were once dear to me on earth; whose sorrows it was my labour to soothe, and whose joys, especially in thee, it was the delight of my heart to promote. I praise thee for the blessedness of every saint, and of every angel, that surrounds thy throne above; and I praise thee with accents of distinguished pleasure for that reviving hope which thou hast implanted in my bosom, that I shall ere long know, by clear sight, and by everlasting experience, what that felicity of theirs is, which I now only discover at a distance, through the comparatively obscure glass of faith. Even now, I am " wait ing for thy salvation," Gen. xlix. 18, with that ardent desire on the one hand which its sublime greatness cannot but inspire into the believing soul, and that calm resignation on the other, which the immutability of thy promise establishes.

And now, O my God, what shall I say unto thee

What, but that I love thee above all the powers of language to express! That I love thee for what thou art to thy creatures, who are in their various forms, every moment deriving being, knowledge, and happiness from thee, in numbers and degrees far beyond what my narrow imagination can conceive.   But, O, I adore and love thee yet far more for what thou art in thyself, for those stores of perfection, which crea tion has not diminished, and which never can be ev hausted by all the effects of it which thou impartest to thy creatures; that infinite perfection, which makes thee thine own happiness, thine own end; amiable, infinitely amiable and venerable, were all derived excellency and happiness forgot.

O thou first, thou greatest, thou fairest of all objects! thou only great, thou only fair, possess all my soul! and surely thou dost possess it.   While I thus feel thy sacred Spirit breathing on my heart, and exciting these fervours of love to thee, I cannot doubt it any more than I can doubt the reality of this animal life, while I exert the actings of it, and feel its sensations.   Surely if ever I knew the appetite of hunger, my soul hungers after righteousness, Matt. v. 6, and longs for a greater conformity to thy blessed nature, and holy will.   If ever my palate felt thirst, " my soul thirsteth for God, even for the living God," Psal. xlii. 2, and panteth for the more abundant communication of his favour.   If ever this body, when wearied with labours or journeys, knew what it was to wish for the refreshment of my bed, and rejoiced to rest there, my soul, with sweet acquiescence, rests upon thy gracious bosom, O my heavenly Father, and returns to its repose in the embraces of its God, who hath dealt so bountifully with it, Psal. cxvi. 7.   And if ever I saw the face of a beloved friend with complacency and joy, I rejoice in beholding thy face, O Lord, and in calling thee my Father in Christ.   Such thou art, and such thou wilt be, for time and for eternity. What have I more to do, but to commit myself to thee for both? leaving it to thee to choose mine inheritance, and to order my affairs for me, Psal. xlvii.

4, while all my business is to serve thee, and all my delight to praise thee. " My soul follows hard after God, because his right hand upholds me," Psal. lxiii. 8. Let it still bear me up, and I shall press on to wards thee, till all my desires be accomplished in the eternal enjoyment of thee. Amen.

CHAPTER XXVIII.

THE ESTABLISHED CHRISTIAN URGED TO EXERT HIMSELF FOR PURPOSES OF USEFULNESS.

A sincere love to God will express itself, not only in devotion, but in benevolence to man, 1. 2. This is the command of God, 3. The true Christian feels his soul wrought to a holy conformity to it, 4, and therefore will desire instruction on this head, 5. Accordingly directions are given for the improvement of various talents; particularly, (1.) Genius and learning, 6. (2.) Power, 7. (3.) Domestic authority, 8. (4.) Esteem, 9. (5.) Riches, 10. Several good ways of employing them hinted at, 11. Prudence in expense urged for the support of charity, 12, 13. Divine direction in this respect to be sought, 14. The Christian breathing after more extensive usefulness.

1. Such as I have described in the former chapters, I trust are, and will be, the frequent exercises of your souls before God. Thus will your love and gratitude breathe itself forth in the divine presence, and will, through Jesus the great Mediator, come up before it as incense, and yield an acceptable savour. But then you must remember, this will not be the only effect of that love to God, which I have supposed so warm in your heart. If it be sincere, it will not spend itself in words alone; but will discover itself in actions, and will produce, as its genuine fruit, an unfeigned love to your fellow-creatures, and an unwearied desire and labour to do them good continually.

2. " Has the great Father of mercies," you will say, " looked upon me with so gracious an eye; has he not only forgiven me ten thousand offences, but

enriched me with such a variety of benefits; O! what shall I render to him for them all! Instruct me, O ye oracles of eternal truth! Instruct me, ye elder brethren in the family of my heavenly Father! instruct me above all, O thou Spirit of wisdom and of love, what I may be able to do to express my love to the great eternal Fountain of love, and to prove my fidelity to him who hath already done so much to engage it, and who will take so much pleasure in owning and rewarding it!"

3. This, O Christian, "is the command which we have heard from the beginning," and it will ever continue in unimpaired force, "that he who loveth God should love his brother also," 1 John iv. 21; and should express that love, "not in word and profession alone, but in deed and in truth," 1 John iii. 18. You are to "love your neighbour as yourself; to love "the whole creation of God;" and, so far as your influence can extend, must endeavour to make it happy.

4. "Yes," will you say, "and I do love it. I feel the golden chain of the divine love encircling us all, and binding us close to each other, joining us in one body; and diffusing, as it were, one soul through all. May happiness, true and sublime, perpetual and ever-growing happiness, reign through the whole world of God's rational and obedient creatures in heaven and on earth! And may every revolted creature, that is capable of being recovered and restored, be made obedient. Yea, may the necessary punishment of those who are irrecoverable, be overruled by infinite wisdom and love, to the good of the whole!"

5. These are right sentiments; and if they are indeed the sentiments of your heart, O reader, and not an empty form of vain words, they will be attended with a serious concern to act in subordination to this great scheme of divine Providence, according to your abilities in their utmost extent. And to this purpose they will put you on surveying the peculiar circumstances of your life and being, that you may

discover what opportunities of usefulness they now afford, and how those opportunities and capacities may be improved. Enter, therefore, into such a survey; not that you may pride yourself in the distinctions of divine Providence or grace towards you, or "having received, may glory as if you had not received," 1 Cor. iv. 7, but that you may deal faithfully with the great Proprietor, whose steward you are. and by whom you are intrusted with every talent, which, with respect to any claim from your fellow creatures, you may call your own. And here, "having gifts differing according to the grace which is given unto us," Rom. xii. 6, let us hold the balance with an impartial hand, that so we may determine what it is that God requires of us; which is no thing less than doing the most we can invent, con trive, and effect, for the general good. But, O how seldom is this estimate faithfully made! and how much does the world around us, and how much do our own souls suffer, for want of that fidelity!

6. Hath God given you genius and learning? It was not that you might amuse or deck yourself with it, and kindle a blaze which should only serve to attract and dazzle the eyes of men: it was intended to be the means of leading both yourself and them to the Father of lights. And it will be your duty, according to the peculiar turn of that genius and capacity, either to endeavour to improve and adorn human life, or, by a more direct application of it to divine subjects, to pl d the cause of religion; to defend its truths; to en' rce and recommend its practice; to deter men from courses which would be dishonourable to God and fatal to themselves; and to try the utmost efforts of all the solemnity and tenderness with which you can clothe your addresses, to lead them into the paths of virtue and of happiness.

7. Has God invested you with power, whether it be in a larger or smaller society? Remember, that this power was given you that God might be honour ed, and those placed under your government, whethei domestic or public, might be made happy. Be con-

cerned therefore, whether you be intrusted with the rod, or the sword, it may "not be borne in vain," Rom. xiii. 4. Are you a magistrate? have you any share in the great and tremendous charge of enacting laws? Reverence the authority of the supreme Legislator, the great Guardian of society: promote none, consent to none, which you do not in your own conscience esteem, in present circumstances, an intimation of his will; and in the establishment of which you do not firmly believe you shall be "his minister for good," Rom. xiii. 4. Have you the charge of executing laws; put life into them by a vigorous and strenuous execution, according to the nature of the particular office you bear. Retain not an empty name of authority. Permit not yourself, as it were, to fall asleep on the tribunal. Be active, be wakeful, be observant of what passes around you. Protect the upright and the innocent. Break in pieces the power of the oppressor. Unveil every dishonest art. Disgrace, as well as defeat, the wretch that makes his distinguished abilities the disguise or protection of the wickedness which he ought rather to endeavour to expose, and to drive out of the world with abhorrence.

8. Are you placed only at the head of a private family? Rule it for God. Administer the concerns of that little kingdom with the same views, and on the same principles, which I have been inculcating on the powerful and the great; if by any unexpected accident any of them should suffer their eyes to glance upon the passage above. Your children and servants are your natural subjects. Let good order be established among them, and keep them under a regular discipline. Let them be instructed in the principles of religion, that they may know how reasonable such a discipline is; and let them be accustomed to act accordingly. You cannot indeed change their hearts, but you may very much influence their conduct; and by that means may preserve them from many snares, may do a great deal to make them good members of society, and may "set them, as it were, in the way

of God's steps," Psal. lxxxv. 13, if peradventure passing by he may bless them with the riches of his grace. And fail not to do your utmost to convince them of their need of those blessings; labour to engage them to a high esteem of them, and to an earnest desire after them, as incomparably more valuable than any thing else.

9. Again, has God been pleased to raise you to esteem among your fellow-creatures, which is not always in proportion to a man's rank or possessions in human life? Are your counsels heard with attention? Is your company sought? Does God give you good acceptance in the eyes of men, so that they do not only put the fairest construction on your words, but overlook faults of which you are con scious to yourself, and consider your actions anc performances in the most indulgent and favourable light? You ought to regard this not only as a favour of Providence, and as an encouragement to you cheerfully to pursue your duty, in the several branches of it, for the time to come; but also, as giving you much greater opportunities of usefulness than in your present station you could otherwise have had. If your character has any weight in the world, throw it into the right scale. Endeavour to keep virtue and goodness in countenance. Affectionately give your hand to modest worth, where it seems to be depressed or overlooked, though shining, when viewed in its proper light, with a lustre which you may think much superior to your own. Be an advocate for truth; be a counsellor of peace; be an example of candour; and do all you can to reconcile the hearts of men, and especially of good men, to each other, however they may differ in their opinions about matters which it is possible for good men to dispute. And let the caution and humility of your behaviour in circumstances of such superior eminence, and amidst so many tokens of general esteem, silently reprove the rashness and haughtiness of those who, perhaps, are remarkable for little else; or who, if their abilities were indeed considerable must be des-

pised, and whose talents must be in a great measure lost to the public, till that rashness and haughtiness of spirit be subdued. Nor suffer yourself to be interrupted in this generous and worthy course by the little attacks of envy and calumny which you may meet with in it. Be still attentive to the general good, and steadily resolute in your efforts to promote it; and leave it to Providence to guard or to rescue your character from the base assaults of malice and falsehood; which will often, without your labour, confute themselves, and heap upon the authors greater shame, or (if they are inaccessible to that) greater infamy, than your humanity will allow you to wish them.

10. Once more: has God blessed you with riches? has he placed you in such circumstances that you have more than you absolutely need for the subsistence of yourself and your family? Remember your approaching account. Remember what an incumbrance these things often prove to men in the way of their salvation, and how often, according to our Lord's express declaration, they render it " as difficult to enter into the kingdom of God, as it is for a camel to go through the eye of a needle," Matt. xix. 24. Let it therefore be your immediate, your earnest, and your daily prayer, that riches may not be a snare and a shame to you, as they are to by far the greater part of their possessors. Appropriate, I beseech you, some certain part and proportion of your estate and revenues to charitable uses; with a provisional increase, as God shall prosper you, in any extraordinary instance. By this means you will always have a fund of charity at hand: and you will probably be more ready to communicate, when you look upon what is so deposited as not in any sense your own, but as already actually given away to those uses, though not yet affixed to particular objects. It is not for me to say what that proportion ought to be. To those who have large revenues and no children, perhaps a third or one half may be too little: to those whose ncomes are small, and their charge consider

able, though they have something more than is absolutely necessary, it is possible a tenth may be too
much. But pray that God would guide your mind.
make a trial for one year, on such terms as in your
conscience you think will be most pleasing to him;
and let your observations on that teach you to fix
your proportion for the next; always remembering
that he requires justice in the first place, and alms-
deeds only so far as may consist with that. Yet, at
the same time, take heed of that treacherous, delusive, and, in many instances, destructive imagination,
that justice to your family requires that you should
leave your children very rich; which has, perhaps,
cost some parsimonious parents the lives of those dar-
lings for whom they laid up the portion of the poor;
and what fatal consequences of divine displeasure
may attend it to those that yet survive, God only
knows; and I heartily pray that you or yours may
never learn by experience.

11. And that your heart may be yet more opened,
and that your charity may be directed to the best
purposes, let me briefly mention a variety of good
uses, which may call for the consideration of those
whom God has in this respect distinguished by an
ability to do good. To assist the hints I am to offer,
look round in the neighbourhood in which you
live. Think how many honest and industrious, per
haps too, I might add, religious people, are making
very hard shifts to struggle through life. Think what
a comfort that would be to them, which you might
without any inconvenience spare from that abun
dance which God has given you.—Hearken also to
any extraordinary call of charity which may happen,
especially those of a public nature; and help them
forward with your example and your interest, which,
perhaps, may be of much greater importance than
the sum which you contribute, considered in itself.
Have a tongue to plead for the necessitous, as well
as a hand to relieve them; and endeavour to discoun
tenance those poor shameful excuses which covetous
ness often dictates to those whose art may indeed set

some varnish on what they suggest, but so slight a
one, that the coarse ground will appear through it.
—See how many poor children are wandering naked
and ignorant about the streets, and in the way to all
kinds of vice and misery; and consider what can be
done towards clothing some of them at least, and in-
structing them in the principles of religion. Would
every thriving family in a town, which is able to
afford help on such occasions, cast a pitying eye on
one poor family in its neighbourhood, and take it under their patronage, to assist in feeding, and clothing,
and teaching the children, in supporting it in affliction,
in defending it from wrongs, and in advising those
that have the management of it, as circumstances
may require, how great a difference would soon be
produced in the appearance of things amongst us!
—Observe who are sick, that if there be no public
infirmary at hand to which you can introduce them,
(where your contribution will yield the largest increase,) you may do something towards relieving
them at home, and supplying them with advice and
medicines, as well as with proper diet and attendance.
Consider also the spiritual necessities of men; in pro-
viding for which, I would particularly recommend to
you the very important and noble charity of assisting
young persons of genius and piety with what is necessary to support the expense of their education for
the ministry, in a proper course of grammatical or
academical studies. And grudge not some proportion of what God has given you to those who, resign-
ing all temporal views to minister to you the gospel
of Christ, have surely an equitable claim to be supported by you, in a capacity of rendering you those
services, however laborious, to which, for your sakes,
and that of our common Lord, they have devoted
their lives. And while you are so abundantly "satisfied with the goodness of God's house, even of his
holy temple," Psal. lxv. 4, have compassion on those
who dwell in a desert land; and rejoice to do something towards sending among the distant nations of
the heathen world, that glorious gospel which has so

long continued unknown to multitudes, though the knowledge of it, with becoming regard, be life ever-lasting.—These are a few important charities, which I would point out to those whom Providence has en-riched with its peculiar bounties; and it renders gold more precious than it could appear in any other light, that it is capable of being employed for such pur-poses. But if you should not have gold to spare for them, contribute your silver; or, as a farthing or a mite is not overlooked by God when it is given from a truly generous and charitable heart, Mark xii. 42, 43, let that be cheerfully dropped into the treasury where richer offerings cannot be afforded.

12. And that, amidst so many pressing demands for charity, you may be better furnished to answer them, seriously reflect on your manner of living. I say not that God requires you should become one of the many poor relieved out of your income. The support of society, as at present established, will not only permit, but require that some persons should allow themselves in the elegance and delights of life; by furnishing which, multitudes of poor families are much more creditably and comfortably subsisted, with greater advantage to themselves, and safety to the public, than they could be if the price of their la-bours, or of the commodities in which they deal were to be given them as an alms; nor can I imagine it grateful to God that his gifts should be refused, as if they were meant for snares and curses, rather than benefits. This were to frustrate the benevolent pur-poses of the gracious Father of mankind, and, if car-ried to its rigour, would be a sort of conspiracy against the whole system of nature. Let the bounties of Providence be used; but let us carefully see to it that it be in a moderate and prudent manner, lest, by our own folly that which should have been for our wel fare, become a trap, Psal. lxix. 22. Let conscience say, my dear reader, with regard to yourself, what proportion of the good things you possess, your hea-venly Father intends for yourself, and what for your brethren; and live not as if you had no brethren, as

if pleasing yourself in all the magnificence and luxury you can devise, were the end for which you were
sent into the world. I fear this is the excess of the
present age, and not an excess of rigour and mortification. Examine, therefore, your expenses, and
compare them with your income. That may be
shamefully extravagant in you, which may not only
be pardonable, but commendable in another of superior estate. Nor can you be sure that you do not
exceed, merely because you do not plunge yourself
in debt, nor render yourself incapable of laying up
any thing for your family. If you be disabled from
doing any thing for the poor, or any thing proportionable to your rank in life, by that genteel and elegant
way of living which you affect, God must disapprove
of such a conduct; and you ought, as you will answer it to him, to retrench it. And though the divine
indulgence will undoubtedly be exercised to those
in whom there is a sincere principle of faith in Christ,
and undissembled love to God and man, though it
act not to that height of beneficence and usefulness
which might have been attained; yet be assured of
this, that he who rendereth to every one according to
his works, will have a strict regard to the degrees of
goodness in the distribution of final rewards: so that
every neglected opportunity draws after it an irrepa-
rable loss, which will go into eternity along with you.
And let me add, too, that every instance of negligence indulged renders the mind still more and more
indolent and weak, and, consequently more indisposed
to recover the ground which has been lost, or even
to maintain that which has hitherto been kept.

13. Complain not, that this is imposing hard things
upon you. I am only directing your pleasures into
a nobler channel; and indeed that frugality, which
is the source of such a generosity, far from being at
all injurious to your reputation, will rather, amongst
wise and good men, greatly promote it. But you
have far nobler motives before you than those which
arise from their regards. I speak to you as to a child
of God, and a member o Christ; as joined, therefore,

ry the nost intimate union to all the poorest of those
that believe in him. I speak to you as to an heir of
eternal glory, who ought therefore to have sentiments
great and sublime, in some proportion to that expected inheritance.

14. Cast about, therefore, in your thoughts, what
good is to be done, and what you can do, either ir
your own person, or by your interest with others;
and go about it with resolution, as in the name and
presence of the Lord. And as the Lord gives wisdom, and out of his mouth comes knowledge and
understanding, Prov. ii. 6, go to the footstool of his
throne, and there seek that guidance and that grace
which may suit your present circumstances, and may
be effectual to produce the fruits of holiness and usefulness, to his more abundant glory, and to the honour of your Christian profession.

THE ESTABLISHED CHRISTIAN BREATHING AFTER MORE
EXTENSIVE USEFULNESS.

O bountiful Father and sovereign Author of all
good, whether natural or spiritual. I bless thee for
the various talents with which thou hast enriched so
undeserving a creature, as I must acknowledge myself to be. My soul is in the deepest confusion before thee, when I consider to how little purpose I have
hitherto improved them. Alas! what have I done,
in proportion to what thou mightest have reasonably
expected, with the gifts of nature which thou hast
bestowed upon me, with my capacities of life, with
my time, with my talents, with my possessions, with
my influence over others. Alas! through my own
negligence and folly, I look back on a barren wilderness, where I might have seen a fruitful field and a
springing harvest. Justly do I indeed deserve to be
stripped of all, to be brought to an immediate accoun
for all, to be condemned as in many respects unfaith-
ful to thee, and to the world, and to my own soul
and, in consequence of that condemnation, to be cast
into the prison of eternal darkness. But thou Lord,

hast freely forgiven the dreadful debt of ten thousand talents.   Adored be thy name for it.   Accept, O Lord, accept that renewed surrender which I would now make of myself, and of all I have unto thy service.   I acknowledge that it is " of thine own that I give thee," 1 Chron. xxix. 14; make me, I beseech thee, a faithful steward for my great Lord; and may I think of no separate interest of my own in opposition to thine.

I adore thee, O thou God of all grace, if while I am thus speaking to thee, I feel the love of thy creatures arising in my soul; if I feel my heart opening to embrace my brethren of mankind.   O make me thy faithful almoner, in distributing to them all that thou hast lodged in mine hand for their relief.   And in determining what is my own share, may I hold the balance with an equal hand, and judge impartially between myself and them.   The proportion thou allowest may I thankfully take for myself, and those who are immediately mine.   The rest may I distribute with wisdom, and fidelity, and cheerfulness.   Guide my hand, O ever-merciful Father, while thou dost me the honour to make me thine instrument in dealing out a few of thy bounties, that I may bestow them where they are most needed, and where they will answer the best end.   And if it be thy gracious will, do thou " multiply the seed sown," 2 Cor. ix. 10; prosper me in my worldly affairs that I may have more to impart to them that need it; and thus lead me on to the region of everlasting plenty, and everlasting benevolence.   There may I meet with many to whom I have been an affectionate benefactor on earth: and if it be thy blessed will, with many whom I have also been the means of conducting into the path to that blissful abode.   There may they entertain me in their habitations of glory.   And, in time and eternity, do thou, Lord, accept the praise of all, through Jesus Christ, at whose feet I would bow; and at whose feet, after the most useful course, I would at last die, with as much humility as if I were then exerting the first act of faith upon him, and had never had an opportunity, by one tribute of obedience and gratitude in the services of life, to approve its sincerity

---

CHAPTER XXIX.

THE CHRISTIAN REJOICING IN THE VIEWS OF DEATH AND JUDGMENT.

Death and Judgment are near; but the Christian has reason to welcome both, 1. Yet nature recoils from the solemnity of them ; 2. An attempt to reconcile the mind, [I.] To the prospect of death, 3, from the consideration, (1.) Of the many evils that surround us in this mortal life, 4. (2.) Of the remainder of sin which we feel within us, 5. (3.) Of the happiness which is immediately to succeed death, 6, 7. All which might make the Christian willing to die, in the most agreeable circumstances of human life, 8. [II.] The Christian has reason to rejoice in the prospect of judgment, 9. Since, however awful it be, Christ will then come to vindicate his honour, to display his glory, and to triumph over his enemies, 10. As also to complete the happiness of every believer, 11, and of the whole church, 12, 13. The meditation of a Christian, whose heart is warm with these prospects.

1. WHEN the visions of the Lord were closing upon John, the beloved disciple, in the island of Patmos, it is observable, that he who gave him that revelation, even Jesus, the faithful and true witness, con cludes with those lively and important words: " He who testifieth these things, saith, Surely I come quickly:" and John answers, with the greatest readiness and pleasure, " Amen, even so come, Lord Jesus," Rev. xxii. 20. Come as thou hast said, surely, and quickly! —And remember, O Christian, whoever you are, now reading these words, your divine Lord speaks in the same language to you: " Behold, I come quickly." Yes, very quickly will he come by death, to turn the key, to open the door of the grave for thine admittance thither, and to lead thee through it into the now unknown regions of the invisible world. Nor is it long before the Judge, who ' standeth at the door," James v. 9, will appear also for the universal

judgment: and though perhaps not only scores **but** hundreds of years may lie between that period and the present moment, yet it is but a very small point of time to him, who views at once all the uumeasurable ages of a past and future eternity. " A thousand years are with him but as one day, and one day as a thousand years," 2 Pet. iii. 8. In both these senses then does he come quickly; and I trust you can answer, with a glad *Amen*, that the warning is not terrible or unpleasant to your ears, but rather that his coming, his certain, his speedy coming is the object of your delightful hope, and of your longing expectation.

2. I am sure it is reasonable it should be so; and yet perhaps nature, fond of life, and unwilling to part with a long known abode, to enter on a state to which it is entirely a stranger, may recoil from the thoughts of dying; or struck with the awful pomp of an expiring and dissolving world, may look on the judgment-day with some mixture of terror. And therefore, my dear brother in the Lord, (for such I can now esteem you,) I would reason with you a little on this head, and would entreat you to look more attentively on this solemn object, which will, I trust, grow less disagreeable to you, as it is more familiarly viewed. Nay, I hope, that instead of starting back from it, you will rather spring forward towards it with joy and delight.

3. Think, O Christian, when Christ comes to call you away by death, he comes—to set you at liberty from your present sorrows—to deliver you from your struggles with remaining corruption—and to receive you to dwell with himself in complete holiness and joy. You shall " be absent from the body, and present with the Lord," 2 Cor. v. 8.

4. He will indeed call you away from this world; but, O what is this world that you should be fond of it, and cling to it with so much eagerness? How low are all those enjoyments that are peculiar to it; and how many its vexations, its snares, and its sorrows! Review your pilgrimage thus far, and though you

must acknowledge, that "goodness and mercy have followed you all the days of your life," Psal. xxiii. 6, yet has not that very mercy itself planted some thorns in your path, and given you some wise and necessary, yet painful, intimations, that "this is not your rest?" Mic. ii. 10. Review the monuments of your withered joys, of your blasted hopes; if there be yet any monuments of them remaining, more than a mournful remembrance they have left behind in your afflicted heart. Look upon the graves that have swallowed up many of your dearest and most amiable friends, perhaps in the very bloom of life, and in the greatest intimacy of your converse with them; and reflect, that if you continue a few years more, death will renew its conquests at your expense, and devour the most precious of those that yet survive. View the living as well as the dead; behold the state of human nature, under the many grievous marks of its apostasy from God; and say, whether a wise and good man would wish to continue always here.

Methinks, were I myself secure from being reached by any of the arrows that fly around me, I could not but mourn to see the wounds that are given by them, and to hear the groans of those that are continually falling under them. The diseases and calamities of mankind are so many, and, what is most grievous of all, the distempers of their minds are so various and so threatening, that the world appears almost like an hospital; and a man, whose heart is tender, is ready to feel his spirits broken, as he walks through it, and surveys the sad scene; especially when he sees how little he can do for the recovery of those whom he pities. Are you a Christian, and does it not pierce your heart to see how human nature is sunk in vice and in shame, to see with what amazing insolence some are making themselves openly vile, and how the name of Christ is dishonoured by many too that call themselves his people? to see the unlawful deeds and filthy practices of them that live ungodly, and to behold, at the same time, the infirmities at least, and irregularities, of those concerning whom we have better hopes? and do you not wish to escape **from** such a world, where a righteous and compassionate soul must be vexed from day to day by so many spectacles of sin and misery? 2 Pet. ii. 8.

5. Yea, to come nearer home; do you not feel something within you which you long to quit, and which would embitter even Paradise itself? something, which, were it to continue, would grieve and distress you even in the society of the blessed? Do you not feel a remainder of indwelling sin; the sad consequence of the original revolt of our nature from God? Are you not struggling every day with some residue of corruption, or at least mourning on account of the weakness of your graces? Do you not often find your spirits dull and languid when you would desire to raise them to the greatest fervour in the service of God? Do you not find your heart too often insensible of the richest instances of his love, and your hands feeble in his service, even when " to will is present with you?" Rom. vii. 18. Does not your life, in its best days and hours, appear a low, unprofitable thing, when compared with what you are sensible it ought to be, and with what you wish that it were? Are you not frequently, as it were, stretching the pinions of the mind, and saying, " O that I had wings like a dove, that I might fly away and be at rest?" Psal. lv. 6.

6. Should you not then rejoice in the thought that Jesus comes to deliver you from these complaints? That he comes to answer your wishes, and to fulfil the largest desires of your hearts; those desires that he himself has inspired? That he comes to open upon you a world of purity, and joy, of active, exalted, and unwearied services?

7. O Christian, how often have you cast a. longing eye towards those happy shores, and wished to pass the sea, the boisterous, unpleasant, dangerous sea, that separates you from them? When your Lord has condescended to make you a short visit in his ordinances on earth, how have you blest the time and the place, and pronounced it, amidst any other disad

vantages of situation, to be the very gate of heaven? Gen. xxviii. 17. And is it so delightful to behold this gate, and will it not be much more so to enter into it? Is it so delightful to receive the visits of Jesus for an hour, and will it not be infinitely more so to dwell with him for ever? " Lord!" may you well say, " when I dwell with thee, I shall dwell in holiness, for thou thyself art holiness; I shall dwell in love, for thou thyself art love; I shall dwell in joy, for thou art the fountain of joy," as, " thou art in the Father, and the Father in thee," John xvii. 21. Bid welcome to his approach, therefore, to take you at your word, and to fulfil to you that saying of his, on which your soul has so often rested with heavenly peace and pleasure; " Father, I will, that they whom thou hast given me, be with me where I am, that they may behold my glory, which thou hast given me," John xvii. 24.

8. Surely you may say in this view, " The sooner Christ comes the better." What though the residue of your days be cut off in the midst? what though you leave many expected pleasures in life untasted, and many schemes unaccomplished? Is it not enough that what is taken from a mortal life shall be added to a glorious eternity; and that you shall spend those days and years in the presence and service of Christ in heaven which you might otherwise have spent with him and for him in the imperfect enjoyments and labours of earth?

9. But your prospects reach, not only beyond death, but beyond the separate state. For with regard to his final appearance to judgment, our Lord says, Surely I come quickly, in the sense illustrated before: and so it will appear to us, if we compare this interval of time with the blissful eternity which is to succeed it; and probably if we compare it with those ages which have already passed, since the sun began to measure out to earth its days and its years. And will you not here also sing your part in the joyful anthem, " Amen, even so come, Lord Jesus!"

10. It is true, Christian, it is an awful day: a **day** in which nature shall be thrown into a confusion as yet unknown. No earthquake, no eruption of burning mountains, no desolations of cities by devouring flames, or of countries by overflowing rivers or seas, can give any just emblem of that dreadful day: when "the heavens being on fire shall be dissolved," as well "as the earth and all that is therein, shall be burnt up;" 2 Pet. iii. 10—12, when all nature shall flee away in amazement "before the face of the universal Judge," Rev. xx. 11, and there shall be a great cry, far beyond what was known in the land of Egypt, when "there was not a house in which there was not one dead," Exod. xii. 30. Your flesh may be ready to tremble at the view; yet your spirit must surely rejoice in God your Saviour, Luke i. 47. You may justly say, "Let this illustrious day come, even with all its horrors!" Yea, like the Christians described by the apostle, 2 Pet. iii. 12, you may be looking for, and hasting to that day of terrible brightness and universal doom. For your Lord will then come to vindicate the justice of those proceedings which have been in many instances so much obscured, and because they have been obscured have been also blasphemed. He will come to display his magnificence, descending from heaven "with a shout, with the voice of the archangel, and with the trump of God," 1 Thess. iv. 16, taking his seat upon a throne infinitely exceeding that of earthly, or even of celestial princes, clothed with "his Father's glory and his own," Luke ix. 26, surrounded with a numberless host of "shining attendants," when "coming to be glorified in his saints, and admired in all them that believe," 2 Thess. i. 10. His enemies shall also be produced to grace his triumph; the serpent shall be seen there rolling in the dust, and trodden under foot by him and by all his servants: those who once condemned him shall tremble at his presence; and those who bowed the knee before him in profane mockery shall, in wild despair, call to the mountains to fall

upon them, and to the rocks to hide them, from the face of that Lamb of God," Rev. vi. 16, whom they once led away to the most inhuman slaughter.

11. O Christian, does not your loyal heart bound at the thought? and are you not ready, even while you read these lines, to begin the victorious shout in which you are then to join? He justly expects that your thoughts should be greatly elevated and impressed with the views of his triumph: but at the same time he permits you to remember your own personal share in the joy and glory of that blessed day: and even now he has the view before him of what his power and love shall then accomplish for your salvation. And what shall it not accomplish? He shall come to break the bars of the grave, and to re-animate your sleeping clay. Your bodies must indeed be laid in the dust, and be lodged there as a testimony of God's displeasure against sin; against the first sin that was ever committed, from the sad consequences of which the dearest of his children cannot be exempted. But you shall then have an ear to hear the voice of the Son of God, and an eye to behold the lustre of his appearance: and shall " shine forth like the sun," Matt. xiii. 43, arising in the clear heaven, " which is as a bridegroom coming out of his chamber," Psal. xix. 5. Your soul shall be new dressed to grace this high solemnity; and be clothed, not with the rags of mortality, but with the robes of glory; for " he shall change this vile body, to fashion it like his own glorious body," Phil. iii. 21. And when you are thus royally arrayed, he shall confer public honours on you, and on all his people, before the assembled world. You may now perhaps be loaded with infamy, called by reproachful names, and charged with crimes, or with views which your very soul abhors; but he will then " bring forth your righteousness as the light," Psal. xxviii. 6, and "your salvation as a lamp that burneth." Isa. lxii. 1. Though you have been dishonoured by men, you shall be acknowledged by God; and though treated as " the filth of the world, and the offscouring of all

things," 1 Cor. iv. 13, he will show that he regards
you " as his treasure, in the day that he makes up his
jewels," Mal. iii. 17. When he shall " put away al
the wicked of the earth like dross," Psal. cxix. 119,
you shall be pronounced righteous in that full assembly; and though indeed you have broken the divine
law, and might in strict justice have been condemned,
yet being clothed with the righteousness of the great
Redeemer, even " that righteousness which is of God
by faith," Phil. iii. 9. justice itself shall acquit you,
and join with mercy in " bestowing upon you a
crown of life," 2 Tim. iv. 8.—Christ will " confess
you before men and angels," Luke xii. 8.—will pronounce you " good and faithful servants, and call you
to enter into the joy of your Lord," Matt. xxv. 21,
he will speak of you with endearment as his brethren,
and will acknowledge the kindnesses which have
been shown to you as if he had received them in his
own person, Matt. xxv. 40. Yea, then shall you, O
Christian, who may perhaps have sat in some of the
lowest places in our assemblies, though, it may be,
none of the rich and great of the earth would condescend to look upon, or to speak to you, be called to
be assessors with Christ on his judgment-seat, and to
join with him in the sentence he shall pass on wicked men, and rebellious angels.

12. Nor is it merely one day of glory and of triumph; but when the Judge arises and ascends to his
Father's court, all the blessed shall ascend with him,
and you among the rest: you shall ascend together
with your Saviour, " to his Father and your Father,
to his God and your God," John xx. 17. You shall
go to make your appearance in the new Jerusalem,
in those new shining forms that you have received,
which will no doubt be attended with a correspon-
dent improvement of mind; and take up your perpetual abode in that fulness of joy, with which you
shall be filled and satisfied " in the presence of God,"
Psal xvi. 11, upon the consummation of that happiness which the saints in the intermediate state have
been wishing and waiting for. You shall go from

he ruins of a dissolving world to " the new heaven and new earth, wherein righteousness for ever dwells," 2 Pet. iii. 13. There all the number of God's elect shall be accomplished, and the happiness of each shall be completed. The whole society shall be " presented before God as the bride, the Lamb's wife," Rev. xxi. 9, whom the eye of its celestial bridegroom shall survey with unutterable delight, and confess to be " without spot or wrinkle, or any such thing;" Eph. v. 27, its character and state being just what he originally designed it to be, when he first engaged to give himself for it, to " redeem it to God by his blood," Rev. v. 9. So shall you ever be with each other, and with the Lord; 1 Thess. iv. 17, and immortal ages shall roll away, and find you still unchanged; your happiness always the same, and your relish for it the same; or rather ever growing, as your souls are approaching nearer and nearer to him, who is the source of happiness, and the centre of infinite perfection.

13. And now, look around about upon earth, and single out, if you can, the enjoyments or the hopes, for the sake of which you would say, Lord, delay thy coming, or for the sake of which you any more should hesitate to express your longing for it, and to cry " Even so come, Lord Jesus, come quickly!"

THE MEDITATION AND PRAYER OF A CHRISTIAN WHOSE HEART IS WARMED WITH THESE PROSPECTS.

O blessed Lord! my soul is enkindled with these views, and rises to thee in the flame, Judges xiii. 20. Thou hast testified thou comest quickly; and I repeat my joyful assent. Amen, even so come, Lord Jesus, Rev. xxii. 20. Come, for I long to have done with this low life; to have done with its burdens, its sorrows, and its snares! Come, for I long to ascend into thy presence, and to see the court thou art holding above!

Blessed Jesus, death is transformed when I view

it in this light.   The king of terrors is seen no more
as such, so near the King of glory and of grace.   I
hear with pleasure the sound of thy feet approaching
still nearer and nearer; draw aside the veil whenever
thou pleasest!   Open the bars of my prison, that my
eager soul may spring forth to thee, and cast itself
at thy feet; at the feet of that Jesus, "whom having
not seen, I love; and in whom, though now I see
thee not, yet believing, I rejoice with joy unspeakable
and full of glory!" 1 Pet. 1. 8.   "Thou, Lord, shalt
show me the path of life:" thine hand shall guide
me to thy blissful abode, where there is fulness of
joy, and rivers of everlasting pleasure," Psal. xvi. 11.
Thou shalt assign me a habitation with thy faithful
servants, whose separate spirits are now living with
thee, while their bodies sleep in the dust.   Many of
them have been my companions in thy laborious
work, and "in the patience and tribulation of thy
kingdom;" Rev. i. 9, my dear companions, and my
brethren.   O show me, blessed Saviour, how glorious
and how happy thou hast made them!   Show me to
what new forms of better life thou hast conducted
them, whom we call the dead; in what nobler and
more extensive services thou hast employed them,
that I may praise thee better than I now can, for thy
goodness to them.   And, O give me to share with
them in their blessings and their services, and to raise
a song of grateful love, like that which they are
breathing forth before thee!
    Yet, O my blessed Redeemer, even there will my
soul be aspiring to a yet nobler and more glorious
hope, and from this as yet unknown splendour and
felicity shall I be drawing new arguments to look and
long for the day of thy final appearance.   There
shall I long more ardently than I now do, to see thy
conduct vindicated, and thy triumph displayed; to see
the dust of thy servants reanimated, and death, the
last of their enemies and of thine, swallowed up in
victory, 1 Cor. xv. 26, 54.   I shall long for that superior honour that thou intendest me, and that complete
bliss to which the whole body of thy people shall be

conducted. Come, Lord Jesus, come quickly, will mingle itself with the songs of Paradise, and sound from the tongues of all the millions of thy saints, whom thy grace has transplanted thither.

In the mean time, O my divine Master, accept the homage which a grateful heart now pays thee, in a sense of the glorious hopes with which thou hast inspired it! It is thou that hast put this joy into it and hast raised my soul to this glorious ambition whereas I might otherwise have now been grovelling in the lowest trifles of time and sense, and been looking with horror on that hour which is now the object of my most ardent wishes.

O be with me always, even to the end of this mortal life; and give me, while waiting for thy salvation, to be doing thy commandments. May "my loins be girded about, and my lamp burning," Luke xii. 35, and mine ears be still watchful for the blessed signal of thine arrival; that my glowing soul may with pleasure spring to meet thee, and be strengthened by death to bear those visions of glory, under the ecstasies of which feeble mortality would now expire!

CHAPTER XXX.

THE CHRISTIAN HONOURING GOD BY HIS DYING BEHA VIOUR.

Reflections on the sincerity with which the preceding advices have been given, 1. The author is desirous that (if Providence permit) ne may assist the Christian to die honourably and comfortably, 2, 3. With this view it is advised, (1.) To rid the mind of all earth. ly cares, 4. (2.) To renew the humiliation of the soul before God, and its application to the blood of Christ, 5. (3.) To exel. cise patience under bodily pains and sorrows, 6. (4.) At leaving the world, to bear-an honourable testimony to religion, 7. (5.) To give a solemn charge to surviving friends, 8. Especially recom. mending faith in Christ, 9. (6) To keep the promises of God in view, 10, 11. And, (7.) To commit the departing spirit to God, in the genuine exercises of gratitude and repentance, faith and charity, 12, which are exemplified in the concluding meditation and prayer.

1. THUS, my dear reader, I have endeavoured to lead you through a variety of circumstances; and those not fancied and imaginary, but such as do indeed occur in the human and Christian life. And I can truly and cheerfully say, that I have marked out to you the path which I myself have trod, and in which it is my desire still to go on. I have ventured my own everlasting interests on that foundation on which I have directed you to adventure yours. What I have recommended as the grand business of your life, I desire to make the business of my own; and the most considerable enjoyments which I expect or desire in the remaining days of my pilgrimage on earth, are such as I have directed you to seek, and endeavoured to assist you in attaining. Such love to God, such constant activity in his service, such pleasurable views of what lies beyond the grave, appear to me (God is my witness,) a felicity incomparably beyond any thing else which can offer itself to our affection and pursuit: and I would not for ten thousand worlds resign my share in them, or consent even

to the suspension of the delights which they afford, during the remainder of my abode here.

2. I would humbly hope, through the divine bless-ing, that the hours you have spent in the review of these plain things may have turned to some profit-able account, and that in consequence of what you have read, you have either been brought into the way of life and peace, or been induced to quicken your pace in it. Most heartily should I rejoice in being further useful to you, and that even to the last Now there is one scene remaining; a scene through which you must infallibly pass, which has something in it so awful, that I cannot but attempt doing a little to assist you in it; I mean the dark valley of the shadow of death. I would earnestly wish, that for the credit of your profession, the comfort of your own soul, and the joy and edification of your sur-viving friends, you might die not only safely, but honourably too: and therefore I would offer you a few parting advices. I am sensible indeed that Pro-vidence may determine the circumstances of your death in such a manner as that you may have no opportunity of acting upon the hints I now give you. Some unexpected accident from without, or from within, may, as it were, whirl you to heaven before you are aware; and you may find yourself so sud-denly there, that it may seem a translation rather than a death. Or it is possible the force of a distem-per may affect your understanding in such a manner that you may be quite insensible of the circumstances in which you are, and so your dissolution (though others may see it visibly and certainly approaching,) may be as great a surprise to you as if you died in full health.

3. But as it is, on the whole, probable you may have a more sensible passage out of time into eter-nity; and as much may, in various respects, depend on your dying behaviour, give me leave to propose some plain directions with relation to it, to be prac-tised, if God give you opportunity, and remind you of them. It may not be improper to look over the

twenty-ninth chapter again when you find the symptoms of any threatening disorder: and I the rather hope, that what I say may be useful to you, as methinks, I find myself disposed to address you with something of that peculiar tenderness which we feel for a dying friend; to whom, as we expect that we shall speak to him no more, we send out, as it were, all our hearts in every word.

4. I would advise then, in the first place, " that, as soon as possible, you would endeavour to get rid of all further care with regard to your temporal concerns, by settling them in time, in as reasonable and Christian a marner as you can." I could wish, there may be nothing of that kind to hurry your mind when you are least able to bear it, or to distress or divide those who come after you. Do that which, in the presence of God, you judge most equitable, and which you verily believe, will be most pleasing to him. Do it in as prudent and effectual a manner as you can: and then consider the world as a place you have quite done with, and its affairs as nothing further to you, more than to one actually dead; unless as you may do any good to its inhabitants while yet you continue among them; and may, by any circumstance in your last actions or words in life leave a blessing behind you to those who have been your friends and fellow-travellers, while you have been dispatching that journey through it, which you are now finishing.

5. That you may be the more at leisure, and the better prepared for this, " enter into some serious review of your own state, and endeavour to put your soul into as fit a posture as possible, for your solemn appearance before God." For a solemn thing indeed it is to go into his immediate presence! to stand before him, not as a supplicant at the throne of his grace, but at his bar as a separate spirit, whose time of probation is over, and whose eternal state is to be immediately determined. Renew your humiliation before God for the imperfection of your life, though it has in the main been devoted to his service. Re-

new your application to the mercies of God, as promised in the covenant of grace, and to the blood of
Christ, as the blessed channel in which they flow.
Resign yourself entirely to the divine disposal and
conduct, as willing to serve God, either in this world
or the other, as he shall see fit. And sensible of
your sinfulness on the one hand, and of the divine
wisdom and goodness on the other, summon up all
the fortitude of your soul to bear, as well as you can,
whatever his afflicting hand may further lay upon
you, and to receive the last stroke of it, as one who
would obtain the most entire subjection to the great
and good Father of spirits.

6. Whatever you suffer, "endeavour to show yourself an example of patience." Let that amiable grace
"have its perfect work:" James i. 4, and since it
has so little more to do, let it close the scene nobly.
Let there not be a murmuring word; and that there
may not, watch against every repining thought; and
when you feel any thing of that kind arising, look by
faith upon a dying Saviour, and ask your own heart,
"Was not his cross much more painful than the bed on
which I lie? Was not his situation among blood-thirsty
enemies infinitely more terrible than mine amidst the
tenderness and care of so many affectionate friends?
Did not the heavy load of my sins press him in a
much more overwhelming manner than I am pressed
by the load of these afflictions? and yet he bore all
'as a Lamb' that is brought 'to the slaughter.'"
Isa. liii. 7. Let the remembrance of his sufferings
be a means to sweeten yours: yea, let it cause you
to rejoice, when you are called to bear the cross for
a little while, before you wear the crown. Count it
all joy that you have an opportunity yet once more
of honouring God by your patience, which is now
acting its last part, and will in a few days, perhaps
in a few hours, be superseded by complete everlasting blessedness. And I am willing to hope, that in
these views you will not only suppress all passionate
complaints, but that your mouth will be filled with
the praises of God; and that you will be speaking

27

to those that are about you, not only of his justice but of his goodness too. So that you will be enabled to communicate your inward joys in such a manner, as may be a lively and edifying comment upon those words of the apostle, " Tribulation worketh patience; and patience experience; and experience hope; even a hope which maketh not ashamed, while the love of God is shed abroad in our hearts by the Holy Ghost, which is given unto us," Rom. v. 3—5.

7. And now, my dear friend, now is the time when it is especially expected from you that you bear an honourable testimony to religion. Tell those that are about you, as well as you can, (for you will never be able fully to express it,) what comfort and support you have found in it. Tell them, how it has brightened the darkest circumstances of your life; tell them, how it now reconciles you to the near views of death. Your words will carry with them a peculiar weight at such a season: there will be a kind of eloquence, even in the infirmities with which you are struggling, while you give them utterance; and you will be heard with attention, with tenderness, with credit. And therefore, when the time of your departure is at hand, with unaffected freedom breathe out your joy, if you then feel (as I hope you will) a holy joy and delight in God, breathe out, however, your inward peace and serenity of mind, if you be then peaceful and serene: others will mark it, and be encouraged to tread the steps which lead to so happy an end. Tell them what you feel of the vanity of the world; and they may learn to regard it less: tell them what you feel of the substantial supports of the gospel; and they may learn to value it more: for they cannot but know that they must lie down upon a dying bed too, and must then need al. the relief which the gospel itself can give them.

8. And, to enforce the conviction the more, "give a solemn charge to those that are about you, that they spend their lives in the service of God, and govern themselves by the principles of real religion."

You may remember, that Joshua and David, and other good men did so, when they perceived that the days drew near in which they should die. And you know not how the admonitions of a dying friend, or (as it may be with respect to some,) of a dying parent, may impress those who may have disregarded what you and others may have said to them before. At least, make the trial; and die labouring to glorify God, and to save souls, and generously to sow the seeds of goodness and happiness in a world where you have no more harvests to reap. Perhaps they may spring up in a plentiful crop when the clods of the valley are covering your body; but if not, God will approve it; and the angels that wait around your bed to receive your departing soul will look upon each other with marks of approbation in their countenance, and own that this is to expire like a Christian, and to make a glorious improvement of mortality.

9. And, in this last address to your fellow-mortals, whoever they are that Providence brings near you, "be sure that you tell them how entirely and how cheerfully your hopes and dependence in this season of the last extremity are fixed, not upon your own merits and obedience, but on what the great Redeemer has done and suffered for sinners." Let them see that you die, as it were at the foot of the cross: nothing will be so comfortable to yourself, nothing so edifying to them. Let the name of Jesus, therefore, be in your mouth, while you are able to speak; and when you can speak no longer, let it be in your heart, and endeavour that the last act of your soul, while it continues in the body, may be an act of humble faith in Christ. "Come unto God by him: enter into that which is within the veil, as with the blood of sprinkling fresh upon you." It is an awful thing for such a sinner, (as you, my Christian friend, with all the virtues the world may have admired, know yourself to be) to stand before that infinitely pure and holy Being, who has seen all your ways, and all your heart, and has a perfect knowledge of every mixture

of imperfection, which has attended the best of your duties; but venture in that way, and you will find it both safe and pleasant.

10. Once more: " To give you comfort in a dying hour, and to support your feeble steps while you are travelling through this dark and painful way, take the word of God as a staff in your hand." Let books and mortal friends now do their last office for you. Call, if you can, some experienced Christian, who has felt the power of the word of God upon his own heart; and let him bring the Scripture, and turn you to some of those precious promises, which have been the food and rejoicing of his own soul. It is with this view, that I may carry the good office I am now engaged in, as far as possible, I shall here give you a collection of a few such admirable scriptures, each of them infinitely " more valuable than thousands of gold and silver," Psal. cxix. 72. And to convince you of the degree in which I esteem them, I will take the freedom to add, that I desire they may (if God give an opportunity) be read over to me, as I lie on my dying bed, with short intervals between them, that I may pause upon each, and renew something of that delightful relish, which, I bless God, I have often found in them. May your soul and mine be then composed to a sacred silence (whatever be the commotion of animal nature) while the voice of God speaks to us in a language which he spoke to his servants of old, or in which he instructed them how they should speak to him, in circumstances of the greatest extremity!

11. Can any more encouragement be wanting, when he says, " Fear not, for I am with thee; be not dismayed, for I am thy God: I will strengthen thee, yea, I will help thee, yea. I will uphold thee, with the right hand of my righteousness," Isa. xli. 10. And " he is not a man that he should lie, or the son of man that he should repent: hath he said, and shall he not do it? or hath he spoken, and shall he not make it good?" Num. xxiii. 19.--" The Lord is my light, and my salvation, whom shall I fear?

The Lord is the strength of my life, of whom shall I
he afraid?" Psal. xxvii. 1.—" This God is our God
for ever and ever: he will be our guide even unto
death," Psal. xlviii. 14.—" Therefore though I walk
through the valley of the shadow of death, I will
fear no evil: for thou art with me, thy rod and thy
staff they comfort me," Psal. xxiii. 4.—" I have wait-
ed for thy salvation, O Lord," Gen. xlix. 18.—" O continue thy loving kindness unto them that know thee,
and thy righteousness to the upright in heart!   For
with thee is the fountain of life; in thy light shall we
see light," Psal. xxxvi. 9, 10.—" Thou wilt show me
the path of life; in thy presence is fulness of joy, at
thy right hand there are pleasures for ever more,"
Psal. xvi. 11.—" As for me, I shall behold thy face in
righteousness: I shall be satisfied, when I awake,
with thy likeness," Psal. xvii. 15.—" For I know in
whom I have believed, and am persuaded, that he is
able to keep what I have committed unto him until
that day," 2 Tim. i. 12.—" Therefore my heart is glad,
and my glory rejoiceth; my flesh also shall rest in
hope," Psal. xvi. 9.—" For if we believe that Jesus
died, and rose again; those also that sleep in Jesus
will God bring with him," 1 Thess. iv. 14.—" I give
unto my sheep eternal life," said Jesus the good Shepherd, " and they shall never perish, neither shall any
pluck them out of my hand," John x. 28.—" This is
the will of him that sent me, that every one that be
lieveth on me should have everlasting life; and I will
raise him up at the last day," John vi. 40.—" Let
not your heart be troubled; ye believe in God, believe also in me.   In my Father's house are many
mansions; if it were not so, I would have told you,
I go to prepare a place for you.   And if I go and
prepare a place for you, I will come again, and receive you to myself; that where I am, there ye may
be also," John xiv. 1, 2, 3.—" Go, tell my brethren,
I ascend unto my Father and your Father; and to
my God and your God," John xx. 17.—" Father, I
will, that those whom thou hast given me, be with
me where I am, that they may behold my glory which

thou hast given me; that the love wherewith thou hast loved me, may be in them, and I in them," John xvii. 24. 24.—" He that testifieth these things. saith, surely I come quickly. Amen, even so come, Lord Jesus," Rev. xxii. 20.—" O death, where is thy sting ? O grave where is thy victory? Thanks be to God who giveth us the victory through our Lord Jesus Christ," 1 Cor. xv. 55, 57.

12. Thus may that God, " who knows the souls of his children in all their adversities," Ps. xxxi. 7, and in whose sight " the death of his saints is precious," Psal. cxvi. 15, cheer and support you and me in those last extremities of nature! May he add us to the happy number of those who have been more than conquerors in death! and may he give us those sup plies of his Spirit, which may enable us to pour out our departing souls in such sentiments as those I would now suggest, though we should be no longer able to utter words, or to understand them if they were read to us! Let us at least review them with all proper affections now, and lay up one prayer more for that awful moment! O that this, and all we have ever offered with regard to it, may then " come in remembrance before God!" Acts x. 4, 31.

MEDITATION OR PRAYER, SUITED TO THE CASE OF A DYING CHRISTIAN.

O thou supreme Ruler of the visible and invisible worlds! thou Sovereign of life and of death; of earth and of heaven! Blessed be thy name, I have often been taught to seek thee. And now once more do I pour out my soul, my departing soul, unto thee. Bow down thy gracious ear, O God, and let my cry come before thee with acceptance!

The hour is come when thou wilt separate me from this world, with which I have been so long and so familiarly acquainted, and lead me to another as yet unknown. Enable me, I beseech thee, to make the exchange as becomes a child of Abraham, who

being " called of thee to receive an inheritance, obeyed, and went out, though he knew not particularly,
whither he went," Heb. xi. 8, as becomes a child of
God, who knows that, through sovereign grace, " it
is his Father's good pleasure to give him the king
dom," Luke xii. 32.

I acknowledge, O Lord, the justice of that sentence by which I am expiring; and own thy wisdom
and goodness in appointing my journey through this
gloomy vale which is now before me.   Help me to
turn it into the happy occasion of honouring thee,
and adorning my profession! and I will bless the
pangs by which thou art glorified, and this mortal
and sinful part of my nature dissolved.

Gracious Father, I would not quit this earth of
thine, and this house of clay in which I have sojourn-
ed during my abode upon the face of it, without my
grateful acknowledgments to thee, for all that abundant goodness which thou hast caused to pass before
me here, Exod. xxxiii. 19.   With my dying breath
I bear witness to thy faithful care.   I have wanted
no good thing, Psal. xxxiv. 10.   I thank thee, O my
God, that this guilty, forfeited, unprofitable life was
so long spared; that it has been still maintained by
such a rich variety of thy bounty.   I thank thee that
thou hast made this beginning of my existence so
pleasant to me.   I thank thee for the mercies of my
days and nights, of my months and years, which are
now come to their period: I thank thee for the mercies of my infancy, and for those of my riper age;
for all the agreeable friends which thou hast given
me in this house of my pilgrimage, the living and
the dead; for all the help I have received from others,
and for all the opportunities which thou hast given
me of being helpful to the bodies or souls of my brethren of mankind.   Surely goodness and mercy have
followed me all the days of my life, Ps. xxiii. 6, and
I have reason to rise a thankful guest from the various and pleasant entertainments with which my
table has been furnished by thee.   Nor shall I have
reason to repine or to grieve, at quitting them, for

O my God, are thy bounties exhausted? I know that they are not. I will not wrong thy goodness and thy faithulness so much as to imagine, that because I am going from this earth, I am going from happiness. I adore thy mercy, that thou hast taught me to entertain nobler views through Jesus thy Son. I bless thee with all the powers of my nature, that I ever heard of his name, and of his death: and would fain exert a more vigorous act of thankful adoration than in this broken state I am capable of, while I am extolling thee for the riches of thy grace manifested in him; for his instructions and his example, for his blood and his righteousness, and for that blessed Spirit of thine which thou hast given me, to turn my sinful heart unto thyself, and to bring me into the bonds of thy covenant; of that covenant, which is " ordered in all things and sure," 2 Sam. xxiii. 5, and which this death, though now separat. ing my soul from my body, shall never be able to dissolve.

I bless thee, O Lord, that I am not dying in an unregenerate and impenitent state; but that thou didst graciously awaken and convince me; that thou didst renew and sanctify my heart, and didst by thy good Spirit work in it an unfeigned faith, and real repentance, and the beginning of a divine life. I thank thee for ministers and gospel ordinances; I thank thee for my sabbaths and my sacrament-days; for the weekly and monthly refreshments which they gave me I thank thee for the fruits of Canaan, which were sent me in the wilderness, and are now sent me on the brink of Jordan. I thank thee for thy blessed word, and for those exceeding rich and precious promises of it, which now lie as a cordial warm at my heart in this chilling hour; promises of support in death, and of glory beyond it, and of the resurrection of my body to everlasting life. O my God, I firmly believe them all, great and wonderful as they are, and am " waiting for the accomplishment of them through Jesus Christ; in whom they are all yea and amen," 2 Cor. i. 20. " Remember thy word unto thy eervant on which thou hast caused me *to* hope!" Psal. cxix. 49. I covenanted with thee noᵢ for world-ɪy en͡ɔyments, which thy love taught me compara-:ively to despise; but for eternal life, as the gift of thy free grace through "Jesus Christ my Lord," Rom. vi. 23, and now permit me, in his name, to enter my humble claim to it! Permit me to consign this departing spirit into thine hand; for thou hast redeemed it, O Lord God of truth! Psal. xxxi. 5. "I am thine, save me," Psal. cxix. 94, and make me happy!

But may I indeed presume to say, I am thine? O God, now I am standing on the borders of both worlds; now I view things as in the light of thy presence and of eternity; how unworthy do I appear, that I should be taken to dwell with thy angels and saints in glo-ry! Alas, I have reason to look back with deep hu-miliation, on a poor unprofitable, sinful life, in which I have daily been deserving to be cast into hell. But I have this one comfortable reflection, that I have fled to the cross of Christ; and I now renew my ap-plication to it. To think of appearing before God in such an imperfect righteousness as my own, were ten thousand times worse than death. No, Lord, I come unto thee as a sinner; but as a sinner who hath believed in thy Son for pardon and life : I fall down before thee as a guilty polluted wretch; but thou hast made him to be unto thy people for wis-dom and righteousness, for sanctification and redemp-tion, 1 Cor. i. 30. Let me have my lot among the followers of Jesus! Treat me as thou treatest those who are his friends and his brethren! for thou know-est my soul has loved him, and trusted in him, and solemnly ventured itself on the security of his gospel. And "I know in whom I have believed," 2 Tim. i. 12. The infernal lion may attempt to dismay me in this awful passage : but I rejoice that I am in the hands of the good Shepherd; John x. 11, 28, and I defy all my spiritual enemies, in a cheerful depen-dence on his faithful care. I lift up my eyes and my heart to him, who "was dead and is alive again and behold he lives for ever more, and hath the keys of death, and of the unseen world," Rev. i. 18. Blessed Jesus, I die by thine hand, and I fear no harm from the band of a Saviour! I fear not that death which is allotted to me by the hand of my dearest Lord, who himself died to make it safe and happy. I come, Lord, I come, not only with a willing, but with a joyful consent. I thank thee that thou rememberest me for good; that thou art breaking my chains, and calling me to "the glorious liberty of the children of God," Rom. viii. 21. I thank thee, that thou wilt no longer permit me to live at a distance from thine arms; but after this long absence, wilt have me at home, at home for ever.

My feeble nature faints in the view of that glory, which is now dawning upon me; but thou knowest gracious Lord, how to let it in upon my soul by just degrees, and to "make thy strength perfect in my weakness," 2 Cor. xii. 9. Once more, for the last time, would I look down on this poor world, which I am going to quit, and breathe out my dying prayer for its prosperity, and that of thy Church in it. I have loved it, O Lord, as a living member of the body; and I love it to the last. I humbly beseech thee, therefore, that thou wilt guard it, and purify it. and unite it more and more! Send down more of thy blessed Spirit upon it, even the Spirit of wisdom, of holiness, and of love; till in due time "the wilderness be turned into a garden of the Lord," Isa. li. 3, and "all flesh shall see thy salvation!" Luke iii. 6.

And as for me, bear me, O my heavenly Father, on the wings of everlasting love, to that peaceful, that holy, that joyous abode, which thy mercy has prepared for me, and which the blood of my Redeemer has purchased! Bear me "to the general assembly and church of the first-born, to the innumerable company of angels, and to the spirits of just men made perfect," Heb. xii. 22, 23. And whatever this flesh may suffer, let my steady soul be delightfully fixed on that glory to which it is rising! Let faith perform its last office in an honourable manner! Let my few remaining moments on earth be spent for thy glory; and so let me ascend with love in my heart, and praise on my faltering tongue, to the world where love and praise shall be complete! Be this my last song on earth, which I am going to tune in heaven; " Blessing, and honour, and glory, and power, be unto him that sitteth on the throne, and to the Lamb for ever and ever," Rev. v. 13. Amen.

THE END.